AT HOME
WITH THE
PATAGONIANS

WAKI KILLING A PUMA

Travellers, Explorers & Pioneers

AT HOME
WITH THE
PATAGONIANS

GEORGE C. MUSTERS

NONSUCH

First published 1871
Copyright © in this edition 2005
Nonsuch Publishing Ltd

Nonsuch Publishing Limited
The Mill, Brimscombe Port,
Stroud, Gloucestershire, GL5 2QG
www.nonsuch-publishing.com

British Library Cataloguing in Publication Data.
A catalogue record for this book is available from the British Library.

1-84588-008-0

Typesetting and origination by Nonsuch Publishing Limited
Printed in Great Britain by Oaklands Book Services Limited

CONTENTS

INTRODUCTION TO THE
MODERN EDITION

PATAGONIA! Who would ever think about going to such a place? Why you will be eaten up by cannibals!' What on earth makes you choose such an outlandish part of the world to go to? What can be the attraction? Why it is thousands of miles away, and no one has ever been there before, except Captain Musters, and one or two other adventurous madmen!

Such were the words of Lady Florence Dixie, as recounted in *Across Patagonia*, the story of her own voyage across this 'outlandish part of the world'. And there is undeniably some truth in what she says. Patagonia, nestled between Argentina and Chile, shaded by the towering Andes and carved into swathes of desert and glacier, is undeniably at quite a remove from the more urbane of destinations. Neither did the magnetism its barren steppes and lush valleys held for the countless explorers drawn to these distant shores revolve around their accessibility. *At Home with the Patagonians* (1871), George Chaworth Musters extraordinary tale of his time immersed in the culture of the natives, was not, it must follow, born of anything less than a curious derangement, and for it we must remain eternally grateful.

One of the first of the 'adventurous madmen' to whom Lady Dixie must surely be referring was Ferdinand Magellan, who came upon Patagonia in 1520. His navigator, the Italian Antonio Pigafetta did much to raise the profile of the country through his meticulous record of the expedition, and in particular, their first encounter with the local people.

> One day, without anyone expecting it, we saw a giant . . . He was so tall that the tallest of us only came up to his waist; however, he was

well built. He had a large face, painted on his cheeks: he had but
little hair on his head, and it was painted white.

These giants were the Tehuelche Indians, and subsequent reports were to inflate
their stature to at least twelve feet in height. While such assessments were in time
to prove to have been somewhat enthusiastic, they did serve to propel this 'ancient
habitation' into the forefront of the pubic imagination. Musters himself found
that one of the first questions he would be asked by curious friends was 'are they
giants or not?'

The Tehuelche Indians, for their part, wore upon their feet the skin of guanacos,
a deer-like creature, and in so doing left enormous foot-prints on the sand. The
lasting effect of this practise, in tandem with the burgeoning reputation of their
size, was that the name of *Patagons*, or 'big feet', as they were referred to by
Magellan, was to gain a permanent foothold, so to speak.

The legendary *Beagle* expedition came through the Straits of Magellan in
January 1834, and of the Tehuelche Indians, Charles Darwin gave the following
description:

> They are half-civilised – they talk a good deal of Spanish and some
> English. Their appearance is however rather wild – they are all
> clothed in large mantles of the Guanaco, & their long hair streams
> about their faces . . . At tea they behaved quite like gentlemen, used
> a knife & fork & helped themselves with a spoon.

What begins to emerge is a picture of a people that is far more complex than
the myth of the 'noble savage' would have one believe. Augustus Guinnard, whose
Three Years Slavery Among the Patagonians (1871) is an account of time spent
among the Teheulches and other tribes under very different circumstances from
that of Musters, was forced to admit of their sophistication. Their hierarchies and
rivalries, small jealousies and passing kindnesses served to remind him, in truth,
of none so much as himself.

Musters work, however, goes further than any other writer of the time in
examining the reality of the lives of the Tehuelche. Through a combination
of machinations, this retired Royal Navy Commander secures a favourable
introduction, and lived and travelled with them as one of their own. He observes
in this work their rituals and practises, their obsession with cleanliness, and the
elaborate grooming rites which seem so uncannily familiar.

The way in which the Tehuelche raise their children, moreover, is a fascinating
study in itself; of the interplay of respect and honour with which their social group
is interwoven. This work is still held as one of the most authoritative ethnographic
documents of these people, and one made all the more remarkable by the fact that
it predates that same discipline's formation.

At Home with the Patagonians is undoubtedly a work of great historical importance, but it is still more than that. Its reflective qualities and philosophical questioning provides an opportunity for insight, which Musters exemplifies in the following passage:

> One word of advice for the future traveller may conclude this imperfect sketch. Never show distrust of the Indians; be as free with your goods and chattels as they are to each other. Don't ever want anything done for you . . . don't give yourself airs of superiority, as they do not understand it – unless you can prove yourself better in some distinct way. Always be first, as you are unlikely to be encumbered by a wife or gear . . . they will learn by degrees to respect you; in a word, as you treat them so they will treat you.

PREFACE

IN submitting the following pages to the public, I am conscious that some readers who desire exact and scientific descriptions of the geography and geology of Patagonia will be disappointed; but it must be urged as an apology that instruments could not be carried nor safely used under the circumstances. The course travelled was as carefully laid down, by the help of a compass, as was possible; and the map of the country is so far accurate, and, if incomplete, at least is not imaginative. To others who may perhaps eagerly expect tales of stirring adventure and hair-breadth escapes, such as are usually recounted as the every-day occurrences of uncivilised life, I can only express the hope that this faithful record of life with the Indians all the year round, if not very sensational, will serve at least to make them really at home with the Tehuelches. It is a pleasanter task to record my thanks to those by whose assistance the results of my journey have been utilised; foremost of whom is the venerable ex-President of the Royal Geographical Society, Sir RODERICK MURCHISON, whose kindly reception and introduction of the returned traveller to the Society are gratefully acknowledged. My obligations are scarcely less to CLEMENTS MARKHAM, C.B., whose unrivalled knowledge of the early history as well as the geography of South America has been freely placed at my disposal; and to Dr. HOOKER, Director of the Royal Gardens, Kew, for his courteous assistance in identifying some of the plants observed: while to Mr. RUDLER, of the Museum of Mines, I am indebted for a careful classification of the various specimens of rocks and minerals collected in the country. Lastly, the reader will share in my gratitude to Mr. ZWECKER, whose able pencil has created, out of outlines sketched in a pocket-book, the vivid and faithful illustrations which bring before his eyes the scenery and incidents of life in Patagonia.

September 1, 1871., G.C.M.

INTRODUCTION

THREE hundred and fifty years ago the great navigator Magellan anchored in a port on the eastern coast of an unknown shore, part of the seaboard of the vast continent of South America, to which he gave the name of St. Julian. Starting from this point, the pilot Serrano explored the coast to the southward, and discovered a river, which he named Santa Cruz. His ship was wrecked near the mouth, and left her timbers on the rocks, the first of the long list of vessels lost on that ironbound coast which, from the mouth of the Rio Negro to the Straits, offers but one or two safe harbours, while submerged reefs, fierce gales, strong tides, currents, and overfalls combine to render it nearly the most perilous known to navigators.

Magellan remained at Port St. Julian and Santa Cruz from April till October of 1520, when he sailed southward, and discovered the Straits which bear his name. Two months after his arrival at Port St. Julian a man of gigantic stature appeared on the beach, 'larger and taller than the stoutest man of Castile.' Eighteen natives afterwards arrived, dressed in cloaks of skins and shoes of guanaco hide, which made huge footmarks, whence they were called Patagonés, or 'large feet,' by the Spaniards; and thus originated in a nickname the name of the country, Patagonia. These men used bows and arrows, and had with them four young guanacoes, with which they decoyed the wild ones within shot. Two young men were treacherously seized and carried off, howling and calling on their god Setebos. The natives naturally resented this return for their ready friendliness, and, attacking a party sent after them, killed one Spaniard with their arrows. Enough, however, was seen of then to furnish Pigafetta with some details. 'Their tents were light movable frames, covered with skins; their faces were painted; they were very swift of foot, had tools of sharp-edged flints, and ate their meat nearly raw.'

That the first knowledge of Patagonia was diffused in England by Pigafetta's narrative is suggested by Caliban's lines in the 'Tempest:' 'he could command my dam's god Setebos;' but it was not till 1578 that the newly-discovered country was visited by Englishmen.

Sir Francis Drake in that year anchored in Seal Bay—probably a little to the south of Port Desire—and saw several Indians. His chaplain narrates their method of stalking the ostriches: 'They have a plume of ostrich feathers on a long staff, large enough to hide a man behind, and with this they stalk the ostriches.' He further says: 'They would have none of our company until such time as they were warranted by their God "Settaboth." They never cut their hair, which they make a store-house for all the things they carry about—a quiver for arrows, a sheath for knives, a case for toothpicks, a box for fire sticks, and what not; they are fond of dancing with rattles round their waists; they have clean, comely, and strong bodies, are swift of foot, very active, a goodly and lively people. Magellan was not altogether wrong in naming them giants, yet they are not taller than some Englishmen.' Drake next visited Port St. Julian; and, curiously enough, as Magellan had in this place put to death two and marooned a third of his captains who mutinied, so this harbour was the scene of the execution of Mr. Doughty, who chose rather to be beheaded than to be put on shore. The ensuing year Sarmiento was despatched from Callao to examine the Straits in search of the daring Englishman. He saw natives who chased their game on horseback, and brought it down with bolas. But fifty years had elapsed since horses had been imported by the Spaniards of the Rio de la Plata, and already the Indians in the far south had become horsemen, and would seem to have exchanged their bows and arrows for the bolas.

In 1581 Sarmiento was sent from Spain with 2,500 men in twenty-three ships, to found new colonies in the Straits, and established a settlement, leaving 400 men and thirty women, furnished with eight months' provisions. On his way home his ship was captured by the English, and the unhappy colonists were altogether forgotten and neglected by their Government.

Five years after, Thomas Cavendish anchored in a bay to the south of St. Julian, called by him Port Desire, which perpetuates the name of his little craft of 120 tons. Here the natives attacked his men with bows and arrows. Visiting the Straits, he arrived at the settlement, and found only twelve men and three women surviving, the rest having perished of slow starvation and disease; and the name of the place, Port Famine, conferred by him, still recalls the miserable fate of these ill-fated colonists.

On his next voyage, in 1591, Cavendish died; but John Davis twice visited Port Desire, and explored the river for twenty miles. During his stay some 1,000 natives visited the strangers, and Knyvet describes them as being fifteen or sixteen span high.

Passing over the visits of Van Noort and Schouten, in the reign of Charles the Second Sir John Narborough took possession of the country near Port Desire in the name of the King. But few natives were seen, and the mate, Mr. Wood, boastingly declared that he himself was taller than any of them.

In the eighteenth century Byron and Wallis successively visited the shores of Patagonia, and made friends with the natives, whose height was found to be from 5 feet 10 inches to 6 feet, while some were nearly 7 feet high.

In 1774 the Jesuit Father Falkner published his work on Patagonia, containing all the information procured by himself and the other Jesuit missionaries who had attempted to obtain a footing on the western and northern boundaries. His account of the Tehuelches, or Tsoneca Indians, was evidently derived from personal communication with them, although his knowledge of the topography of their country seems to have been procured from the reports of others. By this work, which produced a great sensation, the jealous fears of the Spanish Government were aroused, and they hastened to despatch an expedition to form settlements on the coast of Patagonia.

Of the brothers Viedma, who were sent in command, Francisco founded Carmen at the mouth of the Rio Negro, and Antonio, after first fixing on Port Desire, determined finally on Port St. Julian as the site of another colony. He thence undertook the first exploration of the interior in search of timber for building, in the course of which he reached the great lake at the foot of the Cordillera, from which flowed the Rio Santa Cruz. Both on the coast and in the interior he received much friendly aid from the Indians, of whom he formed a most favourable opinion.

Under his brother's auspices the Rio Negro was ascended as far as the mountains by Villarino, to whose expedition reference will be made in the proper place.

No further knowledge was gained of the interior of Patagonia until the survey of the Beagle, so ably performed and so admirably described by Fitzroy and Darwin; during which the ascent of the Santa Cruz river for 200 miles enabled the latter to observe the remarkable formations which he has so aptly described in his work on the Geology of South America.

This brief but perhaps tedious account has been given to show that although the coasts of Patagonia had been explored and surveyed, yet the interior of the country, though pierced by the expeditions of Viedma and Fitzroy, remained up to a late date still almost unknown. Its inhabitants, the Tehuelches, had been often communicated with, their stature noted, and their friendly disposition commended; but their real manners of life as they wandered through the country, and their relations with, or difference from, the Araucanian and Pampa Indians, had remained almost as much a mystery as they were in the last century.

During the last thirty years the Governments of Chili and of Buenos Ayres have shown themselves inclined to claim the possession of the coast, the former trying to advance from the Straits, and the latter from Patagones; and the natives have acknowledged the influence of either Government as they happened to be in the northern or southern parts respectively. Our missionaries also have not left the Patagonians without some efforts to instruct and evangelise them; and although these efforts have been necessarily limited to the coast, yet the fruits of Mr. Schmid's Sojourn with the Tehuelches remain both in their friendly feelings and in the lasting record of the vocabulary of the Tsoneca language published by him. And the intercourse of these Indians with Argentines and Chilians, and more especially with English officers, sealers, and missionaries successively all of whom have testified favourably to their character, has tended to make them more open to access, and to give them a knowledge of foreigners; so that in this respect I can feel that to all those who have been mentioned as having thus preceded me, this brief record is due from a traveller who has experienced the friendly feelings of the natives towards strangers, and especially Englishmen.

While engaged in preparing the ensuing pages for the press, I have had an opportunity of perusing the work of M. Guinnard, first published in French, and recently given to the English public in a spirited translation, entitled 'Three Years' Slavery among the Patagonians.' The name necessarily attracted me, but to my great surprise careful perusal led to the distinct conviction that the author's personal experiences were altogether confined to the Pampas Indians north of the Rio Negro. From his own statements and omissions it is quite evident that he was not carried by any of his successive masters across this river, which he clearly and accurately defines to be (p. 40) the northern boundary of Patagonia. The name of Patagonians is, therefore, a complete misnomer; and the curious account (pp. 72-3) of the 'Tchéouelches,' or Foot Nomads, clothed in seal skins and accustomed to live on fish, and literally destitute of horses, is applicable to no tribe whatever east of the Cordillera, the Fuegians being the only race presenting any of the characteristic habits attributed to this so-called Patagonian tribe.

I hope I may not be supposed to be desirous of impeaching the accuracy of M. Guinnard's account of the hardships endured in his captivity, or of the customs of the Indians into whose hands he fell, much of which I can corroborate; but it is to be regretted that he was induced, probably by others, to describe under the name of Patagonians, the Pampas Indians, who, by country, race, language, and character, are marked as being altogether distinct from the Tehuelches of Patagonia.

I

FROM THE STRAITS TO SANTA CRUZ

IN April 1869 chance took me to our remote colony of the Falkland Islands, with the purpose of taking thence a passage to Buenos Ayres to arrange some business matters. During my stay in the settlement, the coast of Patagonia, in the survey of which H.M.S. Nassau was then engaged, formed a frequent topic of conversation. I had formerly, when stationed on the south-east coast of America, read with delight Mr. Darwin's work on South America, as well as Fitzroy's admirable Narrative of the Voyage of the Beagle, and had ever since entertained a strong desire to penetrate if possible the little-known interior of the country. Now, at length, a favourable opportunity seemed to have arrived for carrying out the cherished scheme of traversing the country from Punta Arena to the Rio Negro, Valdivia, or even to Buenos Ayres. The accounts given me of the Tehuelche character and of the glorious excitement of the chase after the guanaco, graphically described by a seaman, Sam Bonner, who had been much on the coast and had resided at the Santa Cruz station, made me more than ever anxious to prosecute this plan; and, having a tolerable acquaintance with Spanish, which language many of the Indians know well, it seemed to me possible to safely traverse the country in company with some one or other of their wandering parties. Accordingly I bestirred myself to obtain information as to the best way of getting such an introduction to the Indians as would probably secure their consent; to which end most material assistance was afforded by Mr. Dean, of Stanley, who kindly provided me with letters of introduction to Captain Luiz Piedra Buena, an intelligent Argentine well known in Stanley, the owner of a schooner, in which he worked the seal fisheries on the coast, and also of a trading station at the Middle Island, on the Santa Cruz river. Mr. Dean was of opinion that I should be almost certain to meet with Don Luiz in the Straits of Magellan, and that he would willingly exert his influence with the Indians to enable me to carry out my plan of travel. I was furthermore provided with letters of credit to the firm of Messrs. Aguirre & Murga, at Patagones, or, as it is most commonly called at Stanley, the Rio Negro.

Thus armed with credentials, and equipped with a guanaco skin mantle, lazo and bolas, I availed myself of the offer of a passage to the Straits made by an old friend who was bound to the westward coast.

In the first week of April we sailed from Stanley, and, after a boisterous passage of eleven days, anchored in Possession Bay, just within the entrance of the Straits, to wait for the turn of the tide, as the extreme velocity with which the tides ebb and flow through these channels renders it impossible for any vessel not possessed of great steam power to proceed except the tide is favourable. Our first view of the Straits did not impress me favourably. On either hand the shores looked bleak and barren, though far away to the south and west the mountains of Tierra del Fuego could be distinctly seen. As we anchored early in the afternoon, a descent on the coast of Patagonia was proposed, and a party speedily volunteered—well provided with guns and other arms, for the purposes of sport and self-defence in case of necessity—and were soon in the boat. As the tide was out, the shoal water did not permit us to reach the shore, so we had to wade some two or three hundred yards over beds of sharp-edged mussels, and, after a climb up the steep cliff, found ourselves on the verge of a barren plain which seemed perfectly destitute of life.

After a tramp of some distance we came to the edge of a gully running down to the coast, where finding the torn carcase a guanaco, we stopped to examine what was to most of us an unknown animal; and our speculations as to the curious hybrid form of the odd-looking 'camel-sheep' were put an end to by the discovery close by of the fresh footprints of a puma. These were eagerly tracked, in the hopes of a little entertainment; but after some tedious searching we abandoned the pursuit, and again resuming our excursion, tramped along through high, coarse grass, and sparsely scattered thorny bushes; some of the sportsmen varying the monotony by an occasional shot at a snipe. The day was very genial, the warmth of the bright sunshine was tempered by a wind just cool enough to make a walk pleasant, and the Patagonian climate was pronounced by all hands to be agreeable. Whilst we were beating a rough bit of ground, to our utter amazement and delight our friend the puma jumped out of a bush; but the first surprise was so great, that the opportunity of giving him a long shot was lost. Away we all started in chase, hoping to be able to keep him in sight from a small adjacent eminence; and after a good breather two of the party succeeded in viewing him to somewhere near the edge of the cliffs, mainly guided by a retriever dog, which seemed as anxious as anybody to see what the catamount hide was made of. On arriving at the cliff, a seaman observed his tracks on the soft clay of the shelving brow, and soon proclaimed his discovery of the puma in a hole or small cave just below, by the exclamation of 'There he is!' at the same time thrusting the stick he had been beating with nearly into the mouth of the 'lion,' which had set our dog, and appeared about to spring on him. Two shots were fired in quick succession, but apparently without effect, as he made good his retreat, affording us a fine view as he went off, springing in great bounds, along the beach. Pursuit was of course organised, but night being near failed to afford us an opportunity of a closer study of this specimen of the feline race; and we accordingly started again for the ship, after firing a shot or two into the numerous flocks of oyster-catchers and shags which were domiciled on the rocks and about the cliffs. The number of these and other sea-birds was incalculable; the numerous beds of mussels furnishing them with constant food.

Next morning we were under weigh with the flood-tide, and rapidly ran through the narrows at a speed of eighteen miles an hour. The scenery on the northern side of the Straits offered little variety until we sighted the Barrancas of San Gregorio, a range of somewhat picturesque hills, rising near the north shore of the bay of the same name, and running along for some miles in an easterly direction. On the southern or Fuegian side of the Straits the land was low for some distance from the coast, and resembled the northern shore, but high mountains were visible in the background. After passing the second narrows, an hour or two's run with the flood-tide and a good head of steam brought us opposite to the 'Island of San Isabel,' or Elizabeth Island; after passing which the snow-clad peaks of Mount Sarmiento, in the southern part of Tierra del Fuego, came into sight, appearing to rise out of the water, ninety miles distant, if not more. Steaming along the coast through numerous beds of the characteristic kelp seaweed, which in the most forcible way attracted our attention, by fouling the screw, and holding the ship as if anchored for about an hour, we passed Cape Negro, and opened completely different scenery. Instead of undulating plains, hills thickly wooded were seen; at the foot of one of which, on a low piece of flat ground, numerous horsemen, dressed in gay-coloured ponchos, were visible, careering about.

It was the afternoon of Sunday, which in all Spanish South American countries is a gala day, more or less appropriated to horse-racing. However, the sight of a steamer appeared to cause a diversion, and, in fact, a general race to the settlement ensued, all being apparently anxious for anything new or strange. The anchor was soon dropped, near an American schooner lying off the Sandy Point, from which the Chilian settlement of Punta Arenas derives its name.

There was no sign of the Nassau, then engaged in the survey of the Straits, which we had hoped to find in this anchorage; but from the Chilian officer who speedily boarded us, we learned that she had sailed to the westward a day or two before our arrival, and was expected to return immediately. The results of the careful observations made by Mr. Cunningham, of the scenery and natural history of the Straits, have appeared while these pages were in preparation for the press; and it affords me pleasure to refer such as desire more scientific accounts of the botany and zoology, at least of Southern Patagonia, than it was in my power to obtain, to his work.

My own object in visiting Punta Arenas was to proceed thence to Santa Cruz with the Indians, or in whatever way might prove feasible; but, in truth, it was by no means clear to my mind how it was to be accomplished; it was, therefore, with great relief that I learned from the Chilian lieutenant that a small expedition was about to be despatched by the governor to Santa Cruz in pursuit of some runaways from among the deserters who were serving their term of punishment in the colony. He suggested that the Commandante would, doubtless, give permission to accompany this party; and, without delay, I accompanied him on shore, and was introduced to Commandante Señor Viel.

Nothing could exceed the kindness and courtesy with which the Commandante entered into my plans; he at once not only gave me permission to accompany the party, but, unasked, offered me the use of a horse, and told me not to trouble myself about the commissariat for the road. It was possible, however, that the deserters might be overtaken in the Pampas, in which case the party would return without proceeding as far as Santa Cruz; he therefore advised me to secure the services of someone acquainted with the route, who could act as guide in the event of our having to proceed without the rest of our companions.

I was afterwards introduced to Señora Viel, a fair Limena possessing all the proverbial charms of the ladies of Lima, and who bemoaned bitterly the isolation and ennui of life at Punta Arenas; she had literally no equals of her own sex, and scarcely any of the other, to speak to. Señor Viel had formerly commanded a Chilian ironclad, instead of which he had accepted the government of this distant colony; his zeal and energy in discharging the duties of his office were unceasing, and his naval habits asserted themselves in the strictness of discipline maintained, which was absolutely necessary to keep in order the motley population. But as a residence, viewed from a social point of view, Punta Arenas must have been unimaginably dull. The Commandante kindly pressed me to make his house my home, promising quarters for the night—which his own limited accommodation could not supply—in an adjacent house. So after two days, agreeably spent in the interchange of courtesies and visits, I bade adieu to my shipmates, who were to sail at daylight for the Western Straits, and removed myself and traps to a wooden house close to the Cuartel, the quarters of Don Centeno, the engineer in charge of the Government works. The next morning, accompanied by Captain Cushing, of the schooner Rippling Wave, I set out to procure some few necessary supplies, and make inquiries for a guide. We bent our steps to the store of a man named Guillermo, and after purchasing tobacco and other necessaries, the talk turned on gold, of which Don Guillermo showed us some specimens, obtained from the banks of a neighbouring stream. One of the crew of the Rippling Wave grew greatly excited and exclaimed, 'Ah, that's the stuff we used to grub up in a creek in Californy; I guess if the old boat lays her bones on these here shores, I'll stop and turn to digging again.' Hanging up in the store were some Indian bolas and a belt made of beads, studded with silver bosses, which the owner informed me was a woman's girdle, and, with the bolas, had been left in pawn by the Indians. They had not, however, visited the colony, at least for trading purposes, for several months, as they had taken umbrage about a dispute between a Chilian and an Indian, in which they considered their comrade to have been treated with injustice. The party described by Mr. Cunningham evidently arrived with doubtful intentions, and the tact displayed by Señor Viel removed their resentment. This information explained what had previously mystified me, viz., that nothing was to be seen or heard of the Indians with whom I had hoped to make acquaintance. My good fortune in arriving on the eve of the departure of the expedition, and the Commandante's courtesy, were now even more keenly appreciated by me, as otherwise I should have been simply stranded in Punta Arenas. The guide difficulty was not long of solution, although, from the natural dislike of most of the unofficial population to take part in the recapture of runaways, it had seemed rather perplexing. After we had quitted the store, we were accosted by a man named J'aria, who came to offer his services. A short examination of his knowledge and recommendations proving satisfactory, he was engaged on terms which certainly were far from exorbitant, and he deserves to have it recorded that he fully earned his pay. My equipments and preparations for the journey were now made complete by the thoughtful good nature of Captain Cushing, with whom I proceeded on board his vessel, where he provided from his stores, and forced on my acceptance, several most useful articles; and it is pleasant to be able to publish my sense of the kindness received from one of our American cousins, who are always ready to sympathise with and befriend a Britisher, at least according to my experience.

A stroll of inspection round the settlement was extended to the saw-mill, not far distant, worked by water-power; where, under the direction of Mr. Wells, an American, the trees when cut down are converted into boards to build the houses that take the place of the forest. Proceeding thence to the half-cleared outskirts, we found the Commandante supervising numerous labourers, principally of the convict class, who were busily engaged in felling trees, clearing stumps, and otherwise preparing the way for the future development of the settlement.

To anyone unaccustomed to frontier towns, the *coup-d'oeil* of the town presented an irregular and random growth of wooden houses; but the plan which was indicated in outline was laid out after the usual Spanish American fashion, as originally prescribed by the Council of the Indies. A main street ran near and parallel to the beach, crossing a large vacant square—the Plaza, out of which, and at regular intervals from the main street, ran other embryo streets intersecting at right angles, so that the houses, whenever they should be built, would form blocks or 'cuadros.' In the Plaza were the church and a large unfinished school-house. Chilian ideas as to the public duty of education are advanced, and the schoolmaster is a state functionary, combining at this time at Punta Arenas the duties of secretary to the Governor with those proper to his office. The excellent sketch of Staff-Commander Bedwell (Cunningham, 'Straits of Magellan' p. 70) shows the Governor's house nearly at the end of the main street, and beyond it was the Cuartel, a palisadoed inclosure, containing the barracks, the gaol or lock-up, and the guard-house, irreverently termed by the officers of the Nassau 'The Punch and Judy House,' and shown in the same sketch.

From this a constant look-out is maintained, and a light displayed at night. The transverse streets, running up almost to the uncleared forest, were only indicated by scattered houses, and in the line of the main street two or three detached dwellings a mile distant were only separated from the trees by patches of potato ground.

The first penal colony planted in the Straits by the Chilian Government was established in 1843, at Port Famine, the ominous name of which recalls the miserable fate of the colonists left there by Sarmiento in 1581. The superior anchorage was the inducement to select the same place for the modern colony, but the same evil destiny seemed to cling to it. After struggling on for some years, during which the inhabitants were frequently reduced to great distress by the failure of supplies of food from Chili, it was sacked and destroyed by the convicts, who mutinied and killed the Governor and Padre. They afterwards seized a vessel in which they attempted to escape, but were pursued by a man-of-war, and met with deserved punishment.

The colony was subsequently removed to its present position, and in addition to the involuntary immigrants, chiefly deserters from the army, settlers were tempted by liberal grants of land, and a large number of Chilotes or natives of Chiloe were introduced. These men, who are of mixed Spanish and Indian blood, are a hardy, sturdy race, accustomed to the use of the axe in their own thickly-wooded country, whence they export quantities of timber. They are very Paddies in their diet, living almost altogether on potatoes, which grow freely in Chiloe, but in Punta Arenas do not attain large size. Besides land, the Chilotes receive wages from the Government for their labour, and are the most industrious portion of the population: the men are hard working, but also hard drinking, and the women are said to be very lax in their notions of fidelity. Of the convicts, some were allowed, for good behaviour, to live in their own houses, subject to certain restrictions; but many of them were utterly reckless, and needed to be kept under the strictest surveillance, and locked up in the Cuartel every night. Notwithstanding all precautions, escapes are continually contrived, and the runaways face the difficulties of the Pampas, sometimes succeeding in joining the Patagonians, but as often losing their way, and perishing of starvation, or becoming a prey to the pumas. Thus, ten or a dozen had succeeded in escaping just before my visit, necessitating the despatch of the expedition in chase of them. The garrison consisted of some fifty or sixty regular soldiers, besides irregular employés, who hunt wild cattle or deserters, as occasion requires. The number of troops is quite insufficient to defend the place against an attack of the Indians, but the southern Tehuelches are not naturally inclined to raids, and if well and fairly treated are more willing to avail themselves of the trading facilities afforded by the half-dozen stores, the existence of which could only, in my mind, be accounted for by the hopes of Indian barter, for they were far in excess of the wants of the colony. Still the permanent population was certainly a thirsty one, and seemed to do its best to encourage trade, at least in grog: drunkenness in the streets is, however, an offence punishable by imprisonment and at the time of my visit the blacksmith was in durance vile, whence the Irish Doctor had only just been released for this venial offence.

There appeared to be little cultivation, with the exception of potatoes. The climate does not permit wheat or barley to ripen, though, perhaps, oats or rye might succeed. The tame cattle seemed to me stunted and miserable, but in the forests there are others of a wild breed, which are said to be large and of excellent quality; these, as well as the red deer, afford, during some portion of the year, occupation to a few hunters, who obtain high prices for their meat, but the supply is too scanty and irregular to prevent fresh meat from being a rare luxury. The resources and prospects of the colony naturally formed the subject of conversation at Señor Viel's, and Don Centeno, who was in charge of the survey of the newly-discovered coal bed in the vicinity, invited me to join him the next day in a visit of inspection.

Next morning we accordingly set out, and crossing a small stream, shortly arrived at the commencement of the forest, through which a straight road was in course of formation. Numerous groups of Chilotes were employed on all sides, some levelling the way already cleared, others at work felling trees, others applying fire instead of the axe. The timber consists chiefly of Chilian beech (Fagus antarctica) and Winter's bark, described by Mr. Cunningham, the former of which splits readily and is available for most purposes.

After Don Centeno had completed some minor details of surveying, we struck into the dense forest, and followed a winding path until we arrived at the bed of the stream, which debouches at the colony. This we followed up for some time, and eventually arrived at a ravine, the sides of which were as regular as if navvies had been employed to form a cutting, in which, at a point sixty yards above our heads, the seam of coal was visible. Here we dismounted and scrambled up a slippery path to a spot where a shaft, or rather burrow, had been driven into the bed, to the depth of perhaps fifty or sixty feet, made apparently for the purpose of examining the quality, regularity, &c., of the seam. The coal did not appear to me of a very good quality; but I have since heard that it gave exceedingly favourable results. My companion also pointed out to me a place in the opposite bank where some men had been washing for gold, the specimens of which I had seen in the town; and their labours were said to have been attended with good returns. As the day was advancing and rather chilly, a fire was kindled; and after a warm thereat, mounting our horses, we returned homewards down the ravine. On emerging from the forest, we observed a large steamer just on the point of anchoring; so we hurried on to obtain news and despatch our letters if it should prove the Magalhaens—one of the line of packets from Liverpool to Valparaiso. On the beach we found the Commandante and Mrs. Viel, the latter having visited the vessel and obtained some English newspapers. After dinner, accepting the Governor's offer of his boat, I proceeded on board, and found her to be a magnificent steamer of great power and good accommodation. The establishment of this line of steamers will doubtless have a most beneficial effect on the prosperity of Punta Arenas; as, though agriculture and Indian trade are not likely to reward industrious or speculative immigrants, the discovery of the coal-bed is of the most obvious importance as affecting the future of this colony. It will now be possible to maintain powerful steam-tugs to tow sailing-vessels through the Straits, and thus avoid the passage round Cape Horn; whereas up to the present time the navigation of the Straits has been almost closed to sailing-ships; while, owing to the great steam-power required, even steamers, whether war or merchant ships, are frequently obliged to buy wood at Sandy Point; and then, owing to the vast quantity used to keep steam, not unfrequently are obliged to stop again before entering the Pacific to renew their supply wherever they could cut it. Now this will all be changed, and a steam-launch will probably be kept to tow the lighters to and fro, and thus materially facilitate coaling, As population and colonisation increase, encouraged by the accommodation afforded by the Pacific steamers—which at this present date run every month, bringing the Straits of Magellan almost within hail—the interior of the country may become opened up, in which case, probably, other sources of mineral wealth will be discovered and made productive.

Our departure having been definitely fixed for the morrow, I proceeded to review and arrange my equipments for the journey, a list of which may gratify intending explorers of Patagonia. Two saddle-bags contained my kit and necessaries, consisting of a couple of shirts and a jersey or two, a few silk handkerchiefs, and soap, lucifer matches, writing materials, fishing lines and hooks, quinine and caustic, and a small bottle of strychnine. The armoury comprised a rifle in case complete, and two double-barrelled breech-loading pistols, hunting-knives, a small ammunition-case of unfilled cartridges, and a supply of powder. The only instrument ventured on was a small compass. My personal equipment was a shooting suit of tweed and a Scotch cap, and a most excellent pair of boots made by Thomas, to which for comfort were superadded a guanaco skin mantle, two ponchos, and a waterproof sheet. In the evening Señor Viel introduced me to my future travelling companion, Lieutenant Gallegos, who was to command our party. He was a short, thick-set man, with a dark, almost Indian complexion, and looked all over what the Commandante declared him to be, 'a man for hard work.' In his native province of Arauco he had been for many years employed in the frontier wars with the Indians, and could handle the lazo or the lance with wonderful dexterity. He spoke with great cordiality of the officers of the Nassau, and seemed well inclined to the company of one of the same service; indeed, I am strongly inclined to believe that he is introduced into the foreground of Commander Bedwell's sketch— at all events, if any reader wishes to know his appearance, the occupant of the fallen tree presents a strong resemblance to the leader of our party. Our arrangements and prospects were fully discussed; and after bidding farewell to Captain Cushing, who was to sail the next day, and to my most kind and courteous host and hostess, we parted, agreeing to meet at daylight ready for the road.

At an early hour of the morning of the 19th of April I was awoke by J'aria, and with him and my small belongings proceeded to the Corral, where the horses were being caught and loaded. Here we were joined by Gallegos, and when everything was nearly ready for the start adjourned to his house close by for a cup of coffee. The Señora seemed to regard me with great commiseration, and recounted various dismal tales of the dreadful cold winds, hardships, Indians, and other disagreeables to be encountered; her consolations were cut short by the entrance of J'aria with the news that all was ready. After a parting glass of something stronger than water, we got into our saddles, and the cavalcade, consisting of Gallegos, myself, one regular soldier, three irregulars or employés of the Government, and J'aria, with twenty-one horses, left the town. As we passed the cuartel, the guard turned out in the balcony and presented arms, and the bugler executed a musical salute. It was a fine frosty morning, and we rode on in high spirits, accompanied by two or three horsemen, who were going to spend their Sunday festa in duck shooting, and had made an early start to escort us a little way. Scarcely had we crossed the stream when one of the baggage horses kicked his load off; this was soon replaced; but when the bustle was over and the cavalcade reformed, J'aria and one of the employés, to whom I had confidently entrusted a bottle of rum, were missing, and they did not turn up again for some time, and the bottle never again. We rode along the coast until we reached the outpost called Tres Puentes, where a narrow pass, between the forest on one hand and the sea on the other, is barred by a gate house tenanted by two men, posted there to prevent desertion; they turned out, and we lingered for a farewell chat, during which one of the sportsmen stalked and shot some ducks; at the report of his gun the regular soldier's horse, not being used to stand fire, shied and threw him, capsizing his saddle-bags, and strewing the beach with tortillas (cakes) and coffee, with which his no doubt provident and thoughtful 'she' had stored them. Gallegos sat in his saddle and laughed at the scene; but as the others could not catch the horse, he gave us a proof of his dexterity with the lazo. After this little diversion we pursued our course along the beach as far as Cape Negro, where the forests terminated, and our accompanying friends bade us adieu after taking a parting glass all round; J'aria and the other absentee overtaking us in time for this part of the performance.

Our horses' heads were then turned from the coast in a north north-west direction, and after half-an-hour's ride a halt was called for breakfast under the lee of a sheltering hill. To the southward we viewed the counter slope of the wooded hills, below which on the other side lay Punta Arenas. A thick growth of shrubs covered the ground, but beautiful glades of luxuriant pasture were visible; one of which opened just to the south of our camping place, and others appeared east and west like oases of green. Their appearance caused me to remark that as a settler I should choose this location for my hut. Gallegos, however, replied that the pastures could not be used for the cattle of the settlement during the summer, as neither the Indians nor their own men could be trusted; the latter would desert, and the former would steal the beasts. After a pipe we remounted, and having crossed the hill we descended to the valley of a small but deep stream, called the Rio Chaunco, having forded which we ascended the opposite border slope, and entered on the Pampa, which name is universally used in Patagonia to designate the high undulating plains or plateaux, frequently intersected by valleys and ravines, or rising into successive or isolated hills, which generally occupy the crest of the country. The Indians, indeed, who know a little Castilian, apply the word Pampa indiscriminately to any tract of country hunted over by them. After a successful day's sport, and the contentment consequent on a hearty meal, they will ask with great satisfaction, 'Muy buena Pampa? No?' really meaning 'Is not the wild life the best?' But English readers, who have derived their idea of a Pampa from Head's delightful work, or from other experiences of the unlimited grassy or thistle covered plains which roll away for miles in the Argentine States, and offer no obstruction to the stretching gallop of the untiring gaucho, must not transfer that pleasing picture to Patagonia. The Pampas, properly so called, of Patagonia, occasionally indeed present a tolerably even and uniform succession of rolling plains covered with coarse grass, but more frequently the surface, even when unbroken by hills and suddenly yawning ravines, is sterile, with a sparse vegetation, consisting of stunted bushes and round thistle clumps; and even these are often wanting, and nothing clothes the bare patches of clay or gravel; elsewhere it is strewn with huge round boulders, and again rugged with confused heaps or ridges of bare sharp-edged rocks, many of them of volcanic origin: this more particularly applying to the northern part of the country. The only uniformity of appearance is afforded in the winter, when the white sheet of snow covers rocks, grass, and shingle; but one accompaniment is the same, whatever be the nature of the soil or surface; and the word Pampa invariably recalls to one's shuddering memory the cutting blasts which sweep almost without intermission from various points, but chiefly from the west, over the high country, till, reaching the heated atmosphere of Buenos Ayres, the cold Patagonian wind becomes the Pampero, the sudden and terrific blasts of which cause so many disasters among the shipping. The descent from these Pampas to the valleys, or more sheltered and fertile level ground bordering the banks of the streams and rivers, is commonly termed 'Barranca,' or bank, from the scarped slopes, varying in depth from fifty to two or three feet, and in angle from an easy to an almost perpendicular descent, but often fissured by ravines or gullies, affording roads, down all of which, however, the native riders gallop with equal recklessness.

The Pampa we were now traversing presented an expanse of undulating or rolling plains covered with a uniform growth of coarse grass interspersed with barberry bushes, and occasional lagoons in the hollows. No living creatures except ourselves appeared on the waste. To the westward the snow-clad peaks of the mountains bordering the Sarmiento Straits greeted us with an icy blast which made my thoughts longingly revert to the cosy cabin and my late shipmates, who were, no doubt, threading the intricacies of channels. But the good guanaco mantle kept out the wind, and our motley party pushed briskly on in good order. Lieutenant Gallegos has been already introduced: as to the others, J'aria was a small man, of rough exterior, of doubtful extraction, and more than doubtful antecedents, who looked fit for any business except good; but he served me most assiduously, and with unlooked-for care. The soldier was a fine-looking fellow, new to the Pampas, whose carbine, which he duly carried, proved a source of great embarrassment to him; and his horse being by no means too manageable, he was considerably bothered, much to the delight of the rest. Two others were hybrids, between gauchos and sailors, having, like our marines, been equally accustomed to service *per mare, per terram*; but, like the jollies, they were unmistakeably useful and good men. The last of the party was of the J'aria type. All were well mounted, and provided with a spare horse. We carried for provisions biscuit, charqui or dried meat, roasted wheat meal, and coffee and sugar, and were furnished with an unusual but welcome luxury, a small tent, underneath which we cared little for the bitter frost outside.

After riding over the Pampas for three or four hours we encamped for the night in a hollow by the side of a lagoon, having selected a suitable spot for pitching the tent on the sheltered slope, well out of the sweep of the wind. The lagoon was covered with black-necked swans and other wild fowl; so, as soon as the horses had been unloaded and looked after, a fire lit, and all arrangements made for camping, two or three of us went out to try and shoot some wild fowl; but our sporting endeavours were not crowned with much success, and a little before dark we returned to a supper of charqui, and after a talk over the fire, turned in, and slept sound and warm, though outside the frost was severe. My mind was much disquieted, first by the discovery that the box of rifle ammunition which J'aria carried had been dropped by that worthy at the scene of the baggage horse escapade, and secondly, by the mysterious absence from my shot-belt of all my coin, consisting of an onza and a few sovereigns. I said nothing, however, until next morning, when I proceeded quietly to search, remembering that I had taken off my accoutrements before the tent was pitched, and dropped in the grass I found the missing coins. The story afforded J'aria a great theme for jokes, and he often adverted to the chance of inheriting my ounce, in a way that might have made a timid traveller expect foul play, though nothing was farther from my guide's thoughts. At seven o'clock, after coffee and a biscuit, we were again *en route*, and about ten arrived close to the head of Peckett's Harbour. Here one of the party discovered a horse, which was chased into our troop, but as it appeared lame was not pressed into our service; it had probably belonged to the Indians. As in a long voyage, so in a journey of this description, the slightest novelty serves to relieve what it is needless to say becomes the slightly monotonous task of trotting along behind the troop of horses over barren wastes, so we were always on the *qui vive* for something to chase. One of the men had a dog with him, and shortly after the excitement about the horse we started some ostriches, which, however, proved too swift for the cur, and escaped over some muddy plots close to the 'Cabecera del Mar.' This is a large inlet or arm of the sea, running up some miles from Peckett's Harbour, with which it communicates by a very narrow channel, which can only be crossed at low water; it was our good fortune to arrive at this period, thus escaping a long *détour* round the inlet. But our crossing was not effected without trouble; the flood-tide rushing up like a mill-race, and proving almost too much for the steadiness of one of the baggage-horses. After clearing the channel, in our farther progress we passed several small streams with swampy ground, all of which probably discharge themselves into Oazy Harbour, and arrived towards evening at an old Indian encampment situated under a range of hills, running more or less north and south, forming one barrier of a broad and well-watered valley, bounded on the eastern side by the well-known 'Barrancas' of San Gregorio.

Our station was just within the opening of the valley, which, being sheltered from the wind, is the favourite winter quarters of the Southern Tehuelches, whose encampment is usually pitched near Oazy Harbour, called by them 'Ozay Saba.'

Westward the low flats which bordered the shores of the Cabecera del Mar terminated in irregular hills, beyond which higher peaks rose, and they in their turn were overlooked by distant snow-clad summits on the horizon. Among the blue hills of the middle distance floated wreaths of light haze so much resembling smoke that Gallegos, ever on the alert for signs of the deserters, proposed to deviate from our route to investigate, and only my strongly pronounced opinion in favour of haze *versus* smoke induced him to give up the idea. The Argentine Government formerly planned a settlement in this valley, which was not carried out, and the missionaries also proposed to fix a station hereabouts, with Oazy Harbour as a depôt, but the Chilians of Punta Arena set up their claims and compelled the missionaries to desist.

  After camp was arranged, the weather, which since our start had been bright with cold winds and moderate frosts at night, changed to rain, and Gallegos proposed to me that, in the event of its continuing bad, we should remain under the shelter of the tent. However, though the night was rough and rainy, morning broke fair and the sun rose bright and warm, so we started, following a path along the base of the before-mentioned range of hills until about ten o'clock, when, just after passing a beautiful little stream where I noticed fish darting about in the pools, a herd of guanaco, hitherto concealed by a small eminence, came into view. Chase was immediately given, but most of our horses were soon blown, and Gallegos, the soldier, and myself having ascended the hills over which the herd had taken flight, as it appeared useless to continue the chase, stopped on the crest and watched the animals as they streamed up an opposite hill. One of the party was missing, and suddenly an exclamation from the Lieutenant 'What is it?' caused us to turn our eyes in the direction to which he pointed, where some fancied they descried a man. The idea of deserters immediately occurred to their minds, so they started off, asking me to tell J'aria (who had remained with the horses) to travel on to a given spot at the head of the valley. Having descended the hill, which was tunnelled with burrows of the Ctenomys Magellanicus,[1] the crowns of which, yielding to the horses' tread, proved a series of dangerous traps, I rejoined J'aria and we pursued our way for a few miles until we reached a small lagoon at the head of the valley, covered with thousands of widgeon and duck. The sight suggested the thought that no man need starve in this country, so abundant seemed the supplies of animal life. Here we waited, and in the course of half-an-hour the remainder came up with their horses blown, one of the party having a piece of guanaco meat hanging to his saddle. This was José Marinero, one of the hybrids, who had succeeded in lazoing a guanaco, at which he appeared intensely delighted. The 'man,' as I had previously supposed, proved imaginary. I regretted not being up at the death, as it turned out that José had been close to us, but hidden from sight by a rise. After a pleasant and refreshing rest and a draught of café Quillota (parched corn meal and water), we resumed our route north. After leaving the lagoon, a scarcely perceptible slope ascended from the valley, and a more undulating course was traversed until we reached a small cañon, which, after a gradual descent dipped down between walls a hundred feet high, sloping up at either hand, and finishing in a rounded summit leading to the high plain. 'Here,' said J'aria, 'there is no firing, and those *stupid* Indian women actually carry loads of it from the next stage.' But the event proved that the Indians were wiser than ourselves. Following this we arrived at another cañon running at right angles, east and west, on one of the grass-covered sides of which we observed a couple of horses feeding in a hollow which looked more verdant than the rest of the ground, but the animals being caught and examined proved unsound and useless. In the bottom of the cañon there flowed a small but deep stream spreading into lagoons in places. We crossed this and encamped on the northern side, and found J'aria's words, as to no fuel to be found about this valley, verified, much to our discomfort. Towards evening we went out and shot some ducks, but having no fire to cook with, were content to turn in on meal and water. During the night the tent pole, having been first soaked with rain and then frozen, snapped in two, and down came the spread of wet canvas; and altogether we did not spend a very pleasant time.

Misfortunes never come single; at daylight no horses were to be seen, and we had to wait until near ten o'clock before they turned up. During this interval we burnt the tent pegs and some chips from the tent pole, and raised sufficient fire to make coffee. J'aria informed me that this cañon extends from the Cordillera to the sea, but runs in a tortuous manner, and we afterwards again struck either the main line or some cañon leading from it. Having scaled the precipitous banks, we headed towards a range of peaked hills, curiously resembling one another, and after passing down one or two more cañons, where we refreshed ourselves with the berries of a barberry (Berberis axifolia), called by the Chilians califate, and also saw plenty of the red and white tea-berries, so common in the Falklands, we entered a wide plain or valley, at the farther end of which rose a peculiar pointed hill, one of a range that stretched away east and west, pierced by a pass. In the midst of it a huge square flat rock shone white in the sunlight, forming a striking object: it looked like a megalith, deposited by giants to cover the grave of some deceased hero. Others of less dimensions lay strewn here and there, giving somewhat of a graveyard aspect to the scene. As we advanced the ground was encumbered with rocks and scoriæ lying in heaps in all directions, making it very difficult travelling for the horses, and on arriving at the hills themselves their appearance was decidedly volcanic. The whole immediate vicinity of this range of hills presented a peculiarly wild, blasted, and weird appearance; nevertheless ostriches and guanaco were observable in great quantities. My first thought on passing one hill, where, among the other fantastic forms into which the rocks had been tossed, was a natural corral, or circle of huge fragments, built with apparent regularity, but of superhuman dimensions, was, 'What a hell this must have been when the volcanoes were in an active state, belching out the streams of lava and showers of rock, and that perhaps at no distant period!' While at Santa Cruz, Casimiro told me of an active volcano situated at a distance and in a direction which would fix it as belonging to this range. Formerly its neighbourhood had been frequented by the Indians, as the guanaco resorted thither in great numbers during the winter; but the Indians' horses had most of them been poisoned by drinking the water of a stream close to the range, and soon after all the toldos were shaken down by an earthquake or the vibration of an explosion, and since then they had not ventured to go near the place. Casimiro and Gonzalez had, however, subsequently ascended the volcano, and had killed numbers of guanaco in the neighbourhood. It was also mentioned that when they were encamped on the Cuheyli, or Coy Inlet River, tremendous volumes of thick black smoke, rolling from the west, enveloped the Indians and terrified them exceedingly. No signs were afterwards found of burned pasture, and it was conjectured that the Canoe Indians of the Chonos Archipelago had fired the western forests, but it was much more likely to have been due to volcanic eruption. While trotting along the defile through these hills formed by a chasm, with perpendicular walls of rock rising on each hand, as evenly scarped as the sides of a railway cutting, I observed several caves, which J'aria had a tradition the Indians formerly used as dwelling places. This pass led into another valley still more rugged and strewn with sharp angular fragments of rock, amongst which stunted shrubs began to appear; and lagoons, some of which were encrusted round the edges with saltpetre, and contained brackish water, might be seen at intervals. Towards evening we encamped by the side of a small lagoon of circular form, with wall-like cliffs rising some 200 feet from its banks, and nearly surrounding it. I took a stroll, rifle in hand, whilst the men were getting firewood; and plenty of guanaco were visible, but I only succeeded in wounding one, which escaped on three legs. Traces of a puma, in the shape of carrion, were also there, but Leon himself was hidden. So I returned empty-handed to the fire, where I found a cheerful supper of wild duck and guanaco meat just ready. The moon was beautiful, and the air just frosty enough to be bracing and exhilarating, so some of us staid smoking and spinning yarns until the small hours. The stories were chiefly of adventures on the Pampas. José narrated how, when in pursuit of a party of runaways in the depth of winter, when the snow lay thick on the ground, he and his comrade rode into a valley where countless guanaco had taken refuge from the storm in the upper heights, and stood huddled together, too benumbed by the cold to attempt to escape, and were slaughtered like oxen in the shambles. In another hunt the party overtook the deserters, housed in the toldo of an Indian, and a fight ensued, ending in the death of one of the pursuers; the deserter who shot him was pistolled, and J'aria and José carried the dead body of their comrade on horseback to the settlement, sixty miles distant, proceeding without a halt all through the night, and accomplishing their ghastly journey by the next morning. J'aria related how he had been drifted in a launch among the ice in the Straits, and carried over to Tierra del Fuego, where they found rocks so magnetic that iron nails adhered to them. He further amused us by a short dissertation on his domestic arrangements; how, when his last wife died he married a Chilote to be mother for his children and wife for him, and he always called her in conversation the 'Madre Muger'—wife mother.

Next morning we started early, and varying our march with one or two races after foxes, which generally met their death in a very short time, and an engagement with a female puma, which one of the men despatched by a splendid revolver shot through the head, traversed some uneven Pampas, with occasional hills, and arrived at the descent of the valley of the Rio Gallegos, where the very remarkable bench formation, afterwards observed on a smaller or larger scale in other Patagonian rivers, first arrested my attention. To the west, some miles away, a high hill, apparently of basalt, the square summit of which with seemingly regular walls and towers mimicked the distant view of an extensive fortress, served as a landmark for the break in the barranca, which formed a natural road, by which we reached the first or upper bench, a mile and a half in width; from this a drop or scarped slope of 50 feet and upwards descended to another terrace or plain of equal extent, and terminating in another fall, at the bottom of which lay the bed of the river; it is fordable in the summer months, I believe, in many places, but when we crossed the water about reached where one's saddle flaps would be if riding on an English saddle. After crossing the ford a halt took place to smoke a pipe, whilst doing which we watched the gyrations of a huge vulture of the condor species; he hovered for some time, and at length boldly settled on a point of rock about a hundred yards distant; so the soldier, whose carbine was always ready, took a shot, but missed, much to the grief of Gallegos, who asserted that the heart of the vulture is a good remedy for certain diseases. We then mounted, and riding about a mile halted for the night by a spring gushing out of a ravine in the slope between the upper and lower benches, where the pasture was good, as J'aria declared that water was scarce for some leagues farther on. The bivouac arranged, José and myself proceeded to try and shoot a guanaco, but the plain was too open, so, after lighting up a bed of dry grass to attract any neighbouring Indians, we very foolishly indulged in a bathe in the river. The water was intensely cold, and the ill effects of this ill-timed indulgence were felt for a long time after. The soldier meanwhile was away on horseback chasing a large herd, but he returned about dusk empty handed. Next morning we started about 9 o'clock, having been, as usual, delayed by the horses having strayed some distance. Ascending the slope we crossed the higher bench, a barren, dreary waste, for about a league, until we came to a lagoon covered with upland geese, and lying just below what may be termed the barranca of the Upper Pampa. Halting here for a smoke and warm to dispel the effects of the intensely cold wind, we were about resuming our route to ascend the steep slope of the upper plains, when large columns of smoke, in answer to the signal fire we had left behind us, rose up to the sky in a N.E. direction. We moved on, and arriving at the summit of the ascent, looked eagerly round for signs of the fire, but nothing was visible. The plains lay before us apparently destitute of life, excepting a stray guanaco here and there. J'aria then set light to a neighbouring bush, which gave out dense clouds of black smoke, and in a few minutes this was answered in the same direction as that previously observed. A horseman was at length espied galloping towards us, who proved to be an Indian named Sam, son of the chief Casimiro, who has been mentioned in the missionary reports. After conversing for a short time with J'aria and Gallegos, he turned to me and said, in English, 'How do you do?' I speak little Anglishe,' which he had learned during a visit to the Falklands, where also he had acquired his sobriquet of Sam Slick. He then galloped away at full speed, and brought up his companions, who had been concealed from view in a neighbouring hollow; the party consisted of two men and a boy, and two women, all mounted, and apparently having just finished hunting, as they had plenty of fresh guanaco meat with them. We halted by a bush, and in a few minutes had a fire kindled, and the pipe being handed round, I had an opportunity of observing them closely. The men were fine muscular specimens. One, whom they called Henrique, was a Fuegian, formerly, I believe, a captive, but now doctor, or wizard. He travelled with this party separate from the remainder of the tribe on account of some suspicion of his having caused the death of a chief. One of the men, taller than the others, was a Tehuelche. The boy was bright looking and intelligent, and it afterwards appeared that Don Luiz Buena had kept him for some time, vainly endeavouring to teach him Spanish. They were very cordial, and especially forced on me more meat than I could carry; but there was a certain constraint visible in their manners, probably owing to their being conscious of some dealings with the deserters, whom J'aria counselled them to despatch whenever they might meet with them. The women carried bottles of water, which they readily gave us, to our great refreshment and relief, for we were all parched with thirst.

Gallegos asked Sam whether he was willing to guide us to Santa Cruz, J'aria not being over certain of the route. The tracks made by the guanacos are easily mistaken by almost anyone but an Indian for the trail of 'chinas,' or caravans of women and laden horses; and this, combined with the want of landmarks on the Pampas and the confusing succession of hills closely resembling each other, renders it only too easy to lose the right direction. As examples of this, out of ten deserters of whom the party was in search, six were never more heard of. Our guide J'aria himself, when travelling from Santa Cruz to the colony, lost his way, and would inevitably have starved had he not fortunately been fallen in with by a party of Indians. Sam having agreed to come with our party, we bid adieu to the Indians, who, in return for their presents of meat, were gratified with a little tobacco, and rode off. Suddenly a fox started up from a neighbouring bush. The soldier giving chase, Sam shouted, 'Stop, I'll show you:' at the same time putting spurs to his horse, and cutting Reynard off, he put his hand to his waist-belt, drew out his bolas, gave them two turns round his head, and in another minute the fox was lying dead, with his ribs crushed completely in where the metal ball had struck him. Under the directions of our new guide, who rode ahead with me, we traversed a succession of high barren plains, sinking into frequent irregular hollows, without streams, but usually containing lagoons of salt or brackish water, until, about 4 p.m., we descended into the valley of Rio Cuheyli, or the river, which debouches at Coy Inlet. The bench formation, though noticeable, is not here so decidedly marked. For some time we pursued the trail in an orderly march; but an ostrich springing nearly under our horses' feet, and escaping over some marshy swamp, where horses could not follow, roused Sam's hunting propensities, and he proposed to myself, the soldier, and José to leave the path—which he said, with emphatic disdain, was good for women, not for men—and ride up the barranca to see him ball an ostrich; so having regained the Pampa, we formed into line, about two hundred yards apart, to drive a certain area of ground down to a point where there was a gentle slope to the valley, so as to meet the advancing cavalcade of the rest of our party. We saw nothing except one ostrich vanishing at great speed towards the valley at another point, and a pair of doves, which I remarked with interest; so we returned to the track, and as night was closing in, pushed on, wishing to cross the ford of the river and encamp on the other side. At seven o'clock, having reached a nice spring flowing from the barranca, where there was firewood in profusion, Gallegos ordered a halt, although Sam wished to proceed, observing that the moon was so bright it was 'all the same as day.' We accordingly encamped for the night, after making a good supper off guanaco meat, which was a pleasant change after our previous charqui. The valley of the Cuheyli slightly indicates the bench formation, though it does not present so distinctly marked terraces as those which border the Gallegos River; but the lowest or river plain, which is nearly two leagues wide in the neighbourhood of the ford, is of a more fertile character, the pasture being luxuriant and good. One or two of the springs—notably the one the water of which, contrary to our guide's advice and example, we drank—had a strong taste of iron, which caused all the party to suffer from internal derangement; and Sam stated that near our encampment there was a deposit of the black earth with which the Indians paint their bodies. Starting early, after a night of severe frost, we soon struck the ford. Our guide had vanished; but while rearranging the packs, we saw a volume of black smoke rising to the east, caused by Sam, who, having thus signalled his countrymen, rejoined us on the march across the slightly ascending plain. We then observed numerous Indians galloping in our direction, and crossing the stream at various parts, as J'aria remarked, quite regardless of fords. We halted, and were soon surrounded by about forty or more, most of them riding useful-looking horses barebacked. As they appeared very friendly, Gallegos gave them some biscuit and charqui; their chiefs—the head cacique being a nephew of Casimiro—forming them into a semi-circle, in tolerably good order, to receive the present. There were undoubtedly some very tall men amongst them, but what struck me particularly was their splendid development of chest and arms. Although the wind was very sharp, many of them had their mantles thrown back in a careless way, leaving their naked chests exposed to the air, and appeared not the least incommoded. They readily recognised me for an Englishman, coming and examining me closely, and asking for tobacco with a broad grin on their faces, exposing a wonderfully clean and regular set of teeth. My gratifying their importunate requests for tobacco made Sam very jealous, and for some time he bothered me with remarks such as 'Me very cold, no got poncho,' 'Me no got knife, me no got "pellon"' (saddle-cloth), until, finding it useless to beg, he relapsed into sullen silence. A smoke of the pipe, however, brought him back to his usual cheerful temper, and as we galloped along he chanted an Indian song, which consisted of the words 'Ah ge lay loo, Ah ge lay loo,' expressed in various keys.

After a ride of some leagues in a rather more open but still undulating country, a break in the Pampas was reached. Hills of irregular and picturesque outlines, with labyrinthine valleys or ravines, not running in parallel order, but communicating with each other, occupied an extensive district, and though travelling was considerably more difficult, yet the change in the aspect of nature was grateful after the barren monotony of the plains.

We halted in an Indian encampment, situated in a valley underneath a peaked hill called 'Otiti,' where there were pools of fresh and salt water in close proximity. Amongst the incense and thorn bushes, which grow at intervals in these regions, we passed to-day another description of shrub with a thick rough bark, which is readily detached and leaves a long rattail-like sort of twig. From the Rio Gallegos the soil had become generally of a yellower colour than on the south side of that river, although in the valleys and hollows dark peaty earth was generally to be found, and the surface of the Pampas had assumed a more desolate appearance, being strewn with small pebbles, and studded with bushes—generally of a thorny species. Round clumps of prickly thistles, which burn like tinder on applying a lighted match—and a few stray tufts of withered grass, only made more desolate the hungry barrenness of the deserts, over which the wind blew with cutting violence, yet they are the home of large herds of guanaco, ostriches, puma, and armadillo, though the latter were at this period comfortably hybernating.

Next morning no horses were visible, and as time went on till ten o'clock without any appearance we all began to suspect Indian treachery. Sam volunteered the remark that if they (the Indians) had played us such a trick, he would go and clear all their animals out the following evening. This threat there was fortunately no occasion for him to put into execution, as the troop proved only to have strayed into another valley. As we were now nearing Santa Cruz, which the last of the Indians were just leaving, having completed their trade and finished all the grog, we saw numerous columns of smoke, caused by their hunting parties. After passing the broken ground and reaching the high Pampa, Sam and myself rode on ahead, amusing ourselves by fruitlessly chasing guanaco or ostrich, but Sam's dexterity with the bolas was frustrated by his being mounted on a horse belonging to the expedition and unused to this work. Towards evening, after again passing numerous salt lagoons, we came to a descent of 300 or 400 feet leading to a valley containing a large salina, and halting, made our fire by the side of a spring, near which, Sam informed me, were the graves of two Indians, which he mentioned with the deepest respect and in an awe-stricken undertone.

Our signal smoke, which was as much to attract Indians as to give the direction of our route to Gallegos and J'aria, was soon responded to from the opposite hills on the northern side of the valley, and shortly a line of mounted women and children descended the slope in front, making for our fire, which Sam informed me was their intended camping place. We advanced to meet them, and Sam conversed in their tongue, interpreting to me that they had left Santa Cruz two days previously, and that Don Luiz P. B. had quitted his settlement on the island to sail in his schooner to Buenos Ayres; while the Northern Indians, encamped to the north of Santa Cruz, with whom I hoped to proceed to the Rio Negro, had no intention of marching until the ensuing spring. On leaving those ladies, amongst whom was a young and rather pretty girl, I lifted my cap in salute, which called forth, a burst of laughter from the whole group and cries of 'Anglish, Anglish!' amidst which we rode off to join the remainder of our party, who were crossing the valley to the eastward, having intentionally deviated from the straight route; and although Sam used every effort to induce Gallegos to stop at the Indian encampment, the latter wisely determined to proceed about a league farther, knowing that a halt here would cause a considerable inroad to be made in the stock of provisions, which, in view of the return journey, with perhaps an increased party, it was desirable to avoid. We accordingly left the sheltered valley and encamped on the plateau in an exposed situation near a lagoon, the ice of which had to be broken to secure a supply of water. The frost was keen, and the tent afforded but a partial protection from the biting wind; so that the economical foresight of our leader resulted in all the party spending the coldest night hitherto experienced by us.

During the evening we were visited by several Indians, bringing presents of ostrich and guanaco meat. I was presented by the soldier with a piece of the gizzard (the tid bit), which he had cooked on the end of his ramrod; but I must confess I did not appreciate it at the time, though later on in my journey I learnt to relish this and other strange delicacies. Amongst the Indians who gave us the benefit of their company this evening was 'Pedro el Platero,' mentioned in Mr. Gardener's mission book; also an old squaw rejoicing in the name of 'La Reina Victoria' (Queen Victoria), who was the occasion of much chaff, my Chilian friends declaring I ought to salute the sovereign of the Pampas in due form; but having obtained a charge and a light for her pipe, all she required, she was soon lost sight of in the dark. We gladly left the camp early the ensuing morning, the cold continuing unabated; the wind blew strong in our faces, and though from the northward, was so keen that Sam and myself kept galloping on and kindling fires at intervals.

Thus we rode on over a tract of country surpassing in desolation all the districts hitherto traversed. As far as the eye could reach stretched a level waste unrelieved by even an eminence or hollow; the aspect of the low withered shrubs, coarse parched grass, and occasional patches of pebble-strewn ground which for thirty miles wearied the eye with dreary sameness, produced an extraordinary feeling of depression, which was afterwards recalled when journeying through the Travisia, bordering the Rio Negro, which this district resembles, though on a smaller scale. Occasional frozen lagoons, doubtless supplied by rainfall, only added to the desert aspect of this trackless wilderness. The situation was not improved by Sam pulling up and remarking that he was by no means sure that he had not lost himself. The only variety was afforded by an unlucky fox which we chased till he escaped, as he thought, on to the ice of a lagoon, but the treacherous surface gave way, and poor Reynard, after a vigorous struggle, sank out of reach of a lazo. At last, about two o'clock, the desert terminated in a cliff rising from the valley at our feet, and we looked down upon the winding river of the Santa Cruz.

Having waited till the rest came up, we descended by a gorge to the valley, when, after refreshing ourselves by a drink of water, we struck into a trail which followed the river downwards. We were all in high spirits at the prospect of a speedy and felicitous conclusion to our journey; and J'aria was continually questioned as to the distance of the settlement. His answer was invariably 'a league;' and we rode along vainly expecting every moment to see the place, rounding innumerable promontories or points where the barranca advanced into the valley. Each of these projecting cliffs, which stood like outposts of the Pampas, J'aria declared in succession to be the last, Sam all the while maintaining a dignified silence, until at length, at 7.30, when we had almost despaired of ever arriving, we came to the ford opposite the island of the settlement, and a barking of dogs saluted our ears. After Sam had hailed, an answer came back, that if we were going across that night we must look sharp, as the tide was flowing. We accordingly proceeded to cross at once, narrowly escaping having to swim our horses, which on a cold frosty night would have been anything but a pleasant business.

My ideas as to the size and extent of the settlement—and it must he confessed my visions of a 'cheerer,' and even of wine, to put some warmth into my chilled frame—were sadly dispelled by the reality; the thriving, though small, town of my imagination being represented by one house, and all wine and liquor proving to have been exhausted. But this was fully made up for by discovering in Mr. Clarke—or, as the Indians called him, 'Clakalaka'—an old acquaintance, whom I had known some years previously in the Falklands. His utter surprise at the sudden appearance of one whom he thought far away may be imagined. But, to my great delight, he thoroughly approved of the proposed excursion. His cordial welcome and hot coffee soon cheered up our spirits, and when warmed and rested we discussed my plans. It appeared that the Indians had not reported wrong as to Don Luiz Buena's movements and the intentions of the Northern party; but Mr. Clarke believed that the schooner was still detained in the river mouth waiting for a fair wind, and undertook to send off a messenger to communicate with him: my object being to obtain permission to reside in the settlement until the return of the schooner, so as to equip myself with stores as presents for the Tehuelches. After an agreeable 'confab,' I turned in on a shakedown on the floor, well satisfied with having accomplished the first stage, and deriving a good omen for the remainder of the journey from this successful trip to Santa Cruz.

1. Cunningham, p.133

II

SANTA CRUZ

OUR first business next day was to despatch a messenger to board the schooner, if she should prove to be still in the mouth of the river. My Chilian friends had found some of the deserters, who been taken into employment, and subsequently detained as close prisoners by the Mayor Domo, at the instance of a serjeant sent round from Punta Arena in the schooner, to solicit Don Luiz's assistance in their capture. About noon Casimiro, soi-disant chief of the Tehuelches and father of Sam Slick, rode in from a hunting excursion, mounted on a tall, shapely horse, and carrying a guanaco on his saddle. I was formally introduced, and my plans and purpose fully explained to him; and soon after Orkeke, the cacique of the party of Northern Tehuelches, encamped on the Rio Chico, arrived. His consent was necessary to enable me to accompany them in their journey, and by means of Casimiro as an interpreter, as the chief spoke but little Spanish, my request was preferred. He confirmed the statement of Mr. Clarke, that his people intended to winter in their present encampment, and then proceed northwards; but did not seem at all disposed to welcome the addition of an Englishman to his party, urging the difficult nature of the road, length of time, chances of fights, &c., &c. However, I hoped that during the enforced delay opportunities would arise of improving our acquaintance, and obtaining his consent. I was much struck with the grave and dignified bearing of the old chief. Standing fully six feet, and with a well-proportioned muscular frame, no one would have guessed him to have passed his 60th year; and whether vaulting on a bare-backed steed, or leading the chase, he displayed an agility and endurance equal to that of any of the younger men: his thick black hair was slightly streaked with grey; and the bright intelligent eyes, aquiline nose, and thin firm lips were very unlike the popular idea of Patagonian features; a retreating forehead rather marred the expression of his face, which was, however, grave and thoughtful, and at times strikingly intellectual. Months passed in his company gave me afterwards ample opportunity of studying his powers of reflection, which were great, and often found expression in pithy and amusing sayings. Although particularly neat in his dress, and cleanly in his habits, he was troubled, like all the Indians, with vermin; and one night he roused me up to have a smoke, and after sitting for some time, apparently lost in deep thought, he remarked, 'Musters, lice never sleep!' He would sometimes, but rarely, indulge in intoxication, but never quarrelled, and it was an understood thing that either he or his brother Tankelow should on occasions of a general drinking bout remain sober to protect their families. He was himself childless, and had adopted a little terrier named Ako, which enjoyed the place and honours of an only child; but he displayed great affection towards his nephews and nieces, some one or other of whom might often be seen in his arms on a march, or after the return from the chase. During our first acquaintance I was most pleased when, as often happened, he joined our little circle, and in the company of his old friend, Mr. Clarke, unbent from his gravity and laughed and talked in a way that seemed quite foreign to the usually serious chief. It must be confessed that he was jealous and suspicious, and a little stingy, preferring to increase rather than lessen his large stock of horses, gear, and arms; but from the time I became his guest his conduct to myself was irreproachable.

In the evening the messenger returned; he had of course completely mistaken his instructions, and informed Don Luiz that the Englishman desired to proceed in the schooner to Buenos Ayres, and accordingly a boat arrived with the morning flood tide to take me off. Mr. Clarke good naturedly undertook to go himself and explain matters; and returned with a kind message, offering me quarters and every hospitality if I chose to remain in the settlement for the next two months, at the end of which period the schooner might be expected to return. Lieut. Gallegos strongly urged me to accompany him back to Punta Arena, painting in strong colours the tedium and discomfort of a winter at Santa Cruz. But it was plain that the opportunity of cultivating the acquaintance and securing the confidence of Orkeke would thus be thrown away, and with it the prospect of traversing the country. Gallegos believed that this plan was fraught with danger, and indeed almost certain destruction; but as I was immovable, we took an affectionate farewell of each other. He and all his party had treated me, an utter stranger, with the greatest kindness, and I bade adieu to them as true comrades. They departed on their return journey, taking with them the four prisoners, who, however, are destined to appear again in these pages. These men had undergone much hardship to obtain the liberty of which they seemed again deprived; three of them had managed to secure a horse, and walking and riding in turns had found their way to the Indians. Two of them, Olate and Rosa, the latter, though a mere boy, with a thoroughly evil and murderous countenance, were incurably bad; but Mena, a youth of nineteen, attracted one's sympathy by his handsome frank face and cleanly smart appearance; the fourth, Arica, had made his way on foot from Punta Arena to Santa Cruz, without any knowledge of the country, and only guided by a vague notion of the existence of the settlement to the north. He had for twenty-seven days followed the line of the sea-coast, subsisting on shell fish and sea-birds' eggs; the toil and hardships thus undergone must have been indescribable, and his eventual safe arrival was a miracle of patient endurance. He brought in news of the loss of a tender to the schooner, a decked launch, in which Captain Warren and three men had sailed from Staten Land and been no more heard of; of their fate there was now little doubt, as he had found her dingy cast up on the beach, and a piece of the mainsail out of which he had supplied himself with clothes.

The promising *élève* of the mission, Sam Slick, also accompanied the party. Before his departure he offered to give a specimen of his education by singing a hymn, with a broad hint that grog was a fitting accompaniment; but as none was forthcoming, we lost the chance of being edified by his performance.

We watched the cavalcade till it disappeared in the distance on the upper plains, and then returned to the station, where I settled myself to pass the ensuing three months of the Patagonian winter. The settlement or trading station of Santa Cruz consists of only three houses, built on an island called 'Pabon,' marked as Middle Island, in Islet Reach, in Fitzroy's chart. It is owned by Don Luiz P. Buena, who holds it by virtue of a grant from the Argentine Government, which has also conferred on him the commission of captain in the navy, with power to prevent all foreign sealers from trespassing on the valuable seal fisheries on the coast. The island is about a mile and a half long, and has an average breadth of some 350 yards. Access is obtained from the south shore by a ford, about fifty yards across, only passable at low water. The northern channel is wider and deeper, and the swiftness of the current renders it impassable save by a boat, which is moored ready to ferry over Indians desirous of trading, and is also useful for bringing wood for fuel, which is not obtainable on the island. About a hundred yards from the ford stands the principal house, substantially built of bricks, with tiled roof, containing three rooms, and a sort of porch to shelter a nine-pounder, commanding the entrance. It is farther defended by a stockade, over which floats the Argentine flag, and beyond it a fosse, which is filled with water by the spring tides. The object of these fortifications is to afford protection in case of the Indians proving troublesome when under the influence of rum. Though Mr. Clarke narrated some queer scenes he had witnessed, his excellent management had hitherto obviated any danger, and the fairness of his dealings with them had secured their friendship, a regular tariff with equitable prices having been fixed, and scrupulously adhered to, by which their barter of ostrich feathers and peltries was regulated; and although they are keen bargainers often spending two or three hours in debating the

STATION ON PABON ISLAND, RIO SANTA CRUZ

price to be given, they appreciated the fairness with which they were treated. A second house was situated about fifty yards off, and being generally used as a store, bore the name of the Almacen: at this time being empty, one room served as a sleeping-place for some of the men, and the other had been given up for the accommodation of Casimiro and his family. A third house, which stood at the eastern end of the island, was unoccupied. Near it a small plot had been tilled, and potatoes, turnips, and other vegetables had been successfully raised. At the time of my visit no corn had been tried, but a subsequent experimental sowing of one and a half fanegas[1] gave a field, though little pains were bestowed on the crop, of twenty fanegas. As the lower part of the island is liable to be overflowed at high springs, a ditch had been cut across to drain off the water, and there was consequently no lack of irrigation. The ground was covered with stunted bushes, and the small spike-thorn round thistle, and coarse grass. The few sheep appeared to thrive well, but, decreased very sensibly in number during the winter, as on days when game was scarce one fell a victim to the ravenous appetite engendered by the keen air of Patagonia. A numerous troop of horses grazed on the mainland, in a tract below the Southern Barranca, called the 'Potrero,' where the grass, though coarse, grew in rank luxuriance. When wanted for hunting, the entire stud was brought across the river in the morning and driven into the corral; but ordinarily one alone was kept on the island ready for emergencies.

It should be mentioned that a small stock of cattle, and also some pigs, had been imported; these, however, being necessarily left to graze on the mainland, had wandered, and become wild; the cattle probably falling victims to the Indian hunters; but the pigs will no doubt multiply, and become the founders of a race of hogs, destined hereafter to add pig-sticking to the amusements of the future settlers or of the wandering Tehuelches.

Above the island of Pabon there are several smaller islets, but as they are liable to be overflowed by the highest tides, they cannot, without artificial drainage, be made available for tillage. From one which had been occupied and tilled with root-crops, we obtained a quantity of well-grown turnips. It was a singular mistake of the Spaniards to form a settlement at Port St. Julian and overlook the far superior advantages presented by Santa Cruz. The plains and islands of the latter present good grazing grounds and tillage lands, as well as a site for a town secure from sudden Indian surprises; and as regards fitness for a shipping station, there is no comparison between the two localities, as ships can be beached at Santa Cruz in a sheltered place with the flood-tide; while the timber, in search of which Viedma made his expedition, was to be had in abundance by ascending the river. At the present time the knowledge of the navigation of the Straits would make it much easier and cheaper to import timber from Punta Arena than to send lumberers into the Cordillera and raft the timber down to Santa Cruz.

Near the potrero, on the southern shore, there is a natural salt lake or salina, which must have been overlooked by the Beagle expedition, as Mr. Darwin fixes the southern limits of salinas at Port St. Julian. In the summer, and until the winter rains and snow set in, an inexhaustible supply of excellent salt can be obtained. It is at present worked only to furnish, besides the salt for home use, what is required for the annual sealing fishery; but if labour were more abundant, the salt would be found to be a valuable article of export to the Falkland Islands; the salina being situated less than half a mile from the beach, where there is good anchorage.

The river also yields abundant supplies of fish—a species of bass and others—which when cured keep well: some which had been cured over a year proved excellent. These might be profitably exported to Rio Janeiro, &c., where cured fish are always in demand.

Notwithstanding these natural advantages, Santa Cruz could hardly at this period be considered a settlement. Subsequently to my visit, two Frenchmen from Buenos Ayres proposed to try sheep farming in the valley, but with what result I have not heard. As already mentioned, the station existed as a depôt for sealing, and as a trading post, to which the Tehuelches resorted to exchange their ostrich feathers, and puma, guanaco, and ostrich skins, for tobacco, sugar, ammunition, and above all, rum. There was little or no trade going on during the absence of the schooner, as all the stores had been exhausted; but after the summer campaign some of the Tehuelches invariably resort thither, and the vicinity has always been a favourite winter quarters. The missionaries, Messrs. Schmid and Hart, endeavoured to avail themselves of this opportunity for essaying the conversion and civilisation of the Indians. They resided for some time in 1863 at a spot near Weddell Bluff, about ten miles from the mouth of the river. To quote Mr. Sterling's description, the station was at the mouth of a valley which 'retreats towards the south-west for a considerable distance inland; a stream of pure water flows perennially through it, and a broad belt of grass, offering fine pasture for cattle, gives a cheerful, fertile aspect to the low land; the hills on either side are intersected with ravines, or lift up their bronzed faces out of some intervening dale, and refresh the air with the aroma of shrubs and plants growing everywhere about them.'

This was written after a visit in the summer month of January, and the picture drawn presents the landscape in its fairest colours; very different from its bleak aspect as viewed by myself in the winter. This valley still bears the name of Los Misionarios, but this is the only existing trace of their settlement. Mr. Schmid, however, during his sojourn and journeys with a party of the Indians, compiled a vocabulary of the Tsoneca language, as spoken by the southern Tehuelches. Their plan for establishing trade at Santa Cruz, in order to secure the regular visits of the Indians, was not approved of by the managers of the mission, and they were obliged to abandon the scene of their praiseworthy but unsuccessful efforts—to instruct at least 'the little bright-faced Patagonian children,' of whom they speak in their journals with warm affection.

The counter attractions of rum supplied by a trader who visited the river were felt by Mr. Schmid to be very destructive of his influence, but it cannot be doubted that their store, if established, would have had no chance against any rival that supplied rum to his customers; for though there are many exceptions, the Indians too eagerly expend the spoils of their hunting and industry in liquor. Their wives, however, when they accompany them, take care to manage their business with discretion, and reserve sufficient stock to barter for more useful and innocent luxuries as well as necessaries. There is no doubt that in the event of the future development of this settlement, it might serve as a *point d'appui* to raise the Tehuelches to the level of a more cultivated and settled mode of existence; but speculations on this point are not within my province, and it is time to introduce the members of the party with whom my winter was agreeably spent on the island of Pabon. With Don Luiz P. Buena and his amiable and accomplished señora I subsequently made acquaintance, which ripened into friendship; but though his guest, I was at present personally unknown to him. In his absence, his representative, Mr. Clarke, who, as already mentioned, was an old acquaintance, did all he could to make me feel at home. He was a handsome young fellow of twenty-five, and an excellent specimen of the versatile and cosmopolitan New Englander, 'raised' in Salem, Massachusetts, where he had been brought up as a builder, though he afterwards 'shipped himself on board of a ship.' In his nautical life he had been mate of the Snow Squall, in a homeward voyage from Shanghai, when she was chased off the Cape of Good Hope by the Alabama, and but for the pluck of the captain and crew, and the wonderful sailing powers of the craft, another item would have been added to Mr. Adams's 'little bill.' As it was, the beautiful vessel fairly outsailed the swift steamer. The steadiness of the crew, and their well-deserved attachment to the captain, were most strongly proved on this occasion. As there was no alternative between putting in for water at St. Helena—where it was too probable the Alabama would pounce upon the prize—and running home upon half a pint per diem each man, the captain left it to the crew to decide, and they chose the latter course.

Mr. Clarke had spent three months travelling and hunting in company with the Tehuelches, which had made him a most expert hand with lazo or bolas, and well acquainted with the Indian character; and it was pleasant to hear that he entertained a very high opinion of their intelligence and generous dispositions. He treated them with fairness and considerate kindness, and they repaid him by confidence and friendship.

Five other *employés* made up the rest of our party. No social distinctions, however, prevailed, and the inhabitants of Pabon lived in pleasant equality. The charge of the dogs and horses, and the duty of supplying meat, devolved

on two: Gonzalez, a gaucho, a native of Patagones, who was as much at home
in the schooner on a sealing excursion, as in the saddle balling an ostrich;
and Juan Isidoro, a swarthy little man whose sparkling black eyes told
of his Indian blood, a native of Santiago del Estero; he had been sent as a
soldier to Rio Negro, whence he had managed to desert, and make his way
with Orkeke's Indians to the settlement. Next comes Juan Chileno, a bright,
fresh-complexioned youth of nineteen years, to look at whom was refreshing,
after the swarthy and weather physiognomies of the others. Then Antonio, a
Portuguese, by turns gaucho, whaler, or sealer, always ready with a song or a
merry jest, and on occasion equally quick with his knife. Holstein furnished
the last, but by no means least important; a strong-built, good-natured rather
stupid fellow, generally selected as the butt of the rest, who always styled him
'El Cookè,' a sobriquet earned by his many voyages in that capacity on board
various ships. Curiously enough he proved to possess information on a topic to
me of great interest, as he had been one of a party which, about a year previous
to my visit, had ascended the river Santa Cruz to its source. The expedition was
organised by an American well acquainted with the Californian mining, who
proposed to explore the mineral resources of the valley. Unfortunately, during
the ascent of the river, a quarrel broke out, and the American left the others,
and found his way alone to the Indians, thence returning to Santa Cruz. The
loss of the only man capable of scientific observation rendered their journey
almost useless; still the party proceeded, and about midsummer reached the
lake, near which they remained some days, but were unable to penetrate the
thick forests beyond its shores. In the valley they found meat tins and other
traces of Fitzroy's expedition. El Cookè described the river as running from the
lake in many small streams, and flowing over a rocky bed. The lake, which was
covered with wild fowl, had floating ice upon it, and large glaciers were visible
in the neighbouring mountains, while the weather experienced was cold, with
continuous drizzling rain. His account confirmed my own conjectures as to the
cause of the great difference between the periods of the highest floods in the
Rio Gallegos, which is at its height in December and January, and the Santa
Cruz, which is then at its lowest. This is owing to the lateness of the period at
which the ice breaks up in the lake Viedma, situated, as it probably is, on a high
plateau. About the lake the explorers found traces of herds of large deer, and
always in close proximity those of a large fox or wolf, but they did not succeed
in killing any. A specimen of the only mineral brought back appeared to be iron
pyrites embedded in quartz. The journey from the lake to the settlement would
require eleven days for baggage horses, but could be performed by horsemen
within four. Of course the information was not too clear or reliable, but El
Cookè, though not brilliant, seemed to possess the Northern quality of telling
the truth, by the absence of which the Southern and Indian natures are, to say
the least of it, often characterised. El Cookè was fond of hard work, and his

greatest enjoyment was to set out in search of fuel, and lay on with his axe in a way that would have done honour to a Canadian lumberer, but was sadly thrown away on the incense bushes of Santa Cruz.

All these men, who had drifted together from various quarters, and, if truth be told, had all 'run,' for obvious reasons, from their own homes, worked by turns at hunting, trading, sealing, and raising salt from the Salina. They received a fixed salary, which, however, generally proved to be balanced by an account with the store for clothes, &c. In sealing expeditions all went shares, like our own mackerel and herring fishermen; while for working at the Salina, extra pay was given and well earned, especially at this time, since it involved sleeping out in the open for several successive nights, and that in a Patagonian May. Such were the companions of my residence at Pabon, besides whom more than a score of dogs of all sorts slept anyhow and anywhere, and followed anybody, giving their masters the preference.

A short time after our arrival, Mr. Clarke took stock of the stores of provision, which could not be replenished until the return of the schooner. The result was that the amount of biscuits and sugar was found to be about equal to a month's consumption. These articles were accordingly divided into equal portions, and each man received his share, to husband or improvidently use, according to his bent. There was abundance of coffee, black beans, tobacco, and maize, which accordingly were used at discretion. The next thing was to accumulate a good stock of fuel before the snow should render it difficult, if not impossible, to transport it.

Every Sunday all hands except one—the cook of the week—left on guard, went hunting, and, as occasion required, during the week, the gauchos would proceed to supply the larder with guanaco or ostrich, the latter being, however, rare. Idleness was unknown; when not hunting, wood-cutting, or salt-raising, manufactures were the order of the day. We picked stones and worked them round for bolas, and covered them with the hide stripped from the hock of the guanaco, the soga or thong connecting the balls being made from the skin of the neck, the method of obtaining it being as follows:—The head having been cut off, and an incision made just above the shoulder, the skin is dragged off in one piece; and after the wool has been picked off, is softened by hand and carefully cut into strips, which are closely plaited. Of this leather we also made serviceable bridles, lazos, stirrup-leathers, and, in fact, horse-gear generally. Sometimes we would have a fit of making pipes, and all hands would be busy sawing out wood or hard at work boring the bowls; at others, spurs were the rage, made by the simple Indian method of sticking sharpened nails into two pieces of wood, secured together by thongs fastened under the foot and round the leg; or again, we would work silver, and come out with our knife-sheaths glittering with studs. On non-hunting days, I invariably practised the use of the bolas, and caught almost every shrub on the island.

The evenings were passed in playing the American game of brag. Cash being unknown, and no one being disposed to risk the loss of his gear, the stakes were simply so many black beans to a box of matches; and as much excitement prevailed as if each bean or perota had been a five-dollar piece.

Both in our hunting parties and in the house which he had been allowed to occupy, though he occasionally visited the camp on the Chico, I sedulously cultivated the acquaintance of Casimiro. Both the missionaries and Her Majesty's surveyors have made frequent, and often by no means honourable, mention of this Indian, who has always evinced a wish to conciliate the friendship of the English visitors to Patagonia. His history, as I learned it from himself, was a very curious one, and aptly illustrates the conflicting claims of Chilians and Argentines, and the confused politics of the Indians themselves, his father having been killed in an engagement with the Araucanian or Manzaneros Indians. His mother was a Tehuelche: being an inveterate drunkard, whilst visiting the settlements of Rio Negro she bartered the child for a cask of rum to the governor of the fort, a Frenchman named Viba, who was connected with the slave-trade, for at that period Indians seem to have been made slaves of as well as blacks. Viba had Casimiro christened—whence his name Casimiro Viba—and brought up at the Estancia, or sheep-farm, where he learnt to speak Spanish fluently. When thirteen years old he ran away and rejoined the Tehuelches Indians, with whom he remained in obscurity for some years, until being in the Southern district, near the Chilian colony of Port Famine, he gained the friendship of one Santorin, a native of Patagones, who had been taken captive by the Indians, but having adopted their manners and customs, and marrying one of the tribe, had risen to the position of a chief. Together these two performed a voyage to Chili, to negotiate with the Government in some matters regarding the protection of Port Famine from Indian raids. Santorin died during the voyage, but Casimiro was well received at Santiago by the then President, Señor Bulnés,[2] loaded with honours, and given the rank, pay, and rations of captain in the army. He then returned to Port Famine, where he resided, off and on, for some time. By his own account, he was absent on a hunting excursion when the *émeute* took place which resulted in the destruction of the colony. The old wandering habits appeared to have taken possession of him, for he subsequently returned to the Rio Negro, and having entered the service of the Buenos Ayrean Government, again proceeded to the South. During this time he resided occasionally with the missionaries, during their journey in the South, and at their station at Santa Cruz, and entrusted to them his two sons for the purpose of education. The missionaries soon discovered that his objects were purely selfish, and that he had no idea of allowing others to participate in the advantages they could offer; and I am afraid that the labour and cost bestowed on the boys were thrown away, as neither of them appeared to have profited much by their chances. Sam, indeed, could still sing a hymn if there were grog to the fore, and had a lively recollection of material advantages, often saying, 'He was good man, give me gun,' &c. But the youngest, 'Graviel,' who also understood a little English, was one of the laziest of the lazy, and had very undefined notions as to *meum* and *tuum*, as personal experience taught me.

In 1865 Casimiro made a voyage to Buenos Ayres, where the Government on this occasion recognised him as head chief of the Tehuelches, and assigned him the rank and pay of Lieut.-Colonel in the Argentine Army. He was then despatched, in company with an Argentine named Mendoza, to form a settlement at Gregorio Bay. They travelled by land as far as Santa Cruz, at which place Mendoza disappeared, being supposed to have lost himself, but in reality having been killed by an Indian, jealousy being, I believe, the cause of the murder. With his right-hand man gone, Casimiro abandoned himself to drinking, a habit which, as Mr. Cunningham mentions, he had before acquired—perhaps by hereditary development—and ultimately became reduced to the state of poverty in which I found him, owning but two horses for himself, his wife, daughter, and son, with hardly any gear. Indeed, he would have been reduced to great straits but for the kindness of Don Luiz and Mr. Clarke, who, for old acquaintance sake, helped him as much as possible; though his habitual drunkenness made it useless to give him anything valuable whilst there was liquor to be had, as he would exchange anything for drink. As it was my object to have a friend in camp, I made friends with him, and tried to induce him to go north to the Rio Negro, which he at length agreed to do, although he was in great fear of getting into trouble about the loss or death of Mendoza. This man when sober was quick and intelligent, and a shrewd politician. His extensive connections by marriage with all the chiefs, including Rouke and Calficurà, gave him considerable influence. He was also an expert worker in various Indian arts, such as making saddles, pipes, spurs, lazos, and other gear. He was a powerfully built man, standing fully six feet in his potro boots, with a not unpleasing expression of face, although he had a scar or two which did not add to his beauty. Of his personal bravery ample proof will afterwards be given; but, like all drunkards, he was uncertain and not to be depended on. This veritable old Blue Beard informed me that he had been married six times; certainly, if all his wives were of the appearance and disposition of his last venture, it is not to be wondered at if he disposed of the former ones; for an uglier, dirtier, more contumacious old hag never burdened the earth with her weight, owing probably to which latter quality, or quantity, she never, if she could possibly help it, quitted her room. Early in June an Indian, known in Santa Cruz as El Sourdo, or the left-handed man, came across the river and pitched his toldo on the island. He was the husband of two wives, who lived together in perfect felicity and took care of one another's children. This Indian was, as most of them are, very ingenious in working wood and silver, and was a good addition to our hunting parties; he also quickly learned to play at brag. Casimiro would never descend from his lofty pinnacle of self-importance so far as to enter the kitchen when the general revels were held, but occasionally joined Mr. Clarke and myself at supper and sat telling stories for an hour or two.

The sketch of our life at Pabon would be very incomplete without asking the reader to accompany us on a hunting excursion; so I will describe one which took place after El Sourdo had arrived on the island. Game had become very scarce in our immediate vicinity, and our only farinaceous food was black beans varied by maize, which was too troublesome in the preparation to be much used. The meat went wonderfully quickly, so we determined to extend the sphere of the hunting a little more a-field. Accordingly, one fine frosty morning at daylight, the horses were brought up, caught, and saddled; mantles and spurs donned, and eight of us, including the two Indians, Casimiro and El Sourdo, set off to make a circle, i.e. enclose and drive an area of land on the southern shore of the river, finishing at the Missionaries' Valley. Casimiro and Gonzalez accordingly started, and the remainder followed in turn. During our drive down, one guanaco was captured by El Sourdo and Isidoro, and on our arrival near the valley of Los Misionarios I chased a guanaco, but, being without dogs and a tyro with the bolas, failed to capture him. However, on rejoining my companions, who had now finished the circle, I found that they had only killed one ostrich, which, through the carelessness of some of the party, the dogs had mauled to such an extent as to render the greater part of the meat unserviceable. The day had been unusually warm, without any wind. Though a bank of white clouds on the horizon seemed to threaten snow, it was agreed to camp out and try our chance of getting a good supply of meat on the following day; so we proceeded to a sheltered place in the valley, and bivouacked under the lee of a big incense bush, while the horses were turned loose, and a fire was made, on which the remains of the ostrich were soon cooking under the master hand of Casimiro. After supper, which was rather stinted in quantity, we smoked a pipe and lay down to sleep. About three I woke up, feeling, as I thought, a heavy weight pressing on my mantle, and found that above two inches of snow had fallen and that it was still snowing. At daylight it came on to rain, but quickly changed to snow again; so we made a fire and waited for an hour to see if the weather would clear. At last, on a gleam of sickly sunshine appearing, we proceeded to arrange the circle, Casimiro starting first. Emerging from the valley and ascending to the high pampa, we met a terrific gale of wind from the south, driving before it small snow in freezing blasts; but two ostriches jumped up from behind a bush, and Mr. Clarke balled one of them with great dexterity. This was very cheering, as we were all very hungry. But, as it was impossible to face the driving sleet and wind, which prevented us from seeing ten yards before us, we adjourned to the valley, leaving Casimiro, who was not visible, to his own pursuits. Suddenly El Sourdo discovered smoke behind a clump of trees, and, to our great delight, there was our friend before a good fire, nicely sheltered from snow and wind, within an arbour neatly cut out of a bush. We adjourned to the fire and had breakfast; invigorated by which, and encouraged by a lull in the storm, we started off to renew the chase, but soon got separated by the thick snow-storm. Mr. Clarke, El Sourdo, Gonzalez, and myself, who were together, came close upon a herd of guanaco, making for the coast to escape the gale. The dogs gave chase and killed some, others were balled; in fact a regular slaughter took place, and eight or ten carcases were soon lying on the plain. Now came the tedious job of cutting up. I found myself standing alone by a dead guanaco, none of the others being visible, though not fifty yards distant. I proceeded as best I could to arrange the meat, and was about half through the task, with fingers nearly frozen, when I discovered Mr. Clarke and El Sourdo, and shortly after it cleared up, and the remainder of our party, all loaded with meat, arrived. Thus supplied, we turned our faces homewards, and arrived at Santa Cruz a little before sundown, where a steaming kettle of coffee soon dispelled our cold and put us into good spirits.

Mr. Darwin and Admiral Fitzroy have thoroughly described the configuration of the Valley of Santa Cruz and its surroundings, so that a lengthened attempt to portray it is not necessary. I would particularly refer the reader to the accurate and picturesque description by the former of the bench formation which causes the western part of the environs of the river to present the appearance of the shores of former successive estuaries—of a vast river or fiord.

Near the settlement the ascent of the Southern Barranca immediately leads to a level plain extending for the space of couple of miles; then there is another rise of perhaps fifty feet, and another plain, which extends for about the space of a league to a range of successive ridges, which we called the Blue Hills from their peculiar appearance on clear days. These, eastwards, lose their elevations, and merge into the undulations of the high Pampa and a rolling cheerless waste of stones, coarse grass, and incense bushes; its uneven surface often traversed by ravines running in various directions. Amongst these hills there is a large lagoon which Casimiro informed me he used to visit whilst residing with the missionaries for the purpose of procuring wild fowl, of which there were then great numbers, but they had latterly given up this resort. There are other lagoons scattered at intervals in the before-mentioned plains, which, during the winter, were frozen, and the beautifully smooth ice often caused Mr. Clarke and myself to long for a pair of skates; indeed, we tried to manufacture a pair, but without success.

Towards the sea coast from the Blue Hills the slope appears gradual, until nearing the coast, when the plain is intersected by gullies and deep fertile valleys, which render hunting very tedious work, as it is necessary to trust almost entirely to the dogs. Game abounds in this direction, especially during the winter. We made numerous excursions up river, generally staying away from the settlement three or four days, our favourite rendezvous being a place about sixty miles distant, called 'Chickrookaik,' marked by Fitzroy as an Indian Ford or Pass of the river Santa Cruz, which statement both El Sourdo and Casimiro confirmed. At this point the river narrows considerably, and on the south side there are steep cliffs almost over-hanging the water, a cave in which cliffs was always a sure find for a puma. Both above and below this point are large wide plains extending from the 'banks' or cliffs to the river, which may easily be encircled; and the game being hemmed in between the horsemen and the river are readily captured. Sometimes the ostriches take to the water, but in the winter this saves trouble, as their legs get frozen, and on landing they are unable to move. We made an excursion on one occasion some miles higher up the river, and found abundance of game. We had previously on our road had good luck, but, as is often the custom, left the slain animals concealed in bushes, with a poncho or something over them. During the interval of our absence severe weather set in, and on returning to examine our caches the foxes and birds of prey had accounted for the meat. The foxes are a great trouble to the hunters, as, frequently, whilst they are encircling the herds of guanaco, and taking the greatest care to keep out of sight, one of these brutes will jump up, the dogs give chase, and then good-bye to all chance of sport. Fitzroy remarked the number of guanaco bones found in his ascent of the river Santa Cruz, which appear to have puzzled him, but the cause is not far to seek. During the very severe winters which occur I believe about once in three years, these animals, finding no pasture on the high lands, which are covered with snow, are necessarily driven down to the plains fringing the river, where they die from starvation. There is also a disease prevalent amongst them something similar to scab in sheep. On one occasion a hunting party killed ten guanacos, all of which were scabby, or, as we called it, 'sanoso;' and, consequently, unfit for food. Mr. Clarke told me that after one severe winter he found ostriches lying in heaps, dead under the bushes, and also guanacos. The difficulty of getting the horses across the swift and deep stream, with its banks encumbered by ice, prevented us from making frequent excursions to the northern side of the river. A level plain extends from the banks for about a mile, bounded by a chain of irregular hills; near the foot of these I picked up many specimens of a spiral shell, apparently a Turritella, which appeared to have been vitrified; and some were as translucent as glass, and of different colours. Beyond these hills rolled a succession of uneven plains diversified by ridges and hills; the general slope of the ground being apparently from west, to east, and the hills towards the west often assumed the form of abrupt lofty cliffs. Near a laguna at the foot of a cliff a hundred feet high I found boulders incrusted with sulphate of iron, such as had been pointed out to me in the Falklands, and numerous oyster shells and other marine shells occurred in various localities. There are no streams, but frequent lagoons in the hollows, and surrounded by a luxuriant growth of incense bushes. The unbroken plains abound in round thistle, califate, and the curious shrub called 'ratstail,' from the appearance of its twigs when the thick bark is pulled off. When burned it emits a dense black resinous smoke. To the north the horizon is bounded by a lofty range of hills which form the barrier of the valley of the Rio Chico, about sixty miles distant. These northern hills abounded with puma, some of which, killed in our hunts, were of unusual size, measuring fully six feet exclusive of the tail, which is generally half the length of the body. They are, of course, most numerous where the herds of guanaco and the ostriches abound; in the southern part of Patagonia their colour is more of a greyish-brown than that of the species found in the Argentine Provinces. These 'Leones,' as they are universally called in South America, always appeared to me to be the most cat-like of all the felidæ. They are very timid, always running from a man on horseback, and, by day at least, from a pedestrian; they run for a short distance in a series of long bounds, at great speed, but soon tire and stand at bay behind or in the midst of a bush, and sitting upon their haunches, spit and swear just like a monstrous tabby; sometimes endeavouring to scratch with their formidable claws, but rarely springing at the pursuer. Mr. Clarke on one occasion had his mantle torn off in this manner. At another time, when hunting in the vicinity of Santa Cruz, I observed from a distance Gonzalez hacking with his knife at a big incense bush, and, on reaching the spot, found him occupied in clearing away branches to allow him to knock a huge puma on the head with his bolas. He was dismounted and attended by his dogs, which bayed the animal. Still, had the puma not been a cur, he could doubtless have sprung out and killed or severely wounded the gaucho. The Indians affirm that the puma will attack a single man alone and on foot, and, indeed, subsequently, an example of this came under my notice; however, if a person should be benighted or lost, he has only to take the precaution of lighting a fire, which these animals will never approach. They are most savage in the early part of the spring or breeding season, when, according to my experience, they are found roaming over the country in an unsettled manner; they are then also thinner than at other times, but, like the wild horse, they are generally pretty fat at all times of the year. The females I saw were sometimes accompanied by two cubs, but never more. The meat of the puma resembles pork, and is good eating, though better boiled than roasted, but one or two Indians of my acquaintance would not touch the meat. The hide is useful either for saddle-cloths or to make mantles of; and owing to its greasy nature it can be softened with less trouble than that of the guanaco. In Santa Cruz one of the men had a pair of trousers made of lion's skin, which worn with the hair side out was impervious to wet. From the hock and lower part of the hind legs boots may be constructed similar to those made from horse hide, and in common use amongst the Indians and also the gauchos of Plata. These, however, are only made from pumas of large size, and they wear out very quickly. To kill a puma with a gun is rather a difficult matter, as, unless the ball enters his skull, or strikes near the region of the heart, he has as many lives as his relation the cat. I once put three revolver bullets into one, and ultimately had recourse to the bolas as a more effective weapon. When wounded they become very savage, but they are at all times bad customers for dogs, which they maul in a shocking manner. The Indian dogs are trained to stand off and bay them, keeping out of range of the claws; nevertheless they not unfrequently get killed. Perhaps the simplest way of taking the pumas is to throw a lazo over them, as directly they feel the noose they lie down as if dead, and are easily despatched. I was particularly struck, as are all hunters, with their eyes, large, brown, and beautifully bright, but with a fierce glare that does not appeal to any feelings of compassion. I shall never forget the expression in the eyes of one puma, best described by the remark made by one of the Indians as he reined back his horse, expecting a spring: 'Mira los ojos del diablo!' ('Look, what devil's eyes!')

One expedition on the northern shore was long remembered and talked of over the fire; and, indeed, might easily have had a very disastrous conclusion.

Towards the latter end of July I proposed to Mr. Clarke that we should proceed on foot, and investigate more closely the bed of fossil shells mentioned as situated on the hills about a mile from the north bank of the river. Accordingly, one morning we prepared to cross the river, and the remainder of the men, hearing of our intentions, volunteered, together with El Sourdo, to accompany us, and, after having visited the hills, to organise a hunting circle on foot: we started about sunrise and crossed the river to the north side, where we secured the boat above high-water mark; we then all proceeded to the hills, investigated the beds of fossil shells, and gathered many beautiful specimens. The hunt was then formed, so many dogs being apportioned to each person, and the circle being directed to close on a point on the bank of the river about three or four miles west of the settlement. The ground was very favourable for our operations, as the dips, or slightly-depressed valleys, hid us from the view of the game. On emerging on the plain at different points we saw several guanacos and some ostriches; and those nearest them slipped their hounds, following on foot at their topmost speed. Mr. Clarke, Isidoro, El Sourdo, and myself were in the centre, and killed amongst us two guanacos and an ostrich. Antonio, who was pointsman, disappeared to the westward with El Cookè, following their dogs in full chase of a herd of guanacos. Our party lit a fire, ate the ostrich, and conveyed what meat we thought advisable to take back with us towards the boat, following the river bank, which was strewn in many places with cornelians and flint-agates, and occasionally with fossilised shells. On our arrival at the boat we launched her down the beach, and, as the wind had by this time risen to a severe gale and the tide was rapidly ebbing, watched anxiously for the return of the two defaulters; for the navigation of the river is at no time very easy, and when the tide is low, even in daylight, nearly impracticable. At length, after dark, when the squalls of bitterly-cold wind had become very violent, we saw fires in the distance, and, almost half an hour afterwards, our missing men appeared, each with a load of meat on his shoulders. They arrived considerably exhausted, so we gave them a rest, and then dogs and all got into the boat and we shoved off, Mr. Clarke steering. We proceeded all right for a few yards, and then stuck on a bank; after several ineffectual efforts to shove the boat off, we all jumped into the water and fairly hove her over the bank until the water was up nearly to our shoulders, and then got in and pulled across. Owing to the violence of the wind and the strength of the current, we only succeeded in landing fully three-quarters of a mile from the house; here we secured the boat, and ran up as fast as we could to get our now frozen clothes off and a drink of hot coffee. We all agreed that on another expedition it would be advisable either to encamp on the northern shore until daylight, or come back early enough to be able to get across while it was possible to see the banks. But the general conclusion was, not to go again at all.

The weather in July was intensely cold, the lowest reading of the thermometer, which was duly examined every morning, being 8°. Washing our clothes became impossible, as during the process the water froze and the garments became stiff as boards. When crossing the ford, if the potro boots of the rider happened, as was not unfrequently the case, to get filled with water, in a few minutes not only were the boots coated with ice, but the inside resembled an ice-pail. The effect of the river ice piled up on the shore by the tides was very striking. Huge floes had accumulated to the height of fifteen feet and upwards, and, besides rendering the passage difficult, had buried the carefully-stacked wood-pile under a small mountain of ice. This was in the comparatively sheltered valley. On the Pampas, when the fierce south wind blew, as it almost invariably did, it seemed impossible to face it and live. One attempt made nearly resulted in Gonzalez being overcome by the sleep which is a forerunner of death, and the horses of all the party absolutely could not advance. The snow lay eighteen inches deep, and we had flattered ourselves that the guanaco and ostrich would prove an easy prey. *They* could not run—but *we* could not chase, and were thankful to make our way, slowly and laboriously, down from the desolate and storm-swept Pampas.

The Indians from the Rio Chico occasionally visited us, and Orkeke's objections to my company were gradually giving way. He had probably feared that an English Señor would require a considerable amount of attention, and give constant trouble; but during our intercourse he found that the stranger could (and did) groom his own horse, and wait on himself generally, as well as take his part in whatever was being done, even to sleeping out with no shelter but the ample guanaco mantle. Casimiro also, according to promise, visited the camp, and argued in my favour, finally obtaining from the chief a somewhat reluctant permission for me to join his party. Towards the end of July some of his Indians had come to the settlement to inform us that the scarcity of game in their vicinity had compelled them to shift their quarters to a place higher up the Rio Chico. They anxiously enquired if the schooner had arrived; we were as eagerly looking for her, but day after day passed, and the looked-for boat did not appear.

On the 24th of July everybody had gone hunting, except Juan Chileno (who was cook for the week), and myself, whom a hurt received in my foot had compelled to remain quiet. I was employed reading a book, 'Charles Dashwood,' for perhaps the twentieth time, when Juan came in to say that the hunting party had returned. As it was only ten o'clock, my first idea was that the schooner had arrived with Don Luiz. However, this was dispelled by Juan, who had gone out to reconnoitre, rushing in with the news that ten Chileans had arrived on the south side with twenty-one horses. Shortly afterwards Mr. Clarke himself came in and corroborated the intelligence. These men proved to be deserters, who had escaped by night from Punta Arena, taking with them nearly all the horses in the corral. They had left on the 2nd of July at 2 A.M. Four of the number were those previously recaptured in Santa Cruz, who had been kept in irons and closely confined at night; but by a supreme effort they had broken their chains, and, together with the others who had everything arranged outside the cuartel, had effected their escape. The sufferings these men must have undergone during the twenty-two days' journey over the Pampas, exposed without shelter to the fierce winds, and sometimes with the snow up to their horses' girths, must have been something frightful, and many of them were frost bitten. It was out of the question for us to receive them, as our own supplies were failing, and in truth we congratulated ourselves on the horses being secured in the corral, and anxiously watched the movements of the newcomers. The party during the afternoon succeeded in crossing the river to the north side, swimming their horses; and disappeared in the direction of the Rio Chico.

By this time even the kind companionship of Mr. Clarke failed to reconcile me to the tedious monotony of our life. The game also became scarcer and scarcer, and the chance of the schooner's coming appeared so indefinite, that at the beginning of August I began to think it would be better and more amusing to migrate to the Indian camp, where, at any rate, plenty of meat was procurable. Accordingly, when the Indians came over again on a visit on the 7th of August, I bought a horse, or rather changed away a revolver for one (a three year old, newly broken), and started in company with Orkeke, Campan, Cayuke, and Tankelow, four Indians, all of whom were previous acquaintances. Casimiro followed with his family, taking one of the horses from Santa Cruz to assist in the transport of his household. This horse was one I had been accustomed to ride in Santa Cruz, and on arriving at the Indian camp was lent me as a second horse. Shortly after passing the first hills on the northern side, our party not being burdened with women and children, started off at a hand canter, which was kept up until a puma suddenly sprang out of a bush, when chase was immediately given; he, however, got into a thick tangle of incense bushes, from which we tried in vain to dislodge him, and although pelted with stones he lay there spitting like a great cat. Cayuke wished to fire the bush, but Orkeke would not waste time, so we mounted and proceeded on our journey. We continued riding over plains and ridges until about 4 P.M., when we reached a large laguna, close to which grew some high coarse grass and shrubs; here several ostriches were started, and one killed by Orkeke. On reaching the range of hills before described as the southern barrier of the valley of the Rio Chico, we halted, and shortly had the ostrich cooking on a good fire. We looked back for Casimiro, but could not see him, so after supper and a smoke pursued our journey by the soft light of a young moon. As I pointed it out to my companions they all saluted it by putting their hands to their heads, at the same time muttering some unintelligible words. This reminded me of the English custom of turning money at first seeing the new moon. We rode on until about 9 P.M., when we reached the Indian encampment. We had been previously puzzled by seeing fires burning a considerable distance up the valley, and found that our chief, Camillo, had already marched in that direction. One of the first persons who accosted me was Arica, and I shortly discovered that all the Chilians were installed with the Indians in different toldos, which was rather an unpleasant surprise. I was ushered into Orkeke's toldo with due ceremony, and we took our seats by the fire. I had brought a bag of coffee with me, so we set to work and roasted some, after which one of the Chilians was given the task of pounding it between stones, and we all drank what the Indians not inappropriately term 'potwater.' Many Indians crowded in to have a look at us, and amongst others that I noticed was a remarkably pretty little girl of about thirteen years of age, a niece of Orkeke's, who took some coffee when offered in a shy and bashful manner which was delightful to contemplate. In due time we all retired to rest, and a little before daylight I was woke up by the melodious singing of an Indian in the next toldo. Shortly afterwards Orkeke went out and harangued the inmates of the remaining toldos, and presently the horses were brought up, and most of the men started for the chase. Snow had fallen during the night, a biting cold wind was blowing, and Orkeke told me there were very few animals about. I took this as a hint not to ask for a horse, so contented myself with sauntering round and examining the encampment. Some of the men were playing cards, one or two sleeping, whilst the women were almost universally employed in sewing guanaco mantles. About 3 P.M. Casimiro arrived with his family, and proceeded to the tent of a southern

Indian, named Crimè, and shortly afterwards the hunting party returned by twos and threes, but the chase had not been attended with much success. We passed the evening pleasantly enough, making acquaintance with each other, and Keoken, the little girl, instructed me in the Indian names of the various objects about the place. Next morning the order was suddenly given to march. As this was totally unexpected, and I was not prepared for departure, I made up my mind to return at once to Santa Cruz, and fetch my clothes and other small articles; also to take back a colt, promised by an Indian called 'Tchang' to Mr. Clarke. After some little difficulty, as the Indians did not wish me to go alone for fear of getting lost, or any other mischance befalling me, Graviel, the youngest son of Casimiro, started with me. We had to take the colt, what a sailor would term, in tow, that is, drag it for some distance with a lazo. As Graviel's horse was shy, this work fell to my share. Shortly after the start, rain, or rather sleet, came on, and the contrariness of the brute at the end of the lazo claiming all my attention, I could not manage to keep my mantle tight round my shoulders, and getting thoroughly wet, and losing one of my knives, cursed Tchang, colt and all, freely. After a short time, however, when well out of sight of the Indians, I cast off the towing line, and we drove our 'bête noire' before us. We returned by a different route to the one travelled on the outward journey, guided a good deal by my pocket compass. Towards nightfall, deceived by the appearance of a hill, I flattered myself that we were near Santa Cruz. But, alas! it was still miles away, and we got into fresh difficulties with our charge, which, being tired, absolutely refused to go down the hill, and had to be taken 'in tow' again and dragged along, and it must have been nine or ten before we reached the banks of the river. Here, after unsaddling our horses, we vainly attempted to kindle a fire, but everything, like ourselves, was so saturated with snow and wet that all attempts were fruitless; so, fairly tired out, and without fire or supper, we laid down under a bush, and, ensconced under our mantles, were soon in the land of dreams.

Next morning Graviel acted like a dutiful boy for once in his life, and left in search of the horses. Meanwhile the boat came over, and I was anxious to expedite matters; so, after splashing barefooted through several yards of sharp-edged ice on my way to the boat, which had grounded some distance from the shore, I got over to the island, where I was not sorry to get something to eat and a fire to warm my frozen limbs. I packed up my few things, ready for a start later on; but when the flood-tide made, a heavy gale of wind sprang up, and it was with great difficulty that the boat could bring over Graviel and the colt. The cheerful news also awaited me that my horse was missing, and that Graviel and El Cookè had seen a large puma on the river bank, which had probably watched in close proximity to us whilst sleeping the night before. Owing to the gale, it was impossible to cross that evening, so we made up our minds to stop and sleep on the island.

Next day, my horse not appearing, Mr. Clarke lent me one, sending Isidoro to bring the horse back, in the event of our not meeting with the missing steed. About 4 P.M. I bid adieu to my friend, whose kindness during my stay had proved him a friend indeed. Having shaken hands with the remainder of the boys, who one and all heartily wished me luck, we started; and after vainly searching for the missing horse, rode on till about 10 P.M., when we halted and bivouacked by the side of a laguna. Next morning early we arrived at the Rio Chico, which we crossed on the ice, and about 2 P.M. reached the toldos. The men were away hunting, the smoke of their fires being visible, rising from the higher plains to the northward. As we had eaten nothing since our supper the night before, which was furnished by a small skunk (which, though very palatable, was unfortunately very thin), we were in urgent need of something to eat, and Arica hastened to cook some guanaco meat on the asador or iron spit.

When the hunters arrived, Orkeke gruffly asked Isidoro what he had come for, and seemed, naturally enough, the reverse of pleased at the information of the loss of his horse; and, altogether, the old chief's behaviour did not seem auspicious; but, without appearing to notice it, I made myself at home in the toldo, and took up my quarters as one of the family.

1. A fanega contains 100 lbs.
2. Casimiro gave the name as 'Bourne'.

III

THE RIO CHICO

THE morning after we had rejoined the Indian camp was marked by a general breaking up of the party. Camillo and some others had already left, and by this time were several marches in advance; Orkeke and Isidoro started off to Santa Cruz, in search of the lost horse, and charged with some little commissions for me. Finally, Casimiro and all the rest broke up their encampment and started, intending to over-take Camillo. Before leaving, Casimiro came to me, and affecting great interest in my welfare, confidentially urged me to accompany himself and live as an inmate of his (or rather Crimè's) toldo, adding that he had been informed that Orkeke had no real intention of marching northward, but designed to keep me in his toldo until, by some means or other, he could possess himself of my arms and ammunition. As I saw no reason to believe this story, I declined to comply with the proposal of Casimiro, who, having consoled himself by begging a little coffee, took his departure, and the encampment was reduced to the toldo, of which I was to consider myself an inmate, and another, belonging to the only Indians who remained—Tankelow, Orkeke's brother, and his son, a youth of about eighteen. Besides these, there were three of the Chilian deserters who as narrated had escaped from Punta Arena; one was attached to the household of Tankelow, and the other two to that of Orkeke. One of these was Arica, already mentioned, who being a very clever worker in hide, had employed himself in adorning saddles and bridles for the Indians, by which he had acquired a pretty good stock of gear. The condition of all three was, however, not enviable. They had lowered themselves at first by volunteering to discharge the drudgery of fetching wood and water, and by this time were little better than slaves, obliged to perform the menial offices, which before had been the task of the women. These fair creatures, headed by Mrs. Orkeke—a young woman almost six feet in height, and displaying a corresponding breadth across the shoulders—employed themselves in cutting out and sewing guanaco mantles, weaving fillets for the head, and chattering. Tankelow and his son presently started for a hunt; but as I was not offered a mount, and deemed it more reasonable to give my only charger a good rest and feed, I could only accompany them to the river, the frozen surface of which they crossed, and disappeared up a cañon that led up the Barranca, on the northern limit of the valley, to the Upper Pampa. Having wistfully watched them, I reconnoitred the valley of the Rio Chico. Behind me, to the south-east, the river wound through plains covered with withered coarse grass, some eighteen inches high, extending on either bank for several miles till terminated by the rising barranca. Snow lay here and there in patches on some of the higher ground, and increased the dreariness of the prospect. About two leagues below, the river divided into two branches, which reunited beyond an island of some extent. Looking up river in a north-westerly direction, the valley soon narrowed in, the southern barranca sloping down to within a couple of miles of our camp; and the view was closed by two remarkable hills resembling fortresses, which seemed to stand on guard on either side. I made a slight sketch of the outlines of the view, which forms the background of the hunting scene.[1] Having strolled back to the toldo, I was greeted by the women with the usual demand, 'Mon aniwee'—Anglicè, 'Lend us the pipe,' which was duly charged and handed round. We then sat and watched the proceedings of Keoken, Tankelow's pretty little daughter, just budding into womanhood, and a small boy to whom I gave the name of Captain John, who were amusing themselves by catching and riding some of the horses which were tamer than the others. The urchins soon grew tired of their equestrian feats; and, prompted by the spirit of mischief, which seems ever to haunt children, and especially Indian boys, came and begged a match of me. Not suspecting their purpose, I gave them the coveted prize, with which they hurried off in high delight, and in a very few minutes had set fire to the rank, withered herbage, some distance off the toldo, but to the windward. The conflagration was at first unnoticed by us; but at dusk, when Tankelow returned from hunting, with a supply of meat, it was palpably dangerous. So all hands had to set to work, and by dint of tearing up the grass, with great trouble we stopped its progress, which if aided by a breeze in the night would very probably otherwise have consumed the toldo and endangered the inmates. Of the culprits no notice was taken, the occurrence being apparently regarded as all in the day's work. After our supper of guanaco meat, and a smoke, I turned in, and slept soundly on my Tehuelche bed of hides and bolsters which had been carefully arranged by the tall hostess.

    The next day was got through by having a thorough 'wash' of my clothes, and cultivating a closer acquaintance with the Chilian Arica, from whom I obtained a dog in exchange for an old guanaco mantle. But as on the third day no signs of the return of Orkeke appeared, the inaction became insupportable, so after the departure on a hunting excursion of Tankelow and his son, Arica and myself determined to start in pursuit of Casimiro and his party. As Arica had no horse, it would be necessary for us to ride and tie; but even thus we could make quick travelling. Accordingly at 2 P.M. we started, much to the astonishment of the ladies, who protested that we were certain to lose our way or be killed by the pumas. One old lady, Orkeke's sister, after trying in vain to dissuade us, presented me with a slice of charqui, which with a few handfuls of coffee formed our stock of provisions. That day we did not get very far; but in the next march, as the track of the Indians was plain, we had made thirty miles by the time we halted, at nightfall, at a place where another valley from the northward joined that of the Rio Chico. Our charqui had barely sufficed for an evening meal, so this day we satisfied our appetites with a supply of the tuberous roots of a plant which grows in great quantities in most parts of Patagonia.

The plant, which in its growth resembles very closely the balsam bog of the Falkland Islands, and might be easily taken for it but for the absence of the gum, which perhaps was attributable to the quality of the soil or the season of the year, is easily recognisable by its mass of tiny green leaflets, and presents the appearance of a small hillock of earth crowned with delicate moss. By digging down into the heap, one large and several small tuberous roots are found, which when roasted in the ashes prove sufficiently palatable to hungry men.

We went to sleep in the open air, rolled up in our guanaco mantles, but awoke to find that a heavy fall of snow had covered everything a foot deep, and totally hidden all trail of the Indians. In this dilemma, quite uncertain which of the two valleys to ascend, and feeling extremely cold, we first looked out for a place of shelter. This was afforded us by a little dell or recess in the side of the barranca, which was thickly overgrown with incense bushes. Betaking ourselves thither, we speedily had a blazing fire kindled, and while warming our chilled limbs held a council. It was decided that I should mount, and proceed to hunt for some food; and then, if the weather moderated, we could proceed. Arica was left in charge of the fire, with a strong caution from me to keep it up, and to make as much smoke as possible, by way of signal to the Indians. After a good deal of difficulty my horse, which was only half broken, and had a playful way of rearing up and striking with his forefeet, was curbed with the leathern thong which forms the Indian bit. I then proceeded to scale the barranca bordering the river valley, and soon reached the desolate undulations of the higher Pampa. As a necessary precaution against losing my way, I was careful to take two or three bearings of conspicuous hills, visible in the northern limits of the valley; for the monotonous and dreary waste of the Pampa, strewn with boulders and shingle, alternated with tufts of grass, presents no track or landmark to guide the wanderer. It was not long before two or three herds of guanaco were sighted; but the dog, which had probably during the night foraged for himself, and found some half-eaten carcase, would not run, and a gallop of some twelve miles proved fruitless. Just as I was about giving up in despair, I observed a herd in a hollow, which I was able to approach unobserved. Knowing that our chance of food for the day depended on success, I warily approached, and then charged, and to my delight succeeded in entangling one with the bolas. He was soon despatched; and while I was busily cutting off a supply of meat, to my sudden surprise an Indian came galloping up. The newcomer proved to be Tankelow, who was in search of me. He brought word that Orkeke had found the strayed horse, and had returned; and that the party were marching as fast as they could to overtake Casimiro. He had been detached, partly to hunt and partly to find us. In reply to my inquiries about Arica, he assured me that he was all right, and as there seemed no reason for disbelieving the statement, we speedily rode back to the party, and rejoined them on the march; being received with shouts of laughter by the ladies; but as Arica was nowhere to be seen, I expressed my determination to ride back in search of him. This, however, they would not allow, but despatched a mounted Indian and spare horse to bring him in, and a good piece of meat for his refreshment. We then proceeded at a brisk rate, and by nightfall reached the camp. Orkeke at first seemed rather to resent my having started off alone, as if it argued a want of confidence in him; but his delight at having recovered his horse assisted him to recover his good humour. Mr. Clarke had sent me by him some powder, which he *said* he had lost, and some articles, such as linen and tobacco, and my presenting them all to him quite did away with any traces of ill feeling.

The several detachments were all now reunited, and the party mustered altogether, besides the Chilians and myself, eighteen able-bodied Tehuelche or Patagonian men, with a proportionate number of women and children. The most important among the Indians were Orkeke, the actual cacique, and his brother Tankelow, who possessed the greater number of horses; Casimiro, whose leadership was still rather *in posse*; Camillo, Crimè, Cuastro, Cayuke, &c. One more must be mentioned by name, Wáki; a perfect Hercules in bodily frame, and a thoroughly good-natured fellow, with whom I became great friends. Of all these men, who were in the camp by the Rio Chico on August 15, but eight survived to reach the Rio Negro in the following May; the rest had, at one time or another, been killed or had died. The secret feuds, which were before long to endanger the safety of us all, were as yet concealed, and all appeared to be good friends. The whole were housed in five toldos—by which Spanish name the Indian kau, or tents, strongly resembling those of our own gipsies, are known. They were pitched in a sheltered hollow, with their fronts facing the east, to avoid the bitter violence of the prevalent westerly winds.

Fitzroy has given an excellent description of the toldo; but to those readers who are unacquainted with it a brief sketch will not be unacceptable. A row of forked posts about three feet high is driven into the ground in a slightly slanting position, and a ridge pole laid across them; in front of these, at a distance of about seven feet, a second row, six feet high, with a ridge pole; and at the same distance from them a third row, eight feet high, each slanting a little, but not at the same angle. A covering made of from forty to fifty full grown guanaco skins, smeared with a mixture of grease and red ochre, is drawn over from the rear, and the great drag of the heavy covering straightens the poles; it is then secured by thongs to the front poles, while hide curtains fastened between the inner poles partition off the sleeping places, and the baggage piled round the sides of the tent excludes the cold blast which penetrates under the edge of the covering. The fire is kindled in the fore part, or 'mouth of the tent.' In very bad weather, or when encamped for the winter, an additional covering is secured to the front poles and brought down over an extra row of short posts making all snug. It is a common arrangement for relatives or friends to combine their toldos, when, instead of bringing down the coverings to the ground at the side, they are made to overlap, and thus one tent roof will cover two or three distinct domestic interiors.

The furniture of the toldos consists of one or two bolsters and a horse hide or two to each sleeping compartment, one to act as a curtain and the other for bedding. The bolsters are made of old ponchos, or lechus, otherwise called mandils, woven blankets obtained from the Araucanos, who are famous for their manufacture, stuffed with guanaco wool and sewn up with ostrich or guanaco sinews. The bolsters do duty as pillows or as seats, and help to form the women's saddles on the march. Besides these, the women all own mandils for their beds. The men occasionally use the cloths worn under the saddles for seats when the ground is damp, but as a rule all the inmates of the toldo squat upon Nature's carpet, which has the advantage of being easily cleaned, for the Tehuelches are very particular about the cleanliness of the interior of their dwellings, and a patch of sod accidentally befouled is at once cut out and thrown outside by the women.

The cooking utensils are simple, consisting of an asador, or iron spit, for roasting meat, and an occasional iron pot, which serves for boiling and also for trying out ostrich grease and marrow, which is employed both for cooking and for mixing with the paint with which the faces of both sexes are adorned. To these, wooden platters and armadillo shell to serve broth in, are sometimes added. The duty of pitching and arranging the toldos on the halt and striking them for the march, as well as loading the poles, covering, and furniture on the horses, devolves entirely upon the women, who display great strength and dexterity in the work.

About the toldos were innumerable dogs of all sizes and breeds, and Mrs. Orkeke rejoiced in the possession of two fowls brought from the settlement, and the all important possession of the Indians, horses, completed the bustling liveliness of the scene. There were not less than 150 belonging to the various members of the party, Orkeke and Tankelow owning about forty, besides mares and skittish colts of all ages, which ran about so that they could not be counted. The reader can imagine what a scene the march and encampment of such a party presents, and the care with which the Indians must select their route so as to be sure of game for themselves and pasture for their animals. Of the dogs and horses in use by the Tehuelches a fuller description will be given hereafter.

But, to convey a clear understanding of the relations between the tribes which will be mentioned in the ensuing pages, it is as well here briefly to distinguish them. In the various maps and accounts of Patagonia extant, numerous tribes, with different names, are marked and recorded. These accounts, so far as my observations enabled me to judge, have arisen from the custom of parties of the tribe combining to travel or fight under the leadership of a particular chief, and being described by themselves, when met with, by his name. I have been enabled to recognise thus the Moluches, who were so called from Malechou, a hereditary chief of that name; and the celebrated chief Lenketrou united under his leadership men of several tribes, and is said to have commanded 1,500 men in his great raid on the Rio Negro settlements. There are now between the Rio Negro and the Straits about 500 fighting men, giving at a rough estimate a population of about 3,000. The Tehuelches, or Patagonians proper, exclusive of the Foot Indians of Tierra del Fuego—who are distinct, though they may be of the same original stock—are divided into two great tribes, the Northern and Southern. They speak the same language, but are distinguishable by difference of accent, and the Southern men appear to be, on an average, taller and finer men, and are more expert hunters with the bolas. The Northern range chiefly over the district between the Cordillera and the sea; from the Rio Negro on the north to the Chupat, occasionally descending as far as the Santa Cruz River. The Southern occupy the country south of the Santa Cruz, and migrate as far as Punta Arena. The two divisions, however, are much intermixed and frequently intermarry; always, notwithstanding, preserving their clannish division, and taking opposite sides in the frequent quarrels. Our party was composed in almost equal parts of both Northern and Southern, and one inmate of our toldo was a Southern named Hummums, a brother of Mrs. Orkeke. From the Rio Negro as far as the Chupat, another tribe, speaking a different language, is met with, having their head-quarters at the Salinas, north of the Rio Negro. These are the Pampas, called by the Tehuelches 'Penck,' whence I believe the name Pehuelche has been corrupted. Several clans of this nation extend over the plains north of Rio Negro, and make frequent inroads into the Argentine settlements as far as the province of Santa Fé, and even, I believe, to Cordova and Mendoza. The Pampas of the north of Patagonia sometimes keep cattle and sheep, but generally subsist by the chase. A third tribe appear, by their language and physique, to be a branch of the Araucanos of Chili. These are the people called by the Tehuelches Chenna, and also the Warriors; they are otherwise known as Manzaneros, from their head-quarters Las Manzanas, so named from the groves of apple trees; once a station of the early Jesuit missionaries, who vainly endeavoured to convert and civilise these tribes. They are less migratory and more civilised in their habits than the Tehuelches, and are said to keep herds of cattle and sheep in the sheltered valleys of the Cordillera, and sometimes till a little maize. I do not know whether the Jesuit Fathers taught their disciples the art or no, but from the apples of Las Manzanas these Indians brew a very tolerable cider, besides making an intoxicating liquor from the beans of the algarroba. The Tehuelches altogether depend for their stimulants on the chance supplies of rum procured in trade at the settlements, and this and disease, small-pox especially, are rapidly diminishing their numbers.

We remained in our encampment by the Rio Chico for one day, during which the missing Arica arrived. He was received with very black looks by Orkeke, who from this time, although still allowing him a place in his toldo, and a horse to ride, seemed to have conceived a violent aversion to him, which argued badly for the Chilian's future safety. It appeared that during my absence he had given way to the desire of providing something to eat, and had left the fire to burn out, while he foraged for roots. On returning he saw a huge puma couched by the extinct ashes of the fire. Just, however, as Arica was about to fire the revolver which I had lent him, the beast bounded away into the bushes. But as he was convinced that the puma was close at hand waiting for an opportunity to attack, he spent several hours on the watch with his revolver ready. His delight may be imagined when, worn out with want of food and rest, he was relieved by the arrival of the Indian with the meat and a horse for him to ride.

The next day we made a short march up the river valley, the caravan of women and horses, as usual, proceeding along the track, while the men hunted in the adjacent plains. I was fortunate enough in the hunt to kill a guanaco and an ostrich, and duly shared them with Casimiro. The order of march and method of hunting which constitute the daily routine are as follows: the Cacique, who has the ordering of the marching and hunting, comes out of his toldo at daylight, sometimes indeed before, and delivers a loud oration, describing the order of march, the appointed place of hunting, and the general programme; he then exhorts the young men to catch and bring up the horses, and be alert and active in the hunt, enforcing his admonition, by way of a wind up, with a boastful relation of his own deeds of prowess when he was young. Sometimes the women, while the chief is haranguing, rekindle or blow up the embers of the fire and prepare a slight breakfast, but not invariably. Some cold meat is also occasionally reserved from the evening meal, and placed in a hide bag to be carried with them on the march, to be given to the children when they are hungry. But the general custom for the men is to wait until the day's hunt has supplied fresh meat. When the Cacique's 'oration'—which is very little attended to—is over, the young men and boys lazo and bring up the horses, and the women place on their backs the bolsters of reeds, tied with hide thongs, mantles, and coloured blankets, which form their saddles; others are strapping their belts on, or putting their babies into wicker-work cradles, or rolling up the skins that form the coverings of the toldos, and placing them and the poles on the baggage-horses; last of all the small breakers, which are carried on the march, are filled with water. The women mount by means of a sling round the horses' necks, and sit astride of their bolster-saddles; their babies—if they possess any—and their pet dogs are hoisted up, the babies being stowed in the cradles behind them; then they take their baggage-horses in tow and start off in single file. The men, who generally wait until all are ready, then drive the spare horses for a short distance, and having handed them over to the charge of their wives or daughters, retire to a neighbouring bush, where a fire is kindled, pipes are lighted, and the hunt commenced in the following manner:—Two men start off and ride at a gallop round a certain area of country, varying according to the number of the party, lighting fires at intervals to mark their track. After the lapse of a few minutes two others are despatched, and so on until only a few are left with the cacique. These spread themselves out in a crescent, closing in and narrowing the circle on a point where those first started have by this time arrived. The crescent rests on a baseline formed by the slowly-proceeding line of women, children, and baggage-horses. The ostriches and herds of guanaco run from the advancing party, but are checked by the pointsmen, and when the circle is well closed in are attacked with the bolas, two men frequently chasing the same animal from different sides. The dogs also assist in the chase, but the Indians are so quick and expert with the bolas that unless their horses are tired, or they happen to have gambled away their bolas, the dogs are not much called into use. Puma are very frequently found in the circles, and quickly despatched by a blow on the head from a ball. On one occasion I saw Wáki completely crush, by a single blow, the skull of an unusually large one. The Indian law of division of the game prevents all disputes, and is as follows: The man who balls the ostrich leaves it for the other, who has been chasing with him, to carry or take charge of, and at the end of the hunt it is divided; the feathers and body from the head to the breast-bone and one leg belonging to the captor, the remainder to the assistant. In the case of guanaco, the first takes the best half in the same manner; the lungs, heart, liver, kidneys, and the fat and marrow bones are sometimes eaten raw. The Tehuelches also cut out the fat over the eyes, and the gristly fat between the thigh joints, which they eat with great gusto, as also the heart and blood of the ostrich. Owing to the entire absence of farinaceous food, fat becomes a necessary article of diet, and can be consumed in much larger quantities than in more civilised countries. That this is not merely owing to the inclemency of the climate is proved by the appetite for fat which the gauchos in the Argentine provinces acquire. When the hunt is finished, and the birds cut up and divided, fires are kindled, and whilst stones are heating the ostrich is plucked, the wing feathers being carefully tied together with a piece of sinew. The bird is then laid on its back and drawn; the legs are carefully skinned down, and the bone taken out, leaving the skin; the carcase is then separated into two halves, and the backbone having been extracted from the lower half, and the meat sliced so as to admit the heated stones laid in between the sections, it is tied up like a bag, secured by the skin of the legs, with a small bone thrust through to keep all taut, this is placed on the live embers of the fire, a light blaze being kindled when it is nearly done to perfectly roast the outside meat. During the process of cooking it has to be turned frequently to ensure all parts being thoroughly cooked. When ready it is taken off the fire, and the top part being cut off and the stones extracted, the broth and meat are found deliciously cooked. The party, generally consisting of twos or fours, sit round the dish and eat the meat, sopping it in the broth. The back part, which consists nearly altogether of fat (when the ostrich is in good condition), is then divided, pieces being given to each, and reserved as tid bits for the women and children. When the head and breast half are to be cooked, the bone is not extracted, but the wings turned inside and the breast cavity filled with heated stones, and tied up with half of the skin of the legs, which have been divided, additional pieces of meat from the legs having been placed in the breast cavity. The fat of the breast is divided amongst the party at the fireside, the owner in all cases reserving none or a very small piece for himself, as the others who are cooking at the same fire are sure to give him plenty. The cacique generally receives the largest share, or if he is not present, the greatest friends of the owner. The wing feathers are carefully taken to the toldos and stored with others for future trade. The ostrich is most thoroughly eaten; the gizzard, which is large enough to fill both hands, being carefully cooked by the insertion of a hot stone and roasted, the eyes, too, are sucked, and the tripe devoured; but when the birds are thin they are simply skinned, and the carcase left to the pumas. After the meal, concluding the hunt, is finished, a pipe is handed round, saddles are re-adjusted, and the game placed on them, and the party adjourn to the toldos, which by this time have been pitched and arranged by the women.

Guanaco are not much killed, unless a long stay in a place is intended, or an Indian feels inclined for blood, or ostriches, which are always eaten in preference, are scarce. The meat of the guanaco is, however, excellent; the haunches are generally what is termed in Spanish 'charqueared,' which means that the meat is cut off in thin slices, and, after a little salt has been sprinkled over it, is dried in the sun. When thoroughly dried it is roasted in the ashes, pounded between two stones, and mixed with ostrich or other grease; this preparation, like pemmican, is very useful for a man going a long journey, as it can be carried in a small compass, and a mere handful satisfies the appetite.

START FROM THE CAMP AT MÓWAISH OR WINDOW HILL

It would be tedious to describe every day's march, and the routine of hunting, as we made our way slowly up the valley of the Rio Chico, which was still frozen over. The weather was cold, and occasional showers of snow accompanied the strong piercing westerly winds which blew every day. The valley sometimes opened out into wide grass-covered plains, dotted with incense-bushes, then rose again in huge bare ridge and furrow-like undulations. Occasionally there occurred patches of swampy ground with frozen lagoons, and here and there open springs, the resort of numerous water-fowl. The hills on the northern side appeared bare and rugged, rising abruptly out of irregular forms, while the southern heights were lower, and presented more of the steep declivities known as barrancas, interrupted at intervals by high rugged hills of basalt, often assuming the appearance of ruined castles, closing in at the bends of the winding river. To one of these—a remarkable hill under which we were encamped on August 23, about 120 miles from Santa Cruz—I gave the name of Sierra Ventana, from a window-like opening through its peak; the Indians called it Môwaish. (See Illustration.) In many places the bases of these hills were formed entirely of a description of lava, and one of the Chilians informed me that whilst passing over a ridge, he had observed several large masses of pure iron: this, however, I was inclined to disbelieve, as although farther up the country iron ore exists in large quantities, I only observed in this part a species of ore similar to that common at Drobak, in Norway.

On one occasion, while marching, we observed smoke in our rear, which was thought to be caused either by a messenger in search of us announcing the arrival of the schooner, or else by a party of the Southern Indians who had some idea of marching north. However, no scout was sent back to discover the truth, so we remained in ignorance. On the 26th we halted, and encamped by the side of the river in a broad opening of the valley; here there was a lagoon, not completely frozen, in which grew a description of flag, of which the root, or rather lower stem, is eaten by the Indians, and is succulent and juicy, with a pleasant taste. The boys and girls soon brought a large supply into the toldos. The day after our arrival in this place, the attainment of the age of puberty of one of the girls was celebrated according to custom. Early in the morning the father of the child informed the cacique of the event, the cacique thereupon officially communicated the intelligence to the acting doctor or medicine-man, and a considerable shouting was set up, while the doctor adorned himself with white paint and was bled in the forehead and arms with a sharp bodkin. The women immediately set to work to sew a number of 'mandils' together. When the patchwork was finished, it was taken with pomp and ceremony by a band of young men, who marched round the poles—already fixed to form a temporary toldo—singing, whilst the women joined in with the most dismal incantations and howlings. After marching round several times, the covering was drawn over the poles, and lances were stuck in front, adorned with bells, streamers, and brass plates that shook and rattled in the breeze, the whole thing when erected presenting a very gay appearance (its Indian name literally meaning 'The pretty house'). The girl was then placed in an inner part of the tent, where nobody was admitted. After this everybody mounted, and some were selected to bring up the horses, out of which certain mares and fillies were chosen, and brought up in front of the showy toldo, where they were knocked on the head by a ball—thus saving the blood (which was secured in pots) to be cooked, being considered a great delicacy. It is a rule amongst the Indians that anyone assisting to take off the hide of a slaughtered mare is entitled to a piece of meat, but the flesh was on this occasion distributed pretty equally all round. Whilst the meat was cooking, Casimiro, who was ruler of the feast, sent a message for me to come to Crimè's toldo, where I found him busy working at a saddle, in the construction of which he was, by the way, an adept. His wife had a large iron pot bubbling on the fire, containing some of the blood mixed with grease. When the mess was nearly cooked, we added a little pepper and salt, and commenced the feast. Previous to this I had felt a sort of repugnance to eating horse, as perhaps most Englishmen—except, indeed, the professed hippophagists—have; but hunger overcame all scruples, and I soon acquired quite a taste for this meat. On this occasion everybody ate where they liked, in their own toldos. Casimiro informed me, after the meal was concluded, that there would be a dance in the evening. I looked forward with great anticipation to this 'small and early,' and shortly saw some of the women proceed to collect a considerable quantity of firewood, which was placed outside the tent. Presently, towards dusk, a fire was made, first outside the sacred precincts. The women all sat down on the grass round about, but at some distance from the men, who were all seated on the grass, except four and the musicians. The orchestra consisted of a drum made by stretching a piece of hide over a bowl, also a sort of wind instrument formed of the thigh-bone of a guanaco, with holes bored in it, which is placed to the mouth and played, or with a short bow having a horsehair string. When all was ready, some of the old hags all the time singing in their melodious way, the band struck up, and four Indians, muffled up in blankets, so that their eyes only were visible, and their heads adorned with ostrich plumes, marched into the ring, and commenced pacing slowly round the fire, keeping time to the music. After two or three promenades, the time gradually quickened, until they went at a sort of trot; and about the fifth round, dancing fast to the music, they threw away their mantles, and exhibited themselves adorned with white paint daubed all over their bodies, and each having a girdle of bells extending from the shoulder to the hip, which jingled in tune to their steps. The first four consisted of the chiefs Casimiro, Orkeke, Crimè, and Camillo, who, after dancing with great action (just avoiding stepping into the fire), and bowing their plumed heads grotesquely on either side to the beats of the drum, retired for a short time to rest themselves, after which they appeared again and danced a different step. When that was over four more appeared, and so on, until everyone, including the boys, had had a fling. Sometimes, to give greater effect, the performers carried a bunch of rushes in one hand. About 9 P.M., everybody having had enough, Casimiro gave the sign. The band stopped playing, and all retired to bed. The dancing was not ungraceful, but was rendered grotesque by the absurd motions of the head. It was strictly confined to the men, the women being only allowed to look on.

On the second day's march from the scene of my first Indian ball we crossed a rocky ridge abounding with a description of vesicular lava; the ridge ran out from the southern limits of the valley and terminated in precipitous cliffs, round the base of which wound the river. The surface of the ridge was fissured in many places with deep chasms like Alpine crevasses, on the brink of one of which my horse stopped just in time to escape a fall. The caravan had gone a more circuitous route to take advantage of the lowest and easiest crest. On the other side of the ridge the valley suddenly spread out to the extent of several miles, and on the western horizon a line of snowy peaks was visible, their summits capped with clouds: this was our first view of the Cordillera. The low ground was cut up by streams and small lakelets of water, formed by the overflow of a small fork of the river, which glistening in the afternoon sunshine presented a beautiful silvery appearance, very refreshing to the eye wearied with alternate gazing on withered grass and black volcanic rocks. However beautiful to look at, this scene would clearly prove difficult travelling, so a halt was called, and our course debated on; ultimately it was resolved to cross the river and encamp on the northern bank, where the ground was higher and free from floods, so loads were carefully adjusted, and children transferred to the arms of the men, to give the women more freedom of action; baggage-horses were also taken in tow by the young men, and Casimiro and another volunteering to lead the van and act as pilots, we proceeded to make our way to the river-bank, which rose by a gradual elevation from the lower inundated plain. After much floundering about in water-holes, and various spills, which caused great merriment, especially when Mrs. Orkeke and all her gear came down by the run, an iron kettle of which she was very proud clattering down so as to frighten several of the horses into what threatened to become a general stampede, the bank was safely reached; the river was swollen high, and its rapid current running six or seven miles an hour, was bringing down huge sharp-edged masses of ice. It seemed almost impossible for the women and baggage animals to cross. However, Orkeke, taking a long pole to sound with, led the way, and by watching their opportunity to dodge the floating ice, which cut the horses' and riders' legs cruelly, all got safely over. A wilder scene could hardly be imagined—dogs howling on the bank fearing to pass, women singing out to their various friends and relations, and here and there an adventurous Indian, who scorned to go by the ford with the rest, disappearing for a second in the river, horse and all, but ultimately emerging some distance down the stream. The water was bitterly cold, as may be imagined, and the piercing wind benumbed our dripping bodies; so on arriving at the north bank, where there were some small sandy hillocks, we kindled a large fire, and had a warm and a smoke whilst the women were employed pitching the toldos. It had been decided to remain here some days and then proceed to the vicinity of the Cordillera for the purpose of catching wild horses. But, as will be seen shortly, 'l'homme propose et Dieu dispose.' Looking up towards the Cordillera from our encampment, the valley appeared to expand a few miles up into one immense plain, and the Indians informed me that before reaching the mountains there is a great drop or basin where the wild horses are found. This was probably, at the period of our visit, a vast sheet of water from the melting snows. Lake Viedma lies some miles to the southward from the head of the valley, and I should be inclined to think that the course of the Rio Chico, which undoubtedly flows from it, would be found to come from the south to north, and bend easterly at the head of the valley, where it unites the numerous streams as described by Viedma in his journey in 1580. I am also inclined to think that Viedma being taken twice across the Rio Chico mistook the river at the second crossing for another, which he has marked as the Chalia, a name, by the way, unknown to the Indians, save as applied to an unsavoury parasite only too common among them. The following morning, September 2, we were sitting quietly round the fire discussing a breakfast of boiled ostrich prepared by the lady of the house, when suddenly the clash of knives was heard, and we saw two Indians, destitute of mantles, with naked swords in their hands, run across from Camillo's to Crimè's toldo. In a minute everything was in an uproar; arms were produced, guns and revolvers loaded, and some of the Indians equipped themselves in coats of mail, and others, with the assistance of the women, padded themselves about the chest and upper part of the body with thick blankets and corconillas or saddle-cloths. Knowing what was about to happen, the women, and with them all the Chilian deserters except one, beat a retreat to a safe distance from the toldos. Having assumed my arms, and feeling thoroughly mystified as to the real cause of this excitement, I went to Camillo's toldo, where the scene explained itself. He was lying on his bed dead, with a frightful gash in his side, having been murdered by Cuastro, one of the Indians whom we had seen running to Crimè's tents. On issuing from the toldo Casimiro met me, and asked for a revolver, as he had no firearms, and I lent him one accordingly. The Indians showed by their changed countenances all the fury of fight; their very complexions seemed ghastly, and their eyes glared and rolled, seeming to see blood. The two opposing parties, the Southern Indians—friends of Crimè, who was a cousin of Cuastro—and Orkeke's and Casimiro's people or the Northern party, were soon ranged in open line at some twenty yards distance from each other. Cuastro was conspicuous by his tunic or 'buff coat' of hide studded with silver, while his only weapon was a single sword or rapier. The fight commenced with an irregular discharge of guns and revolvers, which lasted a few minutes, till some of the Northern or Orkeke's Indians, led by Casimiro, closed up, and a hand to hand contest with swords and lances took place, resulting in the death of Cuastro and the severe wounding of two or three Southern Indians. The Northerns then drew off to reload, and were about to renew the action, when Tankelow proposed a truce, which was accepted on the understanding that both parties were to march at once in the same direction. The women and children were then recalled from the bushes whither they had retired, the horses brought up, and the dead buried. The Tehuelches' lance is entirely different to that of the Araucanos or Pampas, and is only used when fighting on foot; it consists of a heavy shaft eighteen feet in length, at the extremity of which a blade is fixed about eighteen inches long, constituting a most formidable weapon in the hands of an expert Indian. Cayuke, whom I have before mentioned, in this fight was armed with the lance, and ran Cuastro through the body, although protected by his mail and endeavouring to parry the point with a sword. This Cuastro was a brave man; when dying, with several bullets in his body, and several lance thrusts, he sprang up to his full height and called out, 'I die as I have lived—no cacique orders me;' his wife then rushed up to him crying and sobbing, but he fell down dead at the same moment. Casimiro had a narrow escape; he parried a blow of a sword with what may be termed the slack part of his mantle, but if the blow had caught him on the head, as intended, it would have ended his career then and there. The casualties were a wound in Crimè's leg, and a lance thrust clean through the thigh of Hummums, a young Indian, who seemed to care very little about it. The fight originated out of a vendetta between Cuastro and Camillo, the latter having some years before caused the death of a member of the family of the former, who had on a previous occasion endeavoured to avenge it on Camillo, and he had only attached himself to our party, in company with Crimè, in order to obtain an opportunity of assassinating Camillo. This Cuastro had been suspected on good grounds of making away with Mendoza, the Argentine sent from Buenos Ayres in company with Casimiro, and who mysteriously disappeared; and he had certainly, when under the influence of rum, at Santa Cruz, murdered his own wife Juana, a daughter of Casimiro, so that brave as he was he had richly deserved the fate he met with.

After the obsequies of the dead had been hurriedly performed—a description of which is reserved for another place—the tents were struck, and all marched off, the men remaining armed, and each party travelling separately. Cayuke was sent back some miles to ascertain if there were any signs of the other Southern Indians, who were half expected to overtake us; but he returned some hours later with no intelligence. We marched a few miles up the valley, rather coasting the northern hills, and encamped by a most beautiful circular spring, the water bubbling up through pure white sand and forming a tiny brook, while little fishes darted across in the basin. The Indians still remained with arms ready to hand—were very silent and ate nothing. Several of the Northerns came into our toldo towards evening, and remained a long time conversing by the embers of the fire, and ever and anon one of the widows of the deceased would break out into a wail of lamentation, sobbing in the most dismal and melancholy manner, the lament at times being taken up by some of the older hags.

On the following day Crimè sent for me to dress his leg, imagining, of course, that I understood surgery; so I washed the wound and bandaged it with cold water bandages, which appeared to be successful, as in a few days it inconvenienced him but little. Thence proceeding to Casimiro's toldo—the smallest I ever saw—I got him to cover my saddle with a guanaco skin I had obtained on the road. The children appeared to be the only members of the party unaffected by the prevailing gloom. They had found a snow-bank in a nook, and amused themselves sliding down it on a bit of wood *à la Russe*. This evening things looked very black again. A consultation was held in Orkeke's toldo, and although it was carried on in a low tone, and I was little conversant with the Tehuelche tongue, I heard my name frequently mentioned in connection with a revolver, and also the Chilians. I was much puzzled at what was going on, but as Mrs. Orkeke brought me some supper in the most gracious and smiling manner, did not trouble myself more than to overhaul my arms quietly, and see they were ready for use. I subsequently found out that a plot had been set on foot amongst the Chilians to rise, rob, and murder the Indians, and escape with the horses. Some, however, my informant among the number, refused to join. The Indians, who are naturally quick-sighted, had conceived a suspicion that all was not right, and were debating whether it would not be better to kill the Chilians at once, before they became more troublesome; but Casimiro prevailed on them to let them remain until they did something to necessitate their destruction; and so they escaped for the present.

September 5th, at an early hour, we were awoke by Orkeke's marching harangue; and after coasting the hills bordering the valley for a few miles, bade adieu to the valley of the Rio Chico, and struck into a gorge of the northern hills, leading into an uneven valley lying between low irregular hills of decomposed lava, which we followed, passing several small lagoons in the lower hollows, around which there was invariably a yellow description of clay. The hills were everywhere covered with scrub, and presented a wild, bleak appearance, the grey rocks only appearing now and then. After some hours' travelling through this dismal district in a north-west course, we emerged on a large plain at the western side, bounded by a range of hills 1,000 feet high, forming a spur of the Cordillera. The weather was stormy, and we could only catch occasional glimpses, through the driving clouds and snow-storms, of the loftier peaks of the more distant mountains. Our expedition in search of wild horses was, of course, after

the recent troubles, abandoned; and forced marches, to escape the Southern
Indians, in the event of their following from Santa Cruz, were the order of the
day. Hunting, however, was resumed by the unwounded, and several ostriches
were caught during the day. Towards evening the encampment was fixed near a
lagoon, the environs of which were barren, and destitute of anything except a
small low shrub which served for firewood. Although the wind was northerly, it
was bitterly cold; and as I had for some days past adopted the native costume—
keeping my 'store clothes' stowed away under charge of Mrs. Orkeke—I felt
it exceedingly. The 6th, 7th, and 8th of September were occupied in making
forced marches northward, accompanied by the usual hunting; and although
both parties continued armed, and appeared to be rather suspicious of each
other, things went on pretty smoothly. The country traversed on the 6th and
7th was a large arid plain, dotted with a few stunted shrubs, enclosed by the
before-mentioned spur of the Cordillera on the western side, and on the east
by a low range of sandy-looking hills. The whole of this plain was strewn with
small pebbles of porphyry, quartz, silica, and obsidian; also with small pieces
of silicified wood. On the 8th we crossed the spur by a pass walled on either
hand with rocks of vesicular lava. Here we halted for a quarter of an hour, and
everyone broke off pieces of stone suitable for making hand-balls for bolas.
The descent on the western side was no easy matter, the declivity being strewn
with large masses of rock and loose boulders, and the wind blowing bitterly
cold, and with such force that some of the women's horses could hardly face
it. Ultimately all managed to reach a spacious elevated pampa, on the western
side of which, some fifteen leagues off, rose the Cordillera of the Andes. In the
pass I observed several large pieces of obsidian, so clear and peculiarly round-
shaped that I at first imagined that a demijohn had been carried thither by
some previous party and broken. Of this the women gathered some pieces,
to serve as scrapers for cleaning guanaco skins. We traversed the usual barren
high pampa—interspersed with low shrubs, coarse grass, and here and there an
incense bush of considerable size, which afforded a moment's shelter from the
cutting wind—for some distance, till we at length reached a cliff, below which
lay a grassy plain, watered by a small, rapid stream. About thirty miles in the
background were visible the lofty mountains of the Cordillera. The inviting
appearance of the pasture determined us to remain for a couple of days to
rest the horses, after the unusually long marches of the preceding days. The
following day was occupied chiefly in making hand-balls for bolas from the
soft porous stone obtained in the rocky pass. Towards noon a frightful gale of
wind sprang up, which blew down most of the toldos; but ours, thanks to the
strength of arm of Mrs. Orkeke, who had securely fixed the poles, remained
firm, only one or two of the poles being broken. The river, here flowing in an
eastward direction, was the first stream met with since leaving the valley of the
Rio Chico. In the descent to it, the bench formation, although recognisable,

was not so much marked as in many of the other rivers. After two days' rest, we resumed our journey; and having traversed the grassy valley for, perhaps, a mile, ascended a slight ridge to a higher plain of the usual sterile nature, in which the first ostrich eggs met with were found. Our course was directed nearly north-west, to a range of hills 800 feet in height; on their summit was a plateau strewn with large stones and rocks.

We formed another hunt, in which numerous ostriches and several pumas were killed. From the western side of the plateau we overlooked a large plain, extending to the immediate vicinity of the mountains, but near the side of which there appeared to be a cutting or steep descent, just like a railway embankment. As it had been announced in the cacique's address that we were to encamp near a spring on the eastern side, and I had killed an ostrich, which, after giving a sharp run of half a mile, had been turned by the cavalcade of women, I proceeded in company with Casimiro and another to have some dinner. We accordingly selected a bush, cooked, and ate our bird, and at the conclusion of our meal mounted and proceeded to where we expected to find the encampment. But, arriving at the spot, we found nobody, and looking over the plain caught a glimpse of a belated woman just vanishing down the cutting above mentioned. We accordingly followed, and an hours' gallop brought us up with the remainder. The sun had set, but the light of a young moon enabled us to make our way to the second bench. I may say the formation altogether much resembled that of the river Cuheyli; but the river which flowed in this valley was of small size, although, as we found, the banks were boggy and almost impracticable. The moon had by this time set, and after a considerable deal of confusion in the dark, all got across, and night being far advanced encamped about a mile to the northward. When daylight enabled us to examine the locality, we found ourselves in a valley, walled in by lofty abrupt cliffs on both sides, while a stream—bordered by marshes, containing numerous snipe and teal—flowed swiftly down the centre of the glen. To the north the valley appeared to bend westwards, so having nothing to do, I strolled up to the turn and found that the high cliffs ceased, and were replaced by the ordinary steep barrancas, covered from the top to the bottom with incense bushes. The valley nowhere exceeded a mile in width, and the gloom and oppressive effect of the prison-like walls of cliff rendered it by no means a desirable place of abode, but the pasture skirting the marsh was green and luxuriantly tender. While I was endeavouring to secure some ducks and teal with the bolas, two of the Chilians came up serching for firewood. They bitterly bewailed their lot in having to work and slave for a parcel of savages, but finally forgot their grievances in a slumber under a bush. Not caring to be supposed to have been in their company, I returned to the camp, and examined the rocks, which were different to those previously observed, showing in many places granite, with schistose veins, and what appeared to be a species of grey marble. A stay was made in this place of some four days, and would have been longer, but that on the third day some of the party, chiefly boys, who had strolled away a short distance, balling small birds, came in with the news that Indians were coming from the south. A scout was immediately sent out, horses brought up, and arms got ready. Casimiro came to me for a supply of cartridges for the revolver, saying, 'Now we shall have to fight; for if those Southern Indians beat us, they will spare neither man, woman, nor child.' This was cheering news, seeing that the odds were likely to be about ten to one against our side. However, just as we were mounting, the scout returned with the news that he had found no traces of Indians; the supposed enemy being only a troop of guanaco coming down to water. Cayuke, on its being ascertained that there was really no danger, had one of his horses killed as a thank offering; the meat of course being distributed for food amongst his friends. There is in this place, which is called by the Indians 'Amakaken,' a large spherical boulder of marble, which it is the custom of the Indians to try their strength by lifting. Casimiro informed me that this stone had been there for many years, and the custom was very old. It was so large and heavy that I was just able to grasp it with both arms, and raise it to the level of my knees, but some of the Indians managed to lift it to their shoulders. The night subsequent to the false alarm, snow fell heavily, notwithstanding which on the following day the Indians, who did not appear to feel secure, marched again in a northerly direction. Before quitting this valley, I was fortunate enough to find an ostrich nest with four eggs in it, which we devoured later on, cooked in the ashes by the simple method of placing the egg upright, with a hole broken in the upper surface, through which a piece of stick is inserted to stir round the yolk and white, a little salt being thrown in, and the egg turned to ensure all sides being equally done; the result being an omelette in the shell of most appetising flavour, but a novice in this cookery is apt to burn his fingers in turning the egg. Towards night we entered a dark and gloomy gorge, winding amongst fantastic and confused cliffs and peaked hills, thrown together in utterly chaotic confusion, which appeared to form a barrier east and west. But it was impossible accurately to distinguish the line, so inextricably were the heights jumbled together. My powers of description are utterly inadequate to convey the idea of the formless irregularity of this region of rocky hills.

At a late hour we encamped in a glen, or corrie, apparently without a second outlet, and walled in by frowning cliffs, down the midst of which a torrent foamed in a rocky channel. All the next day our march continued through a barren desert of rocks, frequently intersected by deep ravines with precipitous cliffs, the faces of which in many places displayed beds of red and yellow ochre, visible at a great distance. From some of these the women, after a scramble, replenished their supplies of paint. The whole face of this district was torn and tossed, as if by tremendous explosive force; and, except in some deep-lying clay bottoms, where an occasional shallow lagoon was to be met with, the track was waterless; snow lay on the heights and in some places on the ground traversed by our march, in the course of which a number of the large ibises, called in Chili bandurria (Theristicus melanopis), were seen. The nature of the country rendered hunting laborious and useless. Tankelow, however, found an ostrich and nest, the eggs from which, about thirty in number, he, according to Indian custom, divided among those who came up before, they were removed from the nest; among these lucky individuals was myself; for, seeing him make to the spot, and the male bird get up, and being, moreover, well mounted and exceedingly hungry, I was among the first arrivals. Far away to the right of our track, extending thirty or forty miles eastwards, lies a district called by the Indians 'The Devil's Country,' which, they assured me, is never entered, probably from the barren and impracticable nature of the surface, which seems, from description, to be even worse than the wilderness traversed by us. Beyond this district there is a practicable track, sometimes followed by the Indians, leading northward, probably used as a route to the Chupat; but from that line to the sea the country is so impassable that the Indians say it would require two years to proceed by the sea-coast from Santa Cruz to the Rio Negro. The existence of such tracks as these, and the desolate Travisias encountered near the coast, have probably caused Patagonia to be described as an arid, almost waterless country; but, in reality, after passing the coast barrier most of the interior abounds in lagoons, springs, and frequent streams; and, even in the Travisias, the numerous wild animals met with show that water exists.

Towards evening we left the snow behind us; and descending a lofty hill, which had bounded our view all day, came to a large swelling down, from which the prospect was far more encouraging. Rolling plains extended to the north and north-east, whilst the Cordillera rose like a wall on the western side. This hill is called by the Indians 'God's Hill;' and the tradition, as communicated by Casimiro, relates that from this spot the Great Spirit dispersed the animals which he had made in the caverns. But some of the animals must have remained behind, as, out on the lower slope of the downs, two pumas were chased and killed. An hour's ride over a sandy plain brought us to a valley with a stream flowing through beautifully green pasture. This was the spot chosen for our encamping, and some of the women were already busy planting the poles that form the skeleton of the toldos; so, turning my horse adrift, I started down to the stream, and, after the luxury of a bath, lay down and smoked until the toldos were thoroughly arranged. The following day a short march was made, in a north-west direction, to a valley containing better pasture; here it was intended to give the horses much-needed repose. Meanwhile, however, meat fell short, so a circle was organised; my horse was too tired; but Orkeke, seeing me standing unprepared, said, 'Ask Ako (his pet dog, and adopted child, and in virtue of his office the owner of several horses) to lend you a horse.' As Ako had no objection I was soon mounted, and started for the chase in high spirits.

On our previous journey we had remarked numerous tracks of what appeared to be ostrich near the ground where our present circle was to be formed (viz., in the direction of the Cordillera), and all expected to find plenty of game. The circle was formed, myself going as one pointsman; and, after arriving at the point, I watched anxiously for some time, but the only animal that appeared was a male guanaco, which, as he did not see me crouched behind an incense-bush, until he came within shot, I successfully balled and killed. After waiting a little longer, and the Indians being moderately near at hand, I changed my position a few hundred yards, to a more likely spot; but no animals appeared, so I proceeded in search of Orkeke, whom I shortly discovered smoking on the top of a small eminence. After the pipe had been passed in silence, I asked him what he had killed. 'Nothing,' was the answer; 'let's wait and see; perhaps some other Indian has an ostrich.' A careful survey, however, failed to discover anyone so lucky, although several had killed guanaco. So we retired to where my dead guanaco lay uncovered: at our approach two or three condors rose heavily up; and shortly about twenty or thirty more spread their huge wings, sailed away, and perched on a neighbouring rock. As for the guanaco, in the short half hour of my absence it had been literally torn to pieces; so, after extracting and eating the marrow-bones, we returned to camp, on our way capturing two armadilloes. During the past day or two the temperature had considerably risen, the wind, though westerly, was mild and genial, and the Indians affirmed that farther north it would be so warm that I should require some covering for the head. We found on our return that Arica during our absence had gone off somewhere on foot. As he had that morning asked and obtained some tobacco from me, it seemed probable that he had determined to attempt to make his way alone to reach civilisation at some point or other. During our stay in this valley Casimiro requested me to write a letter for him to the commandante at the Rio Negro, inquiring whether the Argentine Government still allowed him his ration and pay as lieut.-colonel in their service. I also wrote some letters to my friends, but without much hope of their being 'mailed;' though Casimiro assured me that when we joined the Northern Indians they would forward them to the Araucanos, whence they *might* go on by the people who went to Rio Negro to fetch the chief's allowance of cattle; remote, however, as were all these contingencies, still it was a pleasure to write. We quitted the valley after three days' rest, during which Arica had not appeared, and he was concluded either to have fallen a prey to a puma, or to have gone off on his own account. We journeyed all day over a rough hilly country, encumbered with large stones and occasional patches of scrub of considerable height; ostriches abounded, and large quantities of eggs were found. During a long march of about thirty miles no water was seen until we reached the camp at sunset, situated in a cañon; but along the route an occasional patch of snow sufficed to quench our thirst. As I rode along in company with an Indian, named 'Tchang,' he began asking me questions: first, 'Who is cacique of the English?' I explained to him that it was Her Gracious Majesty. 'Is she married?' 'She is a widow.' 'Has she any children, and how many? Has she lots of horses and mares and silver ornaments?' And so on, until I had satisfied him; after which he rode along, repeating, 'A woman cacique! A woman cacique! Four sons and five daughters! Lots of horses, mares, sheep, and cattle!' On the 22nd of September we left the encampment in the cañon about sunrise, and, mounting the ridge on the north side, halted close to the grave of an Indian; the broad and high cairn of stones erected over it denoting him to have been a cacique of importance, which fact was communicated to me in a low whisper by Wáki. Here a fire was made, and a few stones added to the pile. Whilst the Indians were warming themselves the sun rose, and the view of the Cordillera, seen through the clear atmosphere, with the sun's first rays illuminating the snowy mountain summits with a roseate flush, was magnificent. We pursued our route over sandy plains, crossed at intervals by shallow streams of water, and halted near some lagoons in a place called by the Indians 'Kinck.'

The following day we marched again, hunting as usual on the way. A fat ostrich at this time of the year was a rarity, but eggs abounded, and formed the main staple of food; and the armadilloes were also getting into condition, and assisted to furnish a repast at the camp fire. On the 27th we arrived at a place named 'Gelgel,' situated on the banks of a rapid river, probably that debouching at Port Desire. This was the point of divergence from the northern route to Patagones for any party proceeding to hunt in the western plains. During our stay in Gelgel we hunted in the surrounding country, and on several occasions observed columns of smoke to the south, as if made by a party approaching. These at last appeared nearer, and as no distinct answer was made to our signal fires, scouts were sent out, but returned with no information, one, however, asserting that he had found the tracks of many horses, but his known character as an incorrigible liar made his statement valueless. Still everybody became at last convinced that the Northern Indians were at war with the Araucanos, and consequently preparations to fight were commenced. After a watchful night, all fires out, and silence strictly observed, all armed, and mounting their best horses, sallied out. After a while the cause of the whole disturbance turned out to be Arica, who had wandered for eleven days on foot, following our track, subsisting on birds' eggs, and narrowly escaping the pumas, though he had been more than once attacked by them in broad daylight, and had killed one with his knife, his story being vouched for by the boots he had contrived to manufacture out of his deceased enemy's skin. He looked worn and haggard, his feet were sore, and he told me that another night would have finished him. The Indians, who—owing to his desertion and subsequent pursuit of us—had been kept on the alert all night, without fire, and prohibited from conversing, were naturally indignant, and wanted to kill him. But Casimiro and Orkeke interceded for him, and he was brought back to the toldos behind another horseman. Casimiro, *apropos* of these signal fires, related to me a curious story, as follows:—'Many years ago, when I was quite young, I was travelling a few leagues to the northward, under my mother's charge. The party encamped near a large lagoon not far from the Sengel river, and were occupied in hunting in the neighbourhood. On several days in succession smoke was observed in different directions, which approached nearer and nearer each time. Being naturally supposed to be caused by the Indians, it was answered, and scouts were at last sent to ascertain the cause, as no messengers appeared. They returned, however, stating that they could discover nothing. At the end of four days an Indian, tall, gaunt, and emaciated, mounted on a very thin *mule*, arrived in the camp, and asked for a chief whose name was unknown. The stranger was taken, as is customary, to the chief's toldo, and his mule turned loose; but, strange to say, it never moved from the spot where it was unsaddled, and the Indian during the time he remained in the toldo neither ate nor drank. At the end of three days he mounted his mule, which appeared as fresh as when he arrived, and rode away to the northward. On the following day, whilst hunting, a sickness struck the Indians—some falling dead from their horses, while others, though able to return home, only survived a short time. As is usual when disease breaks out, the toldos were removed to some distance from each other, to escape infection, but many men, women, and children died.' Of the fact that a plague or sickness did cause the deaths of many Indians within a few days at some encampment in these plains, I received further and reliable confirmation, my informant, who was in the party, stating that the Pampa tribe was decimated.

In the cliffs above the river on the eastern side of our encampment I observed many balls of sandstone of various sizes. On breaking one in two, a piece of what seemed to be ironstone formed a nucleus, around which layers of sand appeared to have been aggregated. By what process these balls could have been formed was to me a mystery; but they proved very handy for bolas, only requiring to be slightly reduced in size. Hunting to the westward from the encampment, we came across several muddy, or rather clayey bogs, into one of which, when in full pursuit of an ostrich, I rode, and my horse sank deep, throwing his rider a complete summersault; and with much ado I first picked up myself, and then with greater difficulty extricated my horse from the tenacious morass.

After Arica's return, the Chilians manifested a restless spirit, and frequently asked me the direction of the Chupat settlement. I replied that it lay about 150 leagues to the E.N.E. from this point, as far as I could judge; but that it would be better for them to remain with the Indians, and do the women's work of providing wood and water, &c., than to start off into a wild and dreary pampa, where they would inevitably starve without a knowledge of the route or guides.

During our stay here I nearly fell a victim to a matrimonial entanglement. A fair young Indian, whose hair cut across the forehead denoted widowhood, moreover having several mares and considerable possessions, to whom I had perhaps paid some slight attention, proposed that I should set up toldo with her. This was quite out of my programme of the journey, but inasmuch as the alliance might prove useful, as well as agreeable, and feeling lonely in the absence of any particular friend, I half agreed; so a go-between was despatched to arrange the dowry, and it was settled that I should give a revolver in exchange for two horses to be provided by the fair one's friends. However, the evening before the happy day on which we were to have been united, the alarm came, and as she belonged to the Southern Indians, I thought better of giving up my arms; so I assigned as a reason for withdrawing from the bargain, that I did not wish to leave my friend Orkeke's toldo. I have no doubt that her people, desiring the help of my firearms, had suggested the match to secure me to support their side. The lady at first was rather disgusted, but soon got over it, and we remained on our former friendly terms.

In this encampment two disagreements occurred between Indians and their wives, which were the only matrimonial squabbles that came under my notice during my wanderings in their company. One occurred between Tankelow and his spouse in our toldo. It began by Tankelow's striking his daughter, which his wife angrily resented; from words they came to blows, and the squaw was getting rather the best of it, when Mrs. Orkeke interposed with a strong arm, and forcibly put a stop to the disturbance.

The following day Tankelow drove his horses off separately, but towards evening a reconciliation was effected. On the 3rd of October we left Gelgel-aik and marched west in the face of a bitterly cold wind. In the hunt not less than seven pumas were killed, which were, as usual at this time, very fat, and were duly boiled in the iron pots, furnishing an excellent supper, the meat closely resembling boiled pork. During the day seven of the Chilians were missed, and on our arrival at the toldos, it transpired that they had determined to try and find their own way to the Chupat settlement; and as they had left in an underhand manner, which the Indians look upon as tantamount to a declaration of war, some of the people wished to pursue and kill them, but this proposition was overruled by Orkeke and Casimiro. The encampment was sheltered by a hill named 'Téle,' close to a large lagoon, covered with waterfowl, into which flowed a beautiful spring issuing from the hill; along the margin of the clear pure water grew a profusion of a sort of green cress, and at sunset flights of flamingoes (Phœnicopterus tgnipallo) and rose-coloured spoonbills (Platalea ajaja) came to the lagoon to feed. One day's hunting was done in the surrounding plain, which to the west presents several of the remarkable drops or basin-like formations described by Darwin as existing on the eastern side of the Cordillera. On October 5th we broke up the camp and marched in a northerly direction, until a stream of considerable size was arrived at; this some of us crossed at once, although it was deep and the banks rotten and unsound. The women and remainder of the party diverged to a ford, old Orkeke sending one of the Chilians to take care that his little dog (on whom he lavished his paternal affections) did not get wet. In half an hour's time the whole party—Ako included—had crossed in safety, and the camp was pitched on a peninsula between this river and another which joined it lower down. The united streams may or may not form a tributary of the Chupat, as the Indians disagreed on this point, some averring it to be so, others stating that the river flowed into a large lagoon. The weather had changed to drizzling rain, and the wet and sloppy state of the toldos was very disagreeable. It did not, however, much affect our clothing, as it is easy to dry a guanaco mantle by the fire, but care must be taken only to expose the furred side to the heat, otherwise the hide will become dried and apt to tear easily. Whilst in this encampment lookouts were posted, and one came in stating that he had seen smoke in a northerly direction. Consequently, on October 9, having rested our jaded horses, which were rapidly improving in condition, from grazing on the young green grass now springing abundantly in all the valleys, we crossed a barren, clayey pampa, interspersed with bogs and marshes at intervals, and on the 10th arrived at a small range of hills, running east and west, under one of which the toldos were pitched, near to another of those beautiful circular springs which frequently occur in Patagonia; from the centre of the smooth white sand which formed the bottom, the water bubbled up like liquid crystal, and silvery fishes could be seen darting about in the circular basin. The Indians delight in laying their hands and feet in the springs, and will sit there for a long time admiring the beauty of these 'eyes of the desert.' As, on our arrival, the women had not yet completed the domestic arrangements, after throwing the spoils of the chase off our saddles, a party of us ascended an adjacent hill to have a look round. The day was magnificent, and the sun, just setting, bathed the whole country in a flood of red tints. To the N.E. we observed three distinct columns of smoke which the Indians averred to be caused by the five Chilian deserters, and were very bitter against them, as they were supposed to have lost their way, and to be desirous of returning again to the toldos. In this place I found my compass would not act, owing, as I supposed, to having been disabled; but as it subsequently behaved properly, its temporary derangement must have been due to some local attraction. To the northward, as well as I could guess the bearings, ran a long range of hills, terminating in a peculiarly-peaked mountain, below which the Indians pointed out the trees which fringed a river—according to their statements, a tributary of the Chupat. To the west extended rolling plains, which appeared to stretch away into the distance, interrupting the chain of the Cordillera, as though there were a depression or break in the mountains, no hills of large size being visible on the horizon. Whilst lying down smoking on this hill, I picked up several pieces of opal and cacholong combined, and as I was idly forming them into different patterns on the ground, and had arranged a circle resembling a miniature Indian grave, one of my companions observing what I was doing, grew very angry and said, 'That will bring ill, luck,' evidently believing that I was mentally compassing the death of some one by witchcraft. As I had no wish to be killed by way of prevention of any imaginary spells, I quickly gathered up the specimens, many of which were afterwards lost in the ensuing journey. The Indian name for this place is Yaiken-Kaimak, signifying that it is the hill whence they espy the signal smoke denoting the approach of the Indians from the north.

We remained five days in this encampment, a general uneasiness prevailing, and arms being kept ready to hand. In addition to the usual hunting, under the orders of the cacique, we were engaged in performing exercises on horse back; this mounted drill being intended as a preparation in case we should find the northern Tehuelches at war with the Araucanos or Manzaneros Indians. The plains to the westward abounded with guanaco, some thousands being enclosed in the circle at one time. One day that I had not accompanied the hunting party, I was strolling across the camp, having volunteered to occupy the post of the vidette on an adjacent hill, when I observed a guanaco, very tired, coming towards me; so, hiding behind a bush, I waited till he unsuspiciously approached, and then rushing out, balled him with a pair of ostrich bolas. As he was so close to me, his forelegs were perfectly tied up, and I had not much difficulty in despatching him with a blow on the head from another set of bolas. By this time I had attained tolerable dexterity in the use of the bolas, and it was my invariable custom when not otherwise employed to stroll about and practise. Besides their use, my practical training had enabled me soon to acquire the art of manufacturing them, and our many idle hours were employed in plaiting ostrich sinews, so that I contrived to fit up an extensive assortment, some of which I used to barter for tobacco. The weather during our stay here became worse, rain, sleet, and gales of wind prevailing; and the toldos, from the continuous rain and the marshy nature of the ground, became so wet and wretched as to be almost uninhabitable, so that we marched on the 16th over a level pampa—smoke to the eastward being observed and duly answered during the journey. We encamped at night on the north side of a small rapid stream, in a place called 'Pelwecken,' situated a league from the wooded river, the trees of which were visible from the encampment. I here saw a new game played by the Indians which resembled that known amongst schoolboys as 'knucklebones,' being played with small stones in lieu of the bones, and heavy stakes were lost and won on the chances. On Sunday, the 17th, the Indians started to hunt in the vicinity of the wooded river, and Casimiro proposed that I should accompany him to the woods to cut poles for the toldos, and timber for working saddles. Orkeke, however, for some reason or another, recommended me to stay quietly in the toldos; and, as advice is sometimes almost the same as a command, I acquiesced, although longing to enjoy a close view of a tree again after so much wandering over the treeless pampas. As the day was warm and fine, I strolled down the river in search of the eggs of the upland goose (Chloephaga magellanica), yellow-billed goose (Cygnus coscoroba), and other water fowl, and returned about 2 p.m. with plenty of spoil. The women were superintending the cooking of some of these, when one of them rushed into the toldo and cried out that the Indians were returning and a fight had taken place. A glance at the coming horsemen was at once sufficient to convince us that she was right. They came galloping back by twos and threes, swords drawn, mantles hanging off their shoulders, and their faces glowing with fury. They at once proceeded to get their guns and revolvers to renew the fight. Orkeke, however, arrived and made a long speech, and ultimately quiet was restored. One man—a brother of Camillo—had been killed and left on the pampa. The sister of the deceased was frantic at his death, and, arming herself with a knife, attempted to avenge him; but she was soon stopped, disarmed and quieted. The deceased was armed with a six-shooter, and his assailant had only a sword; one shot missed him and the next barrel missed fire, whereupon he closed and ran his adversary through the body. Casimiro returned shortly after the remainder, and when he heard of the fight and the result, was for some time eager to renew it and avenge the slain man, who was a relation of his own, but at last yielded to Orkeke's arguments. The following day the smoke to the east appeared pretty close, and, when we had marched on a little, two young men were despatched in its direction with private instructions from Orkeke, and we proceeded to the wooded river, where we luxuriated for a short time under the shade of a description of birch tree and then forded the stream, which is of considerable width and very rapid. The Indians declared that it was impossible for any man to swim across the river in the deeper portion below the ford, on account of some ferocious beasts which they termed water tigers—'Tigres de l'agua'— which would certainly attack and devour anyone in the water. They described them as yellow quadrupeds, larger than puma. It is certain that two ostriches which, being too poor for use, had been left on the bank, were found by us next day in the shallow water, torn and half devoured, and the tracks of an animal resembling those of a large puma were plainly visible leading down to the water; but a puma invariably drags its prey to a bush; and, though jaguar will take the water readily, I have never known one devour its prey except on land, nor, as far as I know, are they found so far south. The animal may be a species of the large brown otter with orange-coloured fur on the breast, found in the Parana; but the Indians' account is curious as bearing on the name of the lake—'Nahuel Huapi,' or Tigers' Island. It is possible that the aguarra found in the valley of the Rio Negro may also haunt these districts. They further told me that stags had been seen on the banks of the river, but none were heard of during our stay in the neighbourhood. A few miles below the ford the belt of trees ceases, and on the southern side there is a peculiar group of what seem to be square-shaped rocks, which at a distance have very much the appearance of a small town regularly built and walled. This is called by the Indians 'Sengel,' and was the scene of a great fight between the Tehuelches and Araucanos many years ago, relics of which in the shape of bones and skulls still whiten the plain. After crossing the river, the young men who had been sent back returned, bringing with them three horses belonging to the Chilians and one man of their party, who, incredible as it seems, had assisted the Indians to dismount and disable his companions. The particulars of the fate of the others were not divulged though a story was current that some of them had managed to reach the Chupat. I asked no questions, but the blood-stained knife of one of the young men told its own story. This day all the Indians rode on in silence, the last two days' events having roused all their bad passions. I rode alone, feeling that there was danger in the air, and near our halting place joined Orkeke and two others at a fireside for the purpose of cooking some ostrich eggs, which we were busily discussing when a messenger came to say that Casimiro was waiting to see me at a spot which he indicated. I mounted and rode off accordingly, but had not gone far before the two bravos who had been commissioned to do for the Chilians galloped up, one from either side, one brandishing his sword and the other swinging his bolas. I at once put spurs to my horse, and my mantle flying back discovered two revolvers belted round my waist underneath it. They checked their career and sang out, 'Stop! Where are you going?' But, without making any reply, I galloped on, being not further interfered with, and soon joined my old friend. He then informed me that, being utterly disgusted with the late proceedings and general anarchy, he had determined to push forward by himself to meet the Northern Indians, leaving his wife and children under the charge of Cayuke. He therefore wanted the letters which I had written for him and my own, which he undertook to forward at the same time. So I rode back to the toldos for the letters, which I carried to Casimiro without anyone attempting to stop my way.

Having returned to the fire under the bush, I dismounted, and whilst cooking another egg, gave Orkeke a piece of my mind; quietly hinting that I carried ten lives about me. He assured me it was all a mistake, and had happened without any orders from him, the young fellows only wishing to try my mettle by way of joke. I replied that jokes of that sort were sometimes dangerous, and the subject was mutually dropped.

We encamped by the side of a stream, into which many of us soon plunged to take a refreshing bath, always a favourite enjoyment with the Tehuelches, who are powerful swimmers, and dive well. While resting here and sporting in the water a better state of feeling arose, and the mutual suspicion and discord which had so long prevailed was gradually forgotten. Casimiro had left, taking one of the Chilians; and his spouse told me, amid a torrent of abuse of her better half, that he had gone through fear, the other Indians having determined to kill him; and she added that he had the heart of a skunk, a vulture, and an armadillo. These combined would make a very nice mixture. That he was right in making his escape at this particular juncture was very evident, for the next day two young men were sent out, ostensibly as chasquis or messengers, to look for the Northern Indians, but in reality to try and overtake Casimiro and dispose of him; however, they returned without any tidings of the wily old chief.

In the range of hills described as visible from Kaimak, there is a mine or vein of iron ore, about a mile due west from the brook, and marked by a large mass of white quartz. This is used by the Indians in the manufacture of bolas, and an excursion was made to it. We brought back numerous pieces, some of which, now in my possession, have been examined, and pronounced to be brown and magnetic iron ore. The Indians also told me that some leagues to the east of this spot a mass of iron, having, as well as could be gathered from their account, the shape of a bar-shot, lies in the middle of a barren plain, and is regarded by them with superstitious awe. Whether this be an aërolite, or has any connection with the ore on the hill side, it was not in my power to determine, for in the critical state of feeling then prevalent a visit of inspection was impracticable.

On the 22nd of October we marched a few miles, always following the line of hills, and in a northerly course. Ostrich eggs still formed the main staple of food, and furnished a diet sufficiently nutritious, but producing all the effects of a course of 'Banting.' Fortunately this day two of us killed fat pumas, some steaks off which broiled, by way of variety, were an acceptable addition to the evening meal; but from experience I should advise all travellers to boil their puma. We encamped in a small gorge in the hills, directly under a peculiarly pointed rock, which is called Yowlel, or Ship Rock, from its resemblance to a ship under sail, and is regarded with superstition by the Indians, who believe that all who endeavour to ascend it in the calmest weather will, on arriving at the summit, have their mantles blown to pieces by furious gusts of wind.

The next day—a glorious morning, after a night's rain—we proceeded in the same direction; and while waiting for the heavy baggage, in the shape of the women and children, several of us repaired to a regular racecourse—a beaten track six feet wide, extending for almost three miles, level and free from stones, though rather sandy. Here we had trials of the speed of our horses to while away the interval; and, when the women appeared, proceeded to the chase, over a pampa formed by a bend in the range of hills. During the hunt we found the carcase of a guanaco, which had been killed by a puma, carefully covered up in grass and scrub. It was a fat animal, such as the puma always singles out, although I have read in some accounts that he follows the herds and picks up the weakly ones. That this is not the case was proved on various occasions, by finding the carcases left by these cats, which were always those of animals in good condition. Early in the afternoon we arrived at the encampment, by the side of a small river, flowing in an easterly direction from the hills. The women, with the exception of one or two, were not present and might be seen about two miles off, grubbing up a description of potato which grew in the neighbouring hill side. The day was warm, and Orkeke invited me to go to the top of one of the hills to see if any smoke or signs of Indians were visible. We accordingly crossed the stream, and while riding along the northern bank I observed fish swimming lazily on the top of the water. After crossing a marshy patch of ground, we ascended the hills, and dismounting near a bank of blue earth, climbed on foot to the summit, which was composed of a description of quartz, with crystalline veins running through it. Scrambling up this formation, we arrived at the top, whence we had a beautiful view of the encampment and the green pasture bordering the stream. To the northward the view was rather shut in by hills rising to a considerable elevation. Just below us lay a valley, in which several guanaco and ostriches were taking their evening meal. We remained here for some time smoking and enjoying the face of nature generally, but could discern no smoke or signs of Indians. Orkeke remarked that the pasture had a fresher appearance lower down the course of the stream, and proposed that we should inspect it. We accordingly descended from our elevated position, mounted, and proceeded to the valley below; in our descent being lucky enough to kill a fat male ostrich, which was sitting on a nest of twenty-four eggs. We investigated the grass, which was of good quality; and after an *al fresco* meal, in which we were joined by Tchang, returned to the toldos, where the women had just arrived with a considerable supply of potatoes. I again, on our way back, observed fish in the stream, so, turning my horse adrift, proceeded to extract my hooks and line from the baggage under the charge of Mrs. Orkeke. After a little delay all was ready; a piece of meat supplied the place of fly as bait; and dropping it gently into the pool, I soon had a bite, and pulled out a fish about two pounds weight, of the perch class, similar to that called dorado in the River Plate. After half-an-hour's fishing I landed several others as large, and as it was nearly dark, returned to supper off fried fish and boiled potatoes.

I had no opportunity of seeing the plants which produced these tubers, but they exactly resembled those I afterwards obtained in the northern country from a plant, the feathery fern-like leaf of which springs from a long slender stem. The following day we shifted camp down river, to the neighbourhood of the green pasture, and found large quantities of the eggs of the upland geese, ducks, &c. In the neighbourhood one lonely tree grew by the side of the stream, although the banks were lined with driftwood, probably carried down from the wooded slopes of the Cordillera, ten miles farther west, during floods. This day, smoke having been distinctly seen to the northward, Hummums was despatched to ascertain whether it were a signal from the much-looked-for Northern Indians. Three days subsequently, about nine in the evening, whilst I was lying dreaming of home, and had just—in dreamland—taken a glass of sherry, Orkeke woke me up with the intelligence that fires were to be seen to the north, which were no doubt caused by the 'chasqui' or messenger previously despatched. In about three hours' time—somewhere about midnight—Casimiro, Hummums, and another Indian rode into the camp, and our toldo was soon crowded to hear the news from our chasqui, who stated that the Northern Indians were in the wild cattle district, where they had killed several animals; they were also well provided with tobacco and other necessaries from the Rio Negro, where they had been for trading purposes in August, and they would welcome our party, provided that they came in a friendly spirit. The following morning we had a great consultation in Crimè's toldo, at which it was determined that all quarrels should be forgotten, and that we should march at once to effect a junction with the other Indians. This having been resolved on, all marched in an easterly direction to an encampment situated on the borders of the same stream, and under a range of hills called 'Appleykaik.' Here we remained three days; and smoke not previously accounted for having been observed to the east, two scouts were sent out to ascertain the cause, but returned without intelligence. We spent our time, as usual, in hunting, or bathing in the river; and on October 31 marched again, and had not gone very far, in a north-east direction, before Tankelow—who had started earlier than the rest, and constituted himself a *corps d'observation* appeared, with a strange Indian of the Pampa tribe, who stated that his companions were on their way to join the Northern Indians. They had come from the neighbourhood of the Chupat colony, and were, as far as I could make out, mixed Pampas and Tehuelches. It was agreed that they should join us and the others at a place called 'Henno,' to which we were at present marching. We continued our route after this slight interruption, and encamped for the night near the banks of a small stream. The weather had entirely changed, the wind blowing bitterly from the south-west, with squalls of sleet, hail, and snow; and but few of the party found it agreeable to take the evening bath. Casimiro was in high spirits, as many of the Northern Indians were relations of his, and he was to be invested with the supreme command—in prospect of which he had already received presents of horses, and was looking forward to the consultation of the chief, which, he assured me, would have to be conducted with great pomp. During our talk, Casimiro narrated all his adventures after quitting the toldos. He had travelled so fast, knowing that he would probably be pursued, that on the fifth day his horse broke down. As for two days previous he had seen smoke from some encampment to which he was by this time close, though he was uncertain whether it was that of his friends or not, he left his Chilian companion, and proceeded to an eminence to reconnoitre. During his absence the Chilian fell asleep; the grass caught fire and surrounded the sleeping man. The Indians—Hinchel's people—attracted by the smoke, came down and rescued him, all his clothes having been burned off and his body severely scorched. Having heard his story, Hinchel at once sent a party to search for Casimiro. When the latter saw the five mounted Indians' approaching, wrapped in their ponchos, he was uncertain if they were Araucanos or Tehuelches, and drew his revolver, prepared to pick them off in detail; but soon, to his great relief, he recognised in the leader a relation of his own. He also told me that when Hummums, our chasqui, arrived, he was entertained by some friend of his own, to whom, in the evening, he boasted that he and his friends had killed all the Christians in their camp. This story was at once carried to Hinchel and Casimiro, who inquired if 'Muster' had also been killed; to which the tale-bearer unhesitatingly replied that he had. Hinchel, who had previously heard all about the English visitor from Casimiro, was furious at what he considered a grave breach of hospitality, and issued orders forthwith to apprehend the chasqui, and to mount and make ready to avenge my supposed death by killing Orkeke and all his party. Hummums, however, when interrogated as a prisoner, in great terror declared that 'Muster' was safe, and that no one had any idea of killing him, and then the storm blew over. But this account, which was confirmed by the report of the chasqui, accidentally overheard by myself, prepared me to meet Hinchel with feelings of friendliness towards a chief who had evinced so keen a sense of the care to be taken of a stranger who had confided himself to Indian hospitality; and the impression of this chief's character then formed, was fully confirmed on further acquaintance with him.

The two following days our route lay through a succession of rather barren valleys, bordered by ranges of high hills, everywhere strewn with rocks and boulders, and having a very gaunt and weird appearance. The valleys generally contained good pasture on either the northern or southern side of the streams which flowed down every one; but away from the vicinity of the water 'the soil was sandy, with low bushes scattered here and there.

On November 2nd, about 2 P.M., we arrived at a pass or gorge above the rendezvous at Henno. The view of the valley below was very refreshing; green grassy plains stretched for some miles, with a beautiful silvery stream running down the centre. But, much to our disappointment, no signs of Indians were visible; so we descended, and after bathing in a pool, and waiting until the toldos were pitched, lighted a big signal fire, which was shortly answered to the westward, and a messenger was immediately despatched who returned towards nightfall with the intelligence that the expected people would arrive next day; and we had to reconcile ourselves to another night of anxiety, being not at all certain as to the reception to be expected from the new comers.

1. Frontispiece

IV

HENNOKAIK TO TECKEL

AS we were whiling away the next forenoon in fishing and disporting ourselves generally in the water, smoke was descried at various points to the westward, and about 2 p.m. the head of the heavy column of women, children, and innumerable horses came into view on the northern side of the valley. All instantly repaired to the toldos, accoutred ourselves, and got up the horses in preparation for the arrival of the visitors; the meeting of any number of Indians after a separation being recognised as an affair of considerable importance. Shortly after our horses were caught and saddled, and, indeed, before some of our party were ready, the men who had been hunting *en route* appeared, and the ceremonial of welcome was duly observed.

Both parties, fully armed, dressed in their best, and mounted on their best horses, formed into opposite lines.

The Northern Indians presented the gayest appearance, displaying flannel shirts, ponchos, and a great show of silver spurs and ornamental bridles. The chiefs then rode up and down, dressing the ranks and haranguing their men, who kept up a continual shouting of 'Wap, Wap, Wap.' I fell in as a private, though Casimiro had vainly endeavoured to induce me to act as 'Capitanejo' or officer of a party. The Buenos Ayrean colours were proudly displayed on our side, while the Northerns carried a white weft, their ranks presenting a much better drilled aspect than our ill-disciplined forces. Messengers or hostages were then exchanged, each side deputing a son or brother of the chief for that purpose; and the new comers advanced, formed into columns of threes, and rode round our ranks, firing their guns and revolvers, shouting and brandishing their swords and bolas. After galloping round at full speed two or three times, they opened ranks, and charged out as if attacking an enemy, shouting 'Koue' at every blow or thrust. The object of attack was supposed to

CEREMONY OF WELCOME (TCHUELCHES AND ARAUCANIANS)

be the 'Gualichu' or demon, and certainly the demon of discord had need to be exorcised. Hinchel's party then halted and reformed their line, while we, in our turn, executed the same manœuvres. Afterward the Caciques advanced and formally shook hands, making, each in turn, long and complimentary speeches. This was repeated several times, the etiquette being to answer only 'Ahon' or Yes, until the third repetition, when all begin to talk, and formality is gradually laid aside. It was rather a surprise to find etiquette so rigorously insisted on, but these so-called savages are as punctilious in observing the proper forms as if they were Spanish courtiers.

These Northern Tehuelches, under the command of Hinchel, usually frequent the country lying between the Rio Negro and the River Sengel, and once a year, about July, visit the settlement of Patagones, where their stay is generally short, only sufficient for them to barter their furs and feathers, and for the chiefs at the same time to receive their rations of mares, cattle, ponchos, yerba, tobacco, &c., allowed by the Government of Buenos Ayres. By the time we met them in November they had little to show of the gains of their August visit to Rio Negro except a few mares and gay-coloured ponchos. Hinchel, however, owned two or three head of cattle which were said to have been caught at the head of the Chupat valley, being supposed to be stray cattle belonging to the Welsh settlers. Some of the Indians had still also a little yerba left, and tobacco in plenty; and on the occasion of the welcome many were dressed in coloured ponchos, chiripas, and some in leathern boots. With arms they were passably well provided, guns and revolvers being in proportion of about one to four men. During the time that we were occupied in the ceremony the women of the newly-arrived party busied themselves in pitching their toldos; and shortly after we had returned to our camp, which was a little apart from that of the new comers, and appeared very small and insignificant when contrasted with theirs, the Cacique came over, and presented mares, horses, and other gifts to the chiefs of our party; and a grand feast was celebrated in our toldos. Many of the new comers rode over, two or sometimes three mounted on one horse, and would, if not acquainted with the inmates, stop in front of a toldo and look in for a few minutes, then ride on to another, and so on. As these were mostly young men, their real object was probably to reconnoitre the young ladies. One, however, who, though undistinguishable from the Indians in appearance, and who looked like an Araucano, but was really by birth a Spaniard, having been carried off in his childhood from a settlement, brought over a pack of cards, and some of our party were soon deep in a game of siete, at which the stranger being a proficient, soon cleared them out completely.

Next day I paid a visit to Hinchel. He spoke no Spanish, but he managed to converse, and he asked me if the Southern Tehuelches were not a queer lot, for he had heard that they killed men as readily as they would guanaco.

From what Casimiro had reported, I was already inclined to respect this Cacique, who had expressed such readiness to protect or avenge a guest of the Indians, and closer acquaintance only strengthened my regard for him. He was a fine-looking man, with a pleasant, intelligent countenance, which was not belied by his disposition. He never, to my knowledge, exceeded sobriety, and was good-humoured and self-possessed; though if once roused to fight, his resolute and determined courage was well known. He was skilled at all sorts of handicraft, and was always busily employed. He was generous to a fault—ready to give away everything if asked for it, and often without the asking. His great weakness was an inveterate fondness for gambling, which, together with his lavish good nature, eventually impoverished him greatly. At his request I informed Casimiro and Orkeke that he desired to hold a parlemento. Accordingly, the chiefs all proceeded to a place agreed upon between the two camps, where they took their seats in a circle on the grass. After various harangues from Hinchel and others, it was resolved that Casimiro should be elected chief in command of the Tehuelches; and that after the expiration of the young guanaco season, all present, together with those expected from the neighbourhood of the Chupat, should proceed to a place called Teckel, and thence march to Las Manzanas, to unite there with the Araucanian Indians, some of whom had already communicated with us, and had promised to forward my letters, *viâ* Las Manzanas, to Rio Negro.

The relations between the Tehuelches or Tsonecas of Patagonia and the Araucanian Indians of Las Manzanas had been previously by no means of a pacific nature. It has been already mentioned that near the Sengel we passed the scene of a fierce battle between them. Tankelow bore still the scars of seven lance wounds received in a battle when he was left for dead on the field. On the same occasion Orkeke was taken prisoner, but, although mutilated, succeeded eventually in effecting his escape. Casimiro's father also became a prisoner in an unsuccessful assault on an Araucanian stronghold. After two or three years' captivity he succeeded, with two of his comrades, in escaping, and while hurrying to rejoin the Tehuelches in the vicinity of Geylum, met with a solitary Araucanian. He, seeing a fire, approached unsuspicious of danger, and was welcomed and invited to smoke; they then seized him, stripped and bound him hand and foot, and left him lying on the pampa, a helpless prey to the condors and pumas. The two fugitives, having thus gratified their desire for vengeance, succeeded in rejoining their own people, and organised an attack on the Araucanos, in which Casimiro's father was killed. Some wonderful feats of valour were described to me as having been achieved by the Tehuelches; but in fact the Manzaneros proved themselves the superior warriors, and even at the time of our visit to them had Tehuelche slaves. The powerful cacique Lenquetrou succeeded in healing the old feuds, and united all the Indians under his leadership. He was treacherously killed by an Argentine officer at Bahia Blanca during the peace between the Indians and the Christians, and after his death the old quarrels broke out afresh. Casimiro's diplomacy, however, succeeded during the time of my visit in conciliating all parties, and the result appeared in the amicable arrangements concluded at the Parlemento, and afterwards successfully carried out. Had it not been for this, my journey to Las Manzanas, and thence to the Rio Negro, would have been dangerous, if not altogether impossible.

Two days after the arrival of the Northern party the Indians from the Chupat came in, and were duly welcomed by our united forces, the ceremonial on this occasion presenting a very animated scene. They numbered between seventy and eighty men, with women and children, occupying about twenty toldos. Most of them were young men of Pampa, or mixed Pampa and Tehuelche blood, but there were a few pure Tehuelches in their ranks, their chief being a Pampa named 'Jackechan,' or Juan. As I watched them drawn up, or careering round us during the welcome, they appeared to present a different type from that of my first friends, being generally shorter, though as muscular, and even apparently more broadly built, with complexions lighter, and their dress and persons smarter and cleaner. They were all well armed with lances and firearms, and were evidently kept well in hand by the chief. Their range of country lay between the same limits as that of Hinchel's people, but they habitually seemed to have kept more to the sea-coast, where many of them had been accustomed to visit the Welsh colony at the Chupat for trade, and in their opinion, as afterwards expressed to me, the honest Welsh colonists were much pleasanter and safer to deal with than 'the Christians' of the Rio Negro. They seemed to have been especially impressed with the size and excellence of the home-made loaves, one of which would be given in return for half a guanaco, and Jackechan often expatiated on the liberality of the colonists and the goodness of their bread. These men also felt strongly the kindness with which an Indian, if over taken with rum, would be covered up or carried into an out house by the Chupat people; whereas at the Rio Negro the only attention paid to him would be to strip and plunder him completely. During the afternoon the chief, Jackechan, sent a request to the 'Englishman' to pay him a visit, so I repaired to his toldo, and was courteously received by him. He wore a beautifully-wrought silver chain, with a medallion of the Madonna suspended to it, of which he seemed pardonably proud. Having been invited to take a seat, and the pipe having been duly passed round, it became evident that I was to be tested as to my real claims to the character of an Englishman. Jackechan, during his visits to the Chupat, had become acquainted with Mr. Lewis Jones, the Director of the colony, and so had learned the name of the Queen of England, &c., and he proceeded to interrogate me accordingly. I found him to be a most intelligent Indian, speaking Spanish, Pampa, and Tehuelche fluently; and our acquaintance thus commenced ripened into a strong mutual friendship. My answers proving quite satisfactory, he was evidently much pleased, and ordered his wife to produce coffee, a little of which he had still remaining from his store procured at Chupat. Whilst discussing this luxury, we had a long conversation on various topics, and he produced a photograph of Mr. Jones and some letters, one being an order for a ration of animals, mares and cattle, from the Argentine Government. He stated that he had not visited Patagones for some years, on account of a fight that had taken place, but would perhaps now accompany our party. Whilst conversing, his son, a boy of so twelve years of age, came in and startled me by his unlikeness to the other Indian boys, for his brown hair and eyes and fair complexion might easily have caused one to take him for an English boy. His mother was not present, as, for domestic reasons, Jackechan had parted with her; but I subsequently saw her, and she, although a handsome woman, had no European traits about her except that of having quarrelled with her husband. The following day was spent in a second parlemento—or, as the Indians call it, 'aix'—and all agreed to place themselves under the orders of Casimiro, for the purpose of protecting Patagones in the possible event of an invasion by the Indians of Rouke, or 'Calficura,' from the country north of Rio Negro. All present saw the importance of protecting Patagones, as, if that town should be destroyed, there would be no market for their furs, &c.

Our encampment was situated in a large grassy valley watered by a stream flowing to the eastward, which was finally lost in a large marsh. The valley, which may have been about twelve miles in length and perhaps four in width at its broadest part, was confined by hills which, closing, narrowed it in at the eastern and western extremities. To the N.W. and N. the hills—which almost merited the name of mountains—were peculiarly rugged, more especially towards their summits. About N.N.E. by compass from our camp, there was a pass formed by a dip or break in the range leading north, and through the mouth of the pass we could see the smoke of the hunting parties of the Araucanian Indians, who were, however, many leagues distant. Throughout Patagonia smoke is always visible at a great distance, and the practised eyes of the Indians can distinguish it from the clouds, when ordinary persons would be unable to discern it unless pointed out to them. On the southern and eastern sides of the valley lay a range of hills, the rugged summits of which rose from lower slopes of more regular swell, and presenting more even and down-like surfaces than those on the western and northern sides. Immediately above our encampment the hill of Henno, from which the valley is named, rose from the plain. Near the summit of this hill Orkeke and myself, who for amusement had ridden up to it, one day came across the bleached skeleton of a man, perhaps one of two young Argentines who, as I was subsequently informed, had travelled thus far in company with the Indians, and had been for some—or no—reason killed by them near this spot. In the surrounding hills red porphyry frequently cropped out, and also veins of a red agate, unlike the flint agate so common in all the plains of Patagonia. The rocks near the summits of the hills were generally of igneous formation, and on the slopes of these hills frequent springs gushed out, easily discoverable from a distance by the vivid green of the grass growing round them. As we gazed down from the height of Henno, the valley lay before us like a picture; our few toldos were situated in a group to the east, on the south side of the stream; about a quarter of a mile to the north the thirty or forty toldos of the Northern Indians were pitched, and opposite to them, on the north side of the stream, those of the party commanded by Jackechan or Juan. The scene was animated but peaceful: here might be seen a party of young men playing at ball, in another a man breaking a colt, and down by the side of the stream groups of girls bathing, or wandering in the swamps picking the wild spinach which grew all along the margin of the water in great quantities. One day I went on an excursion with the children to pluck spinach and plunder the nests of wild ducks and upland geese, from which we returned laden with spoil, and in the evening a stew, *à la* Tehuelche, was made with ostrich grease, spinach, and eggs, which combination was universally approved of. Another day we went fishing, and after catching several with a hook and line, voted it slow work, so contrived a net by sewing two ponchos together, and wading into the stream dragged the shallow parts, and, notwithstanding the duck weed, which rather impeded us, made several good hauls, the take consisting of the perch-like fish and a black species of cat-fish: the Indians, however, except Casimiro, would not eat the fish, and evidently regarded my enjoyment of them much as an Englishman would at first view their appreciation of blood. Another day we went on an expedition to dig up a species of root somewhat resembling a parsnip but although we grubbed about for an hour our efforts were only scantily rewarded by a few small roots, which were given to the children. One roasted in the ashes, at Mrs. Orkeke's invitation I tasted, and found it rather tasteless and insipid.

During our stay in this pleasant resting-place the weather was bright and sunny, and on calm days warm, and the absence of rain almost made it appear like summer; but whenever the west wind blew, the piercing cold dispelled the passing illusion. The long delay which was necessary to recruit our horses, in anticipation of a campaign against the young guanaco and the wild cattle, was most acceptable to all the members of our party; and after the two preceding months of quarrels, real and suspected dangers, and forced marches, our present peaceable existence, though devoid of adventure, was thoroughly enjoyable. An occasional hunting party, interchange of visits and card parties with the recent arrivals, fishing, foraging for birds' eggs, spinach, &c., with some flirting, and, by way of business, a parlemento or two, made our time pass merrily enough at Henno.

Our hunting parties were under the direction of 'the oldest inhabitant,' an aged cacique called Guenalto, with venerable white hair, and who had been crippled by a lance-thrust, received, to his honour be it said, while endeavouring to mediate between two of his friends. His great age and amiable character commanded universal respect; and on a hunting morning he would sit under a bush and speechify for half an hour, recounting old deeds of prowess, and exhorting us to do our best. The old man was a frequent and welcome visitor at our toldo, where he was encouraged to indulge to his heart's content in long-winded stories. My compass greatly excited his curiosity, and he took it into his head that it possessed a magical power which could effect the restoration of the use of his arm. He accordingly begged to be allowed to hold it in his hand; and sat patiently, with an air of awe and faith combined, for an hour, afterwards declaring that the operation had done him much good. We greatly pleased him by repairing his coat of mail, a complete tunic of heavy iron chains, of unknown antiquity, bound together by strips of hide, and weighing over a hundred weight. This he informed me he only put on to defend himself from 'foolish Indians.'

His use of my compass was rivalled by the custom of other friends, who were wont to borrow it when engaged in a game of cards; their belief being that the magic instrument gave luck to the happy possessor for the time being; and I often thought that it was fortunate I had brought no other instrument, as 'shooting the sun' would have been certainly regarded as a piece of sorcery, and any death or accident happening afterwards would have been visited on the head of the magician. As it was, my taking notes was often regarded with suspicious curiosity, and inquiries made as to what there could possibly be in that place to write about, as although the Tehuelche mind can comprehend writing letters to friends or officials, it by no means understands keeping a journal; and 'some untutored Indian' might probably, if suspicious that 'i' faith he'll prent it,' instead of waiting to cut up the book, anticipate all reviewers by cutting up the intended author himself.

On the 18th of November the camp at Henno was broken up, and all marched a few leagues to the west, crossing successive rocky ridges running parallel to the Cordillera, and divided by well-watered valleys, and encamped near a valley watered by the same river, which between this place and Henno makes a considerable bend. This station was named 'Chiriq,' from a description of bush, with a leaf somewhat resembling that of the sloe, which grows abundantly on the banks of the stream. The wood of this shrub is soft and of little value, but burns well when dry. At this time neither flower nor fruit was visible, but it was described to me as bearing a berry resembling the currant. Since our departure from the wooded river Sengel, a description of cactus, or, as the Spaniards call it, tuna, bearing a tasteless fruit something like the ordinary prickly pear, had been met with occasionally, and found very troublesome, for as it grows close to the ground its spines are very apt to lame the horses if not carefully avoided in the chase. From Chiriq a large plain appeared to extend for some leagues to the westward, bounded north and south by a wooded range of hills, and extending apparently to the bases of the lofty snow-covered peaks of the Cordillera, which appeared to form a complete barrier.

During our stay here an incident occurred which led to the collection and comparison of the traditions concerning the hidden or enchanted city which still are current and believed among the Indians and Chilotes.

One day while hunting we were startled by a loud report, as of the discharge of a cannon, and looking to the west saw a black cloud of smoke hanging above the peaks of the Cordillera. My companion Jackechan told me that on several previous visits to this station the Indians had observed similar columns of smoke in the same direction. On one occasion so convinced were they that it was caused by human agency, that a party set out to endeavour to penetrate the forests and reach the dwellings of the unknown residents, which the smoke was believed to point out. They proceeded some distance into the recesses of the mountain forests, but the extreme difficulties of travelling compelled them at last to abandon their purpose and retrace their steps. It is of course most probable that both the explosion and the smoke proceeded from some unknown active volcano in the range; but the Indians firmly believe in the existence either of an unknown tribe, or of an enchanted or hidden city. The Araucanians when met with farther north had a story current amongst them of having discovered a set of white people, who spoke an unknown tongue, in the recesses of the mountains in the same vicinity. The Chilotes and Chilians from the western side fondly cherish the belief in the existence of La Ciudad Encantada, and the mythical people Los Cesares, to the discovery of which, according to De Angelis—to whose research is due the collection of all the records on the subject—the attention of Buenos Ayres, Lima, and Chili was so long directed. A Chiliote or Valdivian, named Juan Antonio, narrated to me that he knew a man who was acquainted with another who had heard from a third that the last-named deponent was one of a party who visited the coast opposite to Chiloe for the purpose of wood cutting. They ascended in their boat a river, which as described was probably that the upper course of which we afterwards struck in the Cordillera. Having reached the woods, they separated to cut timber. One of their number was missing at the evening camp-fire; his comrades, however, waited for him, but gave him up at last, and were already preparing to return, when he rejoined them, and recounted a strange adventure. Deep in the forest he had come upon a path, which he followed for some distance, till he heard the sound of a bell, and saw clearings, by which he knew himself to be near a town or settlement. He soon met some white men, who made him prisoner, and after questioning him as to the cause of his being there, blindfolded him, and led him away to an exceedingly rich city, where he was detained prisoner for several days. At last he was brought back, still blindfolded, and when the bandage was removed found himself near the place of his capture, whence he made his way back to his comrades. Juan Antonio, the narrator, and Meña, one of the Chilian deserters who was present, fully believed this story, which, however, bears a suspicious resemblance to one told a hundred years before; and both declared that it was all caused by witchcraft or enchantment.

Another curious story was related to me, the hero of which was a mischievous imp of twelve years old, who was afterwards attached to my service as page, and for impudence and uselessness might have been a page of the court of Louis Quatorze. He had been in company with Fayel's tribe of Indians and Valdivians in the neighbourhood of the Cordillera. One day the hopeful boy was missed, and although careful search was made, no traces of him were discoverable. Three months afterwards he turned up again, dressed in the same clothes and in remarkably good condition, his spirits and impudence undiminished. My friend Ventura Delgado, a white Valdivian, who was the camp at the time of his absence and return, vouched from personal observation for so much of the story. When questioned as to his whereabouts and with whom he had been, he answered with confidence, 'With the man on the island in the lake.' There was no known lake nearer than Nahuel-huapi, thirty miles distant, though a chain of lakes must from old accounts exist within the Cordillera; and it certainly was strange how, if he had wandered in the forests for so long a period, subsisting on roots, strawberries, and the plant named talka, he should have preserved his well-fed condition; it was equally puzzling to imagine why if made a captive by strangers he should have been allowed to return.

Another curious fable was told by my guide J'aria, when we were travelling from Punta Arena, *apropos* of the wild animals in Patagonia, on which Lieut. Gallegos was enlarging. J'aria asked if I had ever head of the Tranco, or Trauco, which the Chilotes aver inhabits the western forests of the Cordillera. Gallegos declared that there was no doubt of its existence, and described it as possessing the form of a wild man, covered with a fell of coarse shaggy hair. This nondescript—a specimen of which would no doubt be invaluable to, though not met with on those coasts by Mr. Darwin—is said to descend from the impenetrable forests and attack the cattle, on which it preys. This is possibly a pure invention, emanating from the aguardiente muddled brain of a Chilian, but it seems to have a certain relation to the vague stories of unknown wild tribes dwelling in the unexplored and wooded mountain regions. It is hard to convey the sense of mysterious space and undiscoverable dwelling-places impressed on the spectator by the vast solitudes of the mountains and forests of the Cordillera. The inexplicable sounds of crashing rocks, or explosions from unknown voleanoes, and the still stranger tones which resemble bells and voices, all suggest to the ignorant and superstitious natives confirmation of the strange circumstantial stories handed down for several generations; and it is hard for anyone, even with the assistance of educated reason, to resist the powerful spell of the legends told in sight of these mysterious mountains. My readers will perhaps laugh at the narration of these vagaries of imagination, or will inquire what is the legend of the Cesares, and of the enchanted city. If they have read the delightful pages of 'Westward Ho,' they will not be unacquainted with the shifting mirage of that rich city; which, from Mexico to the Magdalena, mocked the search of so many eager adventurers. The Gran Quivira of New Mexico, the fabled Iximaya, the El Dorado of Guyana, and El Gran Paytiti of Brazil, the baseless fabrics of many a golden vision, are found repeated with change of place and circumstances in this city of Los Cesares. There is a curious combination of three distinct strands of legends in the chain which connects the marvellous stories of the Northern Indians and Chilotes with the accounts so circumstantially deposed to, and firmly believed by, the Spaniards of the last century. The first is the conquest of Los Cesares in 1539. Sebastian Cabot, from his settlement of Carcarañal on the Parana, sent his pilot Cesar with 120 soldiers to explore the river, 60 being left to garrison the fort;[1] this expedition proceeded as far as the junction of the Parana and Paraguay, which latter river they ascended to the Laguna Sta. Anna, on the way defeating the hostile Indians. They reached the boundaries of the Guaranis, with whom they made friendship and returned. They next set out to proceed overland to Peru, and crossed the Cordillera. After making their way against incredible difficulties, they reached a province, the inhabitants of which were rich in cattle, vicuñas, and gold and silver. The ruler of the province, 'a great lord,' at whose capital they at last arrived, received his Spanish visitors kindly, and entertained them with all honour, until at their own choice they were allowed to return enriched with presents of gold and precious stuffs. The Spaniards regained their fort on the Parana only to find it a deserted ruin; the Indians having surprised and massacred the garrison. Cesar thereupon led his party to the settlements, and thence started on another expedition, in which he again crossed the Cordillera, and from a height beheld, as he imagined, the waters of the Pacific and Atlantic on either hand, probably mistaking some large lagoon for the distant Atlantic. He then made his way up the coast to Atacama, and thence to Cuzco, at which city he joined the conquerors just at the period of the capture of the ill-fated Inca Atahuallpa.

This marvellous traverse of all the country was spoken of ever after as the conquest of Los Cesares, and the whole account was set forth by Ruy Diaz Guzman in 1612, whose authority was one of the Conquistadores of Peru, named Arzon, who had learned all the particulars from Don Cesar himself in Cuzco. It does not seem, however, that more than this name, and perhaps the tradition of the rich Indian city, were preserved in the romantic rumours that began to obtain currency in the seventeenth century, and continued to gain credit till 1781, when the Fiscal of Chili, having been charged to make inquiry, summed up in an elaborate state paper all the evidence in favour of the existence of a rich and strong city, situated somewhere between 45° and 56° south, and urged the Spanish Government to authorise an expedition to discover and take possession of it. The city was described by various veracious (?) authorities as 'defended by walls, ditches, and ravelins, the only entrance being protected by a draw-bridge, besides which cautious sentries were always stationed on an adjoining hill to detect intrusive strangers. The buildings were sumptuously constructed, the houses being of wrought stone with azotea roofs; and the churches were covered with glittering roofs of silver, and gorgeously furnished within. Of silver, too, were all utensils, knives, and even ploughshares made; and the inhabitants used golden stools and seats. They were light complexioned, with blue eyes and thick beards, and spoke a language unintelligible to both Spaniards and Indians. They wore jackets of blue cloth, yellow capes, and blue wadmal drawers and loose silk trousers, with large boots and small three-cornered hats! They possessed numerous cattle, marked with brands similar to those of the Spanish colonists; but their principal article of cultivation was pepper, in which they traded with their neighbours, maintaining withal a complete system of exclusive isolation.' By one account the population was composed of the descendants of the crews of several ships which had been wrecked in the Straits of Magellan from 1523 to 1539, the survivors of which had made their way overland and founded a settlement. A wandering padre was said to have received the news of its existence from some Indians, accompanied by a knife as a token, which was recognised as having belonged to the captain of a stranded vessel. The padre set out to discover his countrymen, but lost his life on the road. Another more precise tradition declared that the surviving inhabitants of Osorno, after having maintained a heroic defence against the Araucanians, under the victorious chief Caupolican, in 1539, made good their escape with their families and cattle to a peninsula in a great lagoon thirty miles long and seven or eight wide, situated near Reloncavi, or the volcano called Osorno, where they built a city strongly defended on the landward side by a fosse and drawbridge raised every night. This lagoon was by others said to be that of Payeque, near a rapid stream named Llanqueco. An explorer named Roxas, in 1714, who started from Buenos Ayres, and whose route lay south-west from Tandil and the Volcan, gives most precise distances and landmarks to define the position of the Cesares. He mentions especially a river with a ford only passable during one period of the year, and a hill on which is found much magnetic iron ore. These landmarks, and the rest of his description, point to the locale of that remarkable rock formation mentioned in p.88, which, seen from a distance, might well cheat a traveller into the belief that he beheld a fortified town. Wáki pointed it out to me, and said, jokingly, 'Perhaps Christians live there.' The 'Indians of veracity,' so frequently quoted in these accounts, who were, however, all bound to keep secret the access to the city, doubtless confused their recollections of different settlements visited in their migrations, and the Spaniards, prepared to receive any new wonder, wove into the marvellous tale all the stories told them, and regarded the joint fiction as undoubted fact. But two more remarkable phases of this legend, and then we return to practical Indian life. A military party, who set out in 1777 from Rio Bueno, and marched to Lake Llanquechue, crossed the passes of the Cordillera under Osorno, and passed the night near the snow line. They heard distant artillery, and beheld the head of a great Laguna on the eastern side; they brought back the astounding intelligence that two distinct towns existed, one peopled by a race of Spanish origin, the Auca-Huincas, at war with the Tehuelches; and the other by Englishmen, or Moro Huincas, who lived in amity with the Indians. And the Fiscal of Chili, in his report, insisted strongly on the necessity of rooting out these audacious islanders who had dared to plant themselves in the dominions of 'our Lord the King.' Just as the jealous fear of the encroaching English was thus mixed up in the Spanish version of the mysterious Cesares, so the Indians connected them with the traditionary glories of the great Inca race, and spoke of the Indian Cesares; and the potency of the fable was shown by a proclamation put forth by the heroic and ill-starred Tupac Amaru, who headed the unsuccessful rebellion against the tyrant Christians in 1781, styling himself 'Inca, Señor de los Cesares y Amazonas, con dominio en el Gran Paytiti.' But success mocked his grasp, and he perished by the hand of the executioner, just as the rich and coveted city whose lordship he claimed has eluded many an explorer who has sacrificed his life in the hopeless search. But the patient reader is probably weary of enchanted cities, and glad to return to the daily routine of our Indian life, though it was at this time butcherly enough. It was the all-important season of young guanaco hunting; and though the chase afforded plenty of riding, it could hardly be said to offer sport; but to the Indians it was a matter of business, as their clothing and stock of skins to trade with depended on the number of young guanaco killed at this time. Some notes of the habits of the guanaco and rhea, or ostrich, which furnish the Patagonian Indians with food and clothing, may not be out of place, though all critics are warned that they are not those of a naturalist, but simply the observations of a lover of birds and beasts.

The guanaco, known to the Indians as 'Nou,' is from three to four feet in height, and from four to five in length, measured from the point of the nostrils to the tail. The coat is woolly, but decreases in thickness of wool, or rather becomes hairy, about the head and legs. Its colour is of a yellowish red, intermixed with white in various parts of the body; more especially under the abdomen, down the inside of the legs, and round the lips and cheeks: the white also extends up the inside of the neck and throat. The shoulder is slightly arched; the tail short, and when the animal is in motion slightly elevated. The guanaco abounds over a vast range of country, extending from Peru all down the regions east of the range of the Cordillera of the Andes, over the vast plains from Mendoza to the Straits of Magellan, and even to Tierra del Fuego. As a rule, one male guanaco herds with a troop of about a hundred females, and in the event of their being disturbed he will take up his position on some neighbouring pinnacle of rock, and commence neighing something after the fashion of a horse, keeping himself between the danger and his wives. At the breeding season, however, the males go in flocks by themselves, as do the females. Although it is stated in Monsieur Gay's admirable book on the Zoology of Chili, that the females sometimes bear three fawns, yet this must be a rare case: while we were hunting and killing the young guanaco, the mothers invariably became separated, the young ones lagging behind so as to prevent any appropriation of them to their dams. However, during the time employed in killing the mothers for the purpose of extracting the unborn young from the womb, I never saw or heard of more than one foetus being found. The guanacos are excessively swift of foot, indeed almost unapproachable by horse or dog, as a few buck leaps take them away far beyond the speed of a horse. They frequently wait to allow a pursuer to approach close, and then bound off, and speedily distance him. Their means of defence consist chiefly in the savate, or use of the feet, more especially the fore ones, although they also bite at times, and with their two peculiar canine teeth could inflict a severe wound.[2] I have seen places where a puma and a guanaco have evidently had a severe struggle, always, however, resulting in the victory of the puma, as, on seeing these marks, we invariably searched for and found the body near, carefully covered over by the 'leon.' The flesh of the guanaco is excellent, something resembling mutton; the young guanaco being more like very tender veal. That their wool might be turned to account for mercantile purposes is undoubted, as it is of very fine texture, and is at the present time of value in Chili, where it is woven into ponchos, which are highly prized. Up to the present time few have been domesticated, but they become very tame, and might at a future date be found useful as beasts of burden, as they are similar in most respects to the lama. There is one very remarkable point about the guanaco: at certain times of the year a sort of secretion, condensed into a hard substance like stone, is found in round pieces, varying from ¼ to ½ inch in diameter, in the stomach. To these stones some of the Indians attribute medicinal virtues. The guanaco is of use to the Indians in every way. The skin of the adult is used to make the coverings of the toldos, and that of the unborn or young ones to make mantles for clothes; the sinews of the back furnish them with thread; the skin of the neck, which is particularly tough and durable, with lazos or thongs for bolas, bridles, &c., &c. The skin of the hock supplies them with shoes or coverings for the bolas; from the thigh bone they also cut out dice, or make a musical instrument. On attaining the age of about two months, the coat of the young guanaco begins to become woolly, and the skin is then use less for mantles, but makes sufficiently good saddle cloths. The animal at this early age is very swift of foot, and will give a good chase. They attain their full size the second or third year after birth, and the adult male cannot be better described than as apostrophised by Lieut. Gallegos. As we watched a solitary guanaco standing on a hill above us, and every now and then uttering its shrill warning neigh, 'Ah,' said Gallegos, 'you are a queer animal; you have the neigh of a horse, the wool of a sheep, the neck of a camel, the feet of a deer, and the swiftness of the devil.' The Rhea Darwinii, called by the Indians 'Mekyush,' and by the Spaniards Avestrus or Ostrich, which name is universally applied to it, is peculiar to Patagonia, few being met with north of Rio Negro, and none being found that I am aware of in any other part of the globe; with the exception, perhaps, of the more northern and plain-like parts of Tierra del Fuego, opposite the country extending from Cape Virgin to Oazy Harbour. It is a variety of the Rhea Americana, common in the Argentine provinces of Entre Rios and Santa Fé, also scattered over the Republic of the Banda Oriental, and extending, I believe, as far north as Rio Grande do Sul and the southern Brazilian province. They exist also in Chili, on the plains at the foot of the Cordillera of the Andes. The chief difference between these two species is that the Patagonian Rhea Darwinii is smaller and of lighter colour than the American Rhea. The Patagonian ostriches are very swift of foot, and run with their wings closed, while the other species invariably spread theirs. The former birds also always run in a straight line, except when leaving the nest, when probably, to avoid being tracked, they run in a circuitous manner. Their plumage, that is to say the wing feathers, are an object of commerce, and fetch at present about a dollar a pound in Buenos Ayres. The marrow from the leg bones is also, I believe, of use for making pomade, and was formerly, if not at present, highly prized in Buenos Ayres. To the Indian this bird is invaluable in many ways. Besides furnishing their most favourite food, from the sinews of the leg thongs for bolas are constructed; the neck is used as a pouch for salt or tobacco; the feathers are exchanged for tobacco and other necessaries; the grease from the breast and back is tried out and secured in bags formed of the skin (taken off during the spring season, when the females, like all the Patagonian animals except the puma, are thin); the meat is more nourishing and more relished by the Indians than that of any other animal in the country, and the eggs form a staple commodity of food during the months of September, October, and November. The male bird stands about 2½ feet high, and is to be distinguished from the female by its being of a slightly darker colour, and of greater size and strength; nevertheless, it requires a practised eye to detect the difference at any distance. The male bird is also swifter. Their usual food consists of short grass and the seeds of various shrubs, but more especially of tender grass, which I have on several occasions watched them plucking, from a convenient rock which hid me from their sight. On being alarmed they immediately set off at a great speed; they possess great powers of eyesight. If met or obstructed by horsemen in their line of flight, they not unfrequently squat so closely that they can scarcely be distinguished from the surrounding rocks, as the greyish colour of their plumage so closely resembles the almost universal aspect of the Pampas of Patagonia. These birds, though not web-footed, can swim sufficiently well to pass a river. In the winter season it is not unfrequent for the Indians to drive them into the water, where, their legs getting numbed with cold, they are drifted to the shore by the current, and easily captured, being unable to move. In snowy weather they are also easily taken, as their eyes appear to be affected by the glare of the white snow, and their saturated plumage doubtless becomes heavier. They are polygamous, one male bird consorting with five or six hens, which lay their eggs in the same nest—a hole about two feet six inches in diameter, scooped out of the earth. They begin to lay in the early part of September, the number of eggs in each nest varying from twenty to as many as forty, or more. In the early part of the laying season extraneous eggs were found scattered in different parts of the plain, some of which were of diminutive size. Contrary to the usual rule amongst birds, the male sits on the eggs, and when the chickens are hatched assumes the charge of the brood. The young run immediately, or shortly after emerging from the shell, and are covered with a down of greyish black colour on the back, and whitish on the breast and neck. Their cry resembles the syllables pi, pi, pi, uttered in a sharp, quick manner. The old male, when any dangers appear, feigns to be hurt, like other birds endeavouring to distract the attention of the hunter in order that his brood may escape by hiding in the grass. After the male has sat for some time on the nest (I should place the period of incubation at about three weeks), he gets thin, and the grass closely surrounding the nest is fonnd eaten quite bare. The females by this time are beginning to pick up flesh, which is a fortunate provision of nature for the Indians, who cannot subsist on lean meat. Whilst the females are thin they are killed and skinned, the meat being left, and the skins sewn into mantles for sale at the settlements. These birds at that period are much afflicted with vermin, which invade the toldos and guanaco mantles of the Indians, and cause them infinite annoyance. (A useful hint occurs to me for future travellers amongst the Patagonians—never allow the squaw of the establishment to place ostrich mantles under your sleeping hides.) The young Rhea does not attain its full plumage or size until the second year after its birth, and is never pursued by the Indians unless food is really scarce. The eggs are eaten in all stages, fresh or stale; the Indian not recognising much difference between the unhatched chicken and the unborn guanaco. The inveterate destroyers of these birds are, besides their human enemies, the puma and foxes, the former of which will surprise and kill the sitting bird, which he carefully hides, and then proceeds to eat the eggs with great gusto. We not unfrequently found the eggs broken and scattered by these animals, whilst the bird was generally discovered hard by. The foxes, I think, content themselves with sucking the eggs; but I was assured that near Geylum, where wild cats are common, these latter will kill the bird on the nest, like their relatives the puma. Besides these there are the condors, eagles, and hawks, which no doubt commit extensive ravages on the young broods. With all these difficulties to contend with, the Rhea Darwinii exists in great numbers, and if not kept down to a certain extent by the Indians and other enemies would overrun the whole country. We were, while at Chiriq, busily engaged in the destruction of both guanaco and ostrich, the high rugged range of hills that bounded Chiriq on the eastern side literally swarming with guanaco; and as the females, heavy with young, could not keep up their speed for a long distance, one man not unfrequently captured and killed five and six, or even eight; extracting the young and taking its skin for mantles and the carcase for food, while the hide of the mother served, if needed, to repair the toldo. The marrow bones also were taken as a dainty, but the meat was left for the condors, puma, and foxes. We hunted almost every day, and traversed nearly all the surrounding country. The plains lying to the west afforded beautiful ground to ride over, covered with soft grass, but a few leagues from the Cordillera a sudden dip occurs, which forms a huge basin, lying about 50 feet below the level of the plain, like the bed of a lake, and extending to the mountains; the surface of this was chiefly covered with grass, but in some parts the yellow clay and beds of stones were visible. On the higher ground, before reaching this basin, numerous lagoons occurred, round one of which there was a large gull-rookery and the inhabitants made themselves audible at a long distance. Here also I noticed many of the teru-tero, a spur-winged lapwing, common near Buenos Ayres. I had encountered them even as low as Santa Cruz, but never in such large numbers. Our hunts on the plain were not so successful as those on the hilly range, although in the previous year the Indians asserted that the reverse had been the case. Perhaps the guanaco had gained in experience, and felt themselves safer in the rocky heights where riders were likely to get bad falls. The Northern Indians rode most recklessly, going at full speed down the most precipitous places, and, strange to say, although one or two accidents did occur resulting in broken limbs, they were not numerous. This speaks volumes for the sure footedness of their horses. It is their custom, when hunting in rocky places, to place hide shoes on the horse's fore feet as a safeguard against sharp stones. After hunting, it was the rule every evening for those owning spare horses (and indeed for those who did not) to repair to the race-course a little before sunset, and train or run their horses, or look on at the others, and if there was a race, make bets. The manner of racing is something similar to that in vogue amongst the Gauchos in the provinces of Rio de la Plata, except that it is generally conducted on principles of fair play. The stakes are always deposited before the race comes off: if horses, they are tied out handy; if ornaments, bolas, &c., &c., they are placed in a heap, the winners removing them directly the race is decided. The horses are run bare-backed, the two riders starting themselves after cantering side by side for a few yards. Owing to the great care taken in training the horses, very few false starts ever occur. The races are very often for long distances, four miles or a league being the average, although, of course, with young horses the distance is shorter. The Indian manner of breaking colts is similar to that of the Gauchos; they are, however, more gentle with their horses, and consequently break them better. One rarely sees a horse amongst the Indians that is not perfectly quiet; indeed, the smallest children are nearly always mounted on the racers and best horses, although if a white man approaches or attempts to catch them they show signs of fear and temper. Indeed, there appears to be a sort of instinctive mutual bond between the Indians and their horses. For lameness the cure most prevalent is bleeding in the fetlock with an awl; sometimes the incision is made higher up the leg, and the awl forced nearly through the horse's leg; he is then tied up for a short time, and then let go, and the cure is generally certain. Of course before the bleeding he is tied up several hours without water. The cure for sore backs, which, though rare, sometimes occur owing to an ill-made saddle, is a species of aluminous earth, applied to the wound after it has been cleansed with a knife. This earth is only found in the southern parts of the country, and it is very difficult to obtain any of this much-prized medicine from the Indians. One deposit of it is found in a cliff near Lake Viedma, so high that it can only be got at by throwing stones at the face of the cliff, and so dislodging the earth.

A few lines will suffice to gratify any 'horsey-doggy' friends who may be curious as to the horse flesh and dog shows of the Indians. The horses in use amongst the Southern Indians are, as a rule, of a hardier race than those found amongst the Northern, Araucanian, and Pampas Indians. Their general size is about fifteen hands, or indeed perhaps less, but nevertheless they are of great speed and endurance; when one takes into consideration that the weight of their riders is frequently over fourteen stone, it appears extraordinary that they should be enabled to carry them in the way they do. The horses are, of course, all of Spanish origin, but time, climate, and the different nature of the country have altered them to a considerable degree from the original race. The horses found amongst the Northern Tehuelches are, as a rule, larger than those previously mentioned, with finer heads and smaller legs; they are also extremely swift, and being bred frequently from captured wild mares, are admirably adapted for hunting purposes. The horse, however, most valued is the wild horse captured and tamed; these differ from the others in being, as a rule, of larger size and superior speed. This, I think, only applies to Northern Patagonia, as I have in other parts seen wild horses which in no way equalled those in captivity. The horses vary in colour, those captured from the wild herds generally being a dark bay, black, or brown. Near Port San Julian, I am informed that there are numbers of wild ponies, about the size and make of a shelty, which the children play with. The horses are entirely grass fed, and in consequence of the dry nature of the pasture in the winter season, and the subsequent hard treatment, they generally get very thin in the spring time of the year, but soon pick up condition when given a few days' rest, and allowed to feed on the fresh pasture. The dogs generally in use amongst the Patagonian Indians vary considerably both in size and species. First of all comes a sort of lurcher (smooth haired), bred by the Indians from some obtained in the Rio Negro, the mothers being a description of mastiff, with the muzzle, however, much sharper than that of a mastiff proper; they are also very swift, and have longer and lower bodies. Our chief, Orkeke, kept his breed of this dog, which probably had been derived from the earlier Spanish settlements, pure; and they were, for hunting purposes, the best I saw, running both by scent and view.

Another description of dog observed had long woolly hair, and indeed much resembled an ordinary sheep dog. These were passably common amongst the Indians, but most of the dogs used in the chase—which are nearly all castrated— are so mixed in race as to defy specification. I heard of a dog captured from some Fuegians, which was very swift, and answered perfectly to our description of harrier. These Fuegians are probably those known as the 'Foot' Indians, who, by those who have descended on their coasts, have been observed to use dogs for hunting purposes.

Casimiro informed me that Quintuhual's people formerly hunted on foot, with a large sort of dog, which, from his description, must have resembled a deer hound. The dogs are rarely fed, being allowed generally to satiate themselves in the chase. The hounds belonging to Orkeke, and one or two others, were exceptions to this rule, being fed with cooked meat when it was plentiful. The women keep pet lap dogs of various descriptions, generally a sort of terrier, some of them much resembling the Scotch terrier. 'Ako,' for instance, was to all appearance a thoroughbred dog of that breed. These little lap dogs are the torment of one's life in camp: at the least sound they rush out yelping, and set all the big dogs off; and in an Indian encampment at night, when there is anything stirring, a continual concert of bow-wows is kept up. The dogs are fierce towards strangers, but generally content themselves with surrounding them, showing their teeth and barking, unless set on. That they are ugly customers at night an amusing instance will prove. One morning a dog was found dead near its owner's toldo, which had evidently been knocked on the head with a bola, and finished with a knife; the owner made a great outcry, but no explanation could be had. It subsequently became known to me that a young gallant had sought admission to the toldo of his innamorata by the accustomed method of cautiously lifting the back tent cover from the ground, and dexterously crawling underneath; when half through, he felt his leg seized in a pair of powerful jaws. The lady was highly amused at the predicament of her lover, who, however, extricated himself by a mighty and well-directed kick with his foot in the muzzle of his assailant. When returning from his 'rendezvous' he met his active enemy, and vindictively knocked him on the head, and, to make sure work, cut his throat; but his leg carried after all a deeper scar than his heart as a token of the love-adventure, and when the story was told, and, as may be supposed, excited roars of laughter, it recalled forcibly to my mind,

'He jests at scars who never felt a wound.'

Our camp at Chiriq presented quite the appearance of a town of toldos, and fresh arrivals were still expected from the S.W.; but the Indians of the latter party, with whom we had not yet made acquaintance, sent a chasqui with an invitation to Crimè to join their party, and a message that they would ultimately meet us at Teckel. Accordingly, Crimè, who was now rich in horses and gear, having received many presents, bid us adieu, and set off with an imposing cavalcade. Poor fellow! he had better have remained with us, as the sequel will show.

The weather during the first weeks of our stay in Chiriq was warm and fine, but latterly the wind veered round to the west, and it changed to sleet and cold rain, and the normal Patagonian climate. The humour of the Indians seemed as variable, for old Orkeke grew exceedingly jealous. Jackechan often used to lend me a horse on the hunting excursions, and Orkeke one day asked me in a sullen manner whether I wished to change my toldo, and go with my friend. My reply that I had no wish to do so at present quieted him for the time, and he immediately offered me one of his best horses for the next day, which was a real treat. I am afraid I rather abused his generosity, as we had a great day chasing large herds of guanaco, and with a racer for a mount, one was induced to ride furiously. On the 20th of November it was decided to break up the camp and divide into two parties to hunt, it being considered that our united numbers were too great for successful hunting in one place. When all were packing up and preparing to start, a row nearly broke out between two of our old party: indeed it was with the greatest difficulty, and only through the intervention of Casimiro, Hinchel, and two or three more, that blood was not spilt. Of course, if the fight had commenced between these two, such is the excitability of the Indians that it would soon have become a general battle. This, and a heavy shower of rain coming, prevented our march, so the women unpacked, and horses were let go again. Some few Indians started to hunt, but came back shortly almost empty handed, fairly beaten by the driving sleet and snow. During our stay most of us had refitted all our gear, and were well provided with bolas; many were the necks of guanaco stripped to obtain the hide for them, and for making 'manêos' (straps for securing horses' legs), whips, cinctas (girths), lazos, &c., &c. The work that I preferred was plaiting ostrich sinews for thongs for the ostrich bolas. The ostrich sinews are abstracted by dislocating the lower joint of the leg, the first sinew is then pulled out by hand, and the others drawn out by main force, using the leg bone as a handle. This bone is then separated from the foot, and the sinews left adhering to the foot; they are slightly dried in the sun, after which the extracted bone is used to separate the fibres by drawing it sharply up the sinews. When sufficiently separated they are cut off from the foot, split into equal sizes and lengths, and laid in a moist place to soften; when sufficiently soft they are made into thongs, cooked brains being used to make them more pliable, and lie better in the plaits. These thongs are plaited in four plaits (round sinnet) well known to every sailor, but the ends are doubled in a peculiar manner, which requires practice to manage well. Before leaving Chiriq another disturbance was nearly taking place, caused by one of the Chilians quitting Tchang's toldo, and joining that of a man commonly called Santa Cruz, an Indian well known at Patagones, and allowed a ration of mares from the Government. Tchang, immediately on hearing of his departure, put on his revolver and collared the Chilian's horse. To this Santa Cruz objected, but Tchang kept the horse, and, revolver in hand, defied anybody's claim to it. After this little incident the camp as broken up, and the two parties divided— Hinchel marching S.W. and our party to the N.W.

After a very cold and hungry march in the face of a bitterly piercing wind, we encamped on the shores of a lagoon of some extent, called 'Hoshelkaik,' which signifies 'Windy-hill,' and certainly is worthy of its name; for during our stay a succession of S.W. winds blew with great violence. After our arrival a small boy cut his finger, and, according to custom, a mare was killed. Some of the meat sent to our toldo was thankfully received, as we were all half starved. Having strolled through the camp and visited Cayuke's toldo, I found that Casimiro had not arrived, having started, to my great disgust, with the party travelling to the S.W., and taken with him a specially good horse, which he had given me in exchange for a revolver. I was, however, glad to find that Jackechan, the Pampa chief was there, and we had a confabulation and smoke together. On the 23rd, the previous day having been too rough, the Indians started to hunt the enclosing grassy basin before mentioned as existing at the foot of the mountains. Immense herds of guanaco were driven down, and being encircled by men and fires the sport soon commenced. The Tehuelches had for some reason set light to the grass in every available part, and the wind rising to a furious gale, the fires soon spread and joined in an advancing line. Jackechan, myself, and several other Indians were in the centre of the circle, each employed in skinning the guanaco we had already killed, when suddenly we found that we were encircled in flame and smoke, and that if we did not want to be well scorched we had better look out for means of exit. Leaving our game, we galloped at the spot where the smoke appeared thinnest, but after riding three or four minutes with our faces covered up, found an impassable barrier of flame; so, half-maddened with the hot sand dashed in our eyes by the gale, and nearly suffocated with smoke, we galloped down the line of flame to a spot where, the grass being stunted, we managed to get through without injury, although our horses' legs were singed a little. We were very thankful to breathe pure air, though the atmosphere was still thick with smoke, and nothing could be distinguished of valley or anything else. Jackechan, with unerring Indian instinct, led the way to a stream of water, where we were able to drink and wash some of the hot sand out of our eyes. After a quarter of an hour's rest and a smoke, as the flames had passed on, we determined to ride back over the still smoking ground, and endeavour to discover the bodies of our guanaco. We accordingly emerged from the hollow, where we had sheltered ourselves, and once more plunged into the thick of the driving smoke and heated sand: holding our mantles over our eyes, we penetrated the murky atmosphere till Jackechan discovered two of his animals; but as they were both roasted, or rather burned, and ourselves and horses were nearly suffocated, we beat a hasty retreat. I was very thankful when at length, ascending a steep declivity, we emerged at the top into the pure air. 'Ah!' said Jackechan, looking down on the plains still full of smoke, 'it has been a rough time, but "we are men, not women," though we were fools to remain to the last.' I fully agreed with him in this, as my eyes still smarted very painfully. How he found his way through the smoke was perfectly inexplicable to me: if I had been alone, my travels would have been concluded then and there. Towards the evening of this eventful day the wind abated in violence, and during the night snow fell, and all the ensuing day there were passing squalls of white water or snow, and furious blasts of wind. About this time I came to the conclusion that summer was unknown in these regions, and that the Patagonian year consisted of two seasons—a hard winter and a bad spring. The Indians, however, declared that the climate had grown colder during the last two years. On the 28th of November we broke up camp and marched to a valley situated under one spur of the wooded hills, previously mentioned as bounding the northern side of the valley—killing some young guanaco by the way. I was astonished on galloping up to two to find they did not run away at first, although their mothers had already gone, and had taken up a position on a rocky eminence some distance off. Whilst watching them, however, and meditating on the necessity and cruelty of killing them, the two little things started off; so, as my mantle was fast losing its beautiful appearance, I put compunction on one side, and shortly killed them with a blow on the head. On arriving at the fire where some of the Indians were collected eating ostriches,

I was proceeding to take the skins off, when Tankelow, who presided, stopped me, saying that we would skin them in the toldos, where the blood would be a treat to the women and children. We accordingly reserved the luxury, and after a feed crossed a small stream and piece of marsh, beyond which lay the encampment, where the women soon verified Tankelow's words. Though the flesh of the young guanaco is rather tasteless and soft, the blood has a sweeter taste than that of the adult. The rennet, or milk, which is found curdled into a sort of cheese in the intestines, is also eaten with gusto. The most laborious part of young guanaco hunting consists in taking off the skin, which, after the necessary incisions have been made with a knife, has to be taken off by hand, the thumb being used to separate the hide from the body. The calves, when three days old, run at about the speed of a horse's hand gallop, but sometimes give longer chases. The Indian plan is to kill them with a blow on the head from a ball, and then pass on to another, and so on, afterwards returning to collect them in a heap and skin them. After the hide is taken off it is necessary to expose it to the air for a few minutes before folding it up, otherwise it is liable to get heated, and will tear easily in the subsequent processes. We hunted in the neighbourhood of Jeroshaik, or 'Bad Hill,' several times, with varying success, sometimes proceeding up into the wooded hills, where the timber in some places grew in clumps, as if planted by the hand of man; in others filled up the rocky dells, until the main forests were reached, which appeared to extend far into the Cordillera. Most of the trees were of a species of beech, on which were many small edible fungi, some of which we gathered for use; and traces of red deer were frequently seen, and a few were chased by the Indians, but owing to the thickness of the wood they escaped. Some of the Indians took the opportunity to cut fresh poles for the toldos. The sight of woods and trees was so refreshing that I spent several days consecutively amongst them, very often alone, or with one companion. Nobody, except a sailor after months on the sea, can imagine the pleasure of wandering under trees to one who had passed so long a time in the barren and monotonous plains. The weather, however, still continued wet and inclement. On the 5th of December, some of us wandering on the heights above, made out smoke to the N.E., and Campan went off at speed on horseback to reconnoitre. He returned towards nightfall very drunk, and riding straight to our toldo, proclaimed that El Sourdo, the Indian left behind in Santa Cruz, had arrived at a place close to us, bringing grog in two small barrels, and letters for me: when he had delivered his news, he, with some difficulty, dismounted without coming on his head; then produced a bottle half full of rum from under his mantle, which he dispensed to the attendant company.

Our toldo was soon crowded, and it was proposed that on the following day we should march and meet the visitor, all being eager for a drink. Accordingly, on the morrow we started, in a storm of sleet and rain, and prepared to hunt *en route*.

While hunting, just after Jackechan and myself had killed an ostrich, the former perceived a single toldo, which he knew must be El Sourdo's, so we galloped towards it, accompanied by two other Indians, and were received with open arms by El Sourdo and his two wives, Jackechan being a very old friend. We were made to sit down, and the olla, or boiling-pot, was brought out by the two wives, who acted as Hebes by producing the rum, with which our host filled the pot, and dispensed the liquor in a pannikin. One of the wives then produced my letters, which proved to be from Mr. Clarke and Don Luiz P. B., the schooner having arrived on October 5, all safe. El Sourdo then gave me all the news verbatim—how a fight had taken place at the settlement between Gonzalez and Antonio, in which the latter had been killed or mortally wounded, and the former had escaped to the Pampas, but had subsequently been captured and taken as a prisoner in the schooner to Buenos Ayres; and other news of trivial importance. Meanwhile the grog was fast disappearing, and the pot had to be replenished. This in turn was about half-emptied by the time the other Indians and women arrived, and Jackechan, very inebriated, was vowing eternal friendship to me, while Tchang was howling in my other ear a lovely Tehuelche ditty. As I had drunk in moderation, I thought it about time to clear, so, on the plea of looking after my horse, retired and re-read my letters, which anyone may imagine, although not coming from my relations, were of great interest. After my departure no more liquor was given away, El Sourdo selling two bottles for a young horse or a silver-sheathed knife, so that he soon found himself a rich man. By midnight all the liquor was exhausted and many drunk, but no disturbances occurred worthy of mention, all arms having previously been stowed away safely. I was roused from my first sleep by a lady from a neighbouring toldo, who wished to embrace me, and, with feminine curiosity, wanted to know the contents of my letters. She was, I am sorry to say, in an advanced stage of intoxication, so after giving her a smoke, Orkeke, who had roused up and was dying of laughter, politely showed her the door. Most of the party went out hunting in the morning, the ride no doubt proving beneficial to those suffering from headache, though little game was killed; but the Sourdo, whom I had joined in a morning bowl of coffee, remained at home, as his horses were very much used up, one of his boys going on a friend's mount to procure meat. For four days after this drinking bout we did nothing but slaughter and eat mares, somebody's child having been slightly hurt in some manner. Although I have read in various books that the Indians have a religious festival at which mares are slaughtered as a sacrifice to the Deity at a certain time of the year, I never saw anything of it. Whenever this sort of sacrificial feast took place, there was always a special occasion for it—either a death, or a child hurt, or some escape from a danger, when the animals are killed as a thank-offering. Rather tired of remaining so long in one place, on the 12th we marched due north across the plain, which was called 'Gisk,' and encamped under a hill covered with trees, and the sides furrowed with small gullies, densely filled with vegetation and shrubs of two or three species. Here there were plants of the description of potatoes before mentioned, but growing very deep in such unfavourable ground that few were extracted. On the hill sides a plant bearing a yellow flower grew in abundance, the leaf of which, the Chilians informed me, was an excellent remedy for wounds and bruises, and much used in Chili. Four days' hunting took place here, at the end of which Orkeke, who had some story that the Pampas had been stealing a march by hunting at night, and was rather disgusted at his continual ill-success, proposed that we should separate, and in company with the toldos of Tchang, go westward to a plain below the higher mountains, which he stated to be abounding in guanaco. He also proposed a trip into the Cordillera in search of wild cattle. This plan was eagerly approved, as I anticipated persuading him, if possible, to penetrate to the Chilian shores of the Pacific. We accordingly set out on our travels, but had not gone far before a frightful storm of wind, sleet, and rain set in, which wetted us all completely. We huddled for shelter under a bush for some time, but as it continued there was nothing for it but to push on, and about 3 P.M. the weather cleared up; we then entered a glen with a wooded stream running down it, expanding higher up into an open plain. A short distance up the valley the intended camping-ground lay, so a small circle was made, in which some ostriches and guanaco were killed. We then adjourned across the river under the trees, and soon had a roaring fire blazing, by the side of which we dried ourselves and cooked our dinner. A more romantic-looking spot than this I was never in. On the other side of the stream was a mass of grey rocks, half hid by shrubs, from amongst which here and there a dead tree stood up. On one side the grass was beautifully green, and the trees were growing in scattered round clumps a few yards apart; doves were cooing in their branches, and young ostriches were running about. These, I am sorry to say, were caught by the horsemen, who jumped down and secured them: hunger had no scruples, and two furnished a good meal for each wet and starving traveller. Despite our ducking, we were soon all in high spirits, and some of us, before going back to the toldos, proceeded to search for wild potatoes, a few of which we brought back. The following morning the sun rose bright, with a clear sky, so we continued our march in a westerly direction, arriving about mid-day at a gorge amongst the wooded hills, where I hoped that we were going to encamp; the women, however, diverged to the northward, and proceeding up a ravine or cañon in the barranca of the high pampa, pitched the toldos in a gloomy, prison-like spot. Melancholy as it seemed to me, it afforded abundant pasture for the horses, which between the hills was scarce, so that they were inclined to wander into the woods and be hard to find when wanted, which undoubtedly was the reason of our taking the cañon in preference to the wooded valley. This cañon, a little beyond our camp, divided into two, in one of which was a laguna frequented by avocets. The stream, which in spring poured down the glen, presented only an occasional pool and a dry bed, in which were numbers of rounded white stones of chalky substance, supplying capital materials for bolas, easily reduced to the suitable form: it also occurred to me that the chips pounded to powder might have the curative effects of chalk mixture, as diarrhoea had affected some of the party, and the result of the medicinal experiment was satisfactory, though it was impossible to prevail on the Indians to try the remedy. Whilst the women were pitching toldos, the men, eight in number, started to hunt again. Riding to the west, where the plain was still open, we came upon another of the huge basins previously described, on the western side of which, beyond a lagoon stocked with waterfowl, flowed a broad winding stream fringed with trees. At a short distance from the other side of the stream open glades extended for the space of perhaps a mile to the verge of the interminable forests, rising high up on the lofty sides of mountains, some of whose summits were still partially snow-clad. To the south were two or three round detached hummocks, hardly deserving the name of hills, crowned with trees. In the foreground were immense herds of guanaco, and on the northern side frowned a high range of arid-looking hills, forming a great contrast to the deliciously-refreshing green aspect of the other points of view. Whilst waiting concealed behind a bush for the coming herd, which had been cunningly encircled by Tchang and another Indian, and were to be driven in our direction, we gazed long at the beautiful view before us, and Orkeke pointed out a mountain some distance to the north, underneath which, he said, was the entrance to the scene of our future campaign against the wild cattle. Towards evening we returned to the toldos, pretty well loaded with skins. On another occasion, when hunting, we made a circle, finishing off in the wooded district near the banks of the river. On our return we hunted over a park-like country, with alternate open glades and woods. Here we killed a doe red deer and a large description of fox, apparently identical with the Falkland Island species (Lupus antarcticus). In the vicinity of the woods, the velvety sward was carpeted with the wild strawberry plants, which, however, were only in bloom. On this occasion our enjoyment was marred by one of the party getting a severe fall, which laid him up for a day or two. Before we reached the toldos rain set in heavily, which during the night turned to snow, and the morning sun shone on a white landscape. During our stay the women went to the woods to cut fresh poles for the toldos, and the men brought back from the wooded country a description of fungus, which, when dried, forms an excellent tinder, of considerable value amongst the Indians, as there are only a few spots where it is to be obtained. After some days spent in this pleasant neighbourhood, as the supply of guanaco was failing, we marched over the barren range of hills, and passing a lagoon of considerable extent below the hills, encamped on the other side of them, by the side of a smaller one, in a place called 'Gogomenykaik.'

During the hunt I had singled out a guanaco, and was in full chase across the upper pampa, which was covered with stunted bushes and tufts of grass, when the quarry suddenly disappeared, as if the earth had swallowed him. The next moment my horse halted in mid-gallop, with its fore feet on the edge of a precipitous descent which shelved away without any warning. Below was a long beautiful glen, with a pool of water glistening among the trees which filled it, but did not rear their topmost boughs above the level of the pampa. Here the guanaco had taken refuge, and as the descent was impracticable for a horse, I could only gaze longingly down into the fairy-like scene, and turn away to join the circle, remembering that it was only too easy to lose oneself by delay. Of this an instance occurred the same day, for one of the Chilians did not appear at the fireside when the hunting was completed. At first no heed was bestowed on him, as it was natural to suppose that he had chased a herd of guanaco to some distance, and was detained taking off the skins; but when at sunset he was still missing, some dry grass was fired, for the purpose of directing him to our camp. The following morning he had not appeared when we started to hunt, myself going as pointsman with Orkeke. We galloped for some distance over the plain, and halted in a hollow, where we came on six young skunks outside their parental burrow, into which they quickly vanished on our dismounting; but as their burrows do not penetrate far, Orkeke soon grubbed out a couple. As they were too small to kill for the value of their skins, and too much trouble to carry home as pets for the children, we set them free again, and I proceeded, leaving Orkeke to pursue his way slowly. A slight rise brought me in front of a rocky hill, on the other side of which was a river with wooded banks, across the valley of which river lay my route. I at first considered it to be the same as that seen in the previous encampment, but on reflection it was plainly another, this flowing north-east, whilst the other took a south-west course. Our hunt progressed very fairly. On closing the circle, one of the Chilians, who was running a guanaco with me, and not expert in the use of the bolas, entangled his horse and himself instead of the chase, which lost him his spoils, and caused much merriment amongst the remainder of the party; although I may as well state here that when a horse gets a ball round his legs or under his tail, it is not much of a joking matter for the rider. On our way back to camp, halting by a spring, we found large quantities of wild celery; nettles were also common—the real old English white-flowering one being prevalent. Although my bare legs got considerably stung, I forgot to swear in Tehuelche, and forgave the plant for old acquaintance sake. At the toldos we found the Chilian, who had arrived recently, having run a herd some distance and lost his way, but had been safely directed by our signal fires. In the afternoon some of the party were occupied in breaking their horses, while others were sitting at home lazily watching the performance. Conde's step-father, generally known as 'Paliki,' had a three-year-old iron grey, with a white star, and a very fine animal, tied up ready to be mounted for the first time. Paliki entered our toldo to borrow my cincta, or girth, and chaffed me, asking if I would venture to 'domar' him. Orkeke seconded the proposal, and accordingly, having stripped off mantle and boots, I proceeded to take the lazo and reins and mount. The instant he felt the unwonted incumbrance he buck-jumped for several yards, finally jumping into the middle of the brook and nearly losing his footing. I spurred him out, and once on the bank he commenced to whirl round and round like a teetotum. At last I got his head straight, and after a few more buck-jumps he went off at racing speed, urged by whip and spur. After a stretching gallop of three miles, I rode him quietly back, now and again turning him to accustom him to the bridle-thong, but not venturing to feel his mouth, and then brought him up to the toldo amidst the shouts of the spectators. Orkeke expressed great surprise, and wanted to know where I had learned to 'domar'; and the gratified owner insisted on presenting me with a piece of tobacco. This was most welcome, as my store was almost exhausted, though it had been replenished occasionally by the possessors of guns and revolvers in return for my services in putting the locks to rights; and the fear of being left tobaccoless—the agony of which all smokers will appreciate—was becoming unpleasantly strong. The following day we bade adieu to the lagoon, which, as usual, was covered with swans and other wild fowl, which we never molested, husbanding our powder in the event of future disturbances with other Indians. We marched a few miles, and encamped near the river—indeed, on its very banks, under the shadows of the trees. Here we passed our time away hunting, bathing in the stream, smoking, and lying in the shade for three days. One of my horses being lame, I could not hunt every day, so frequently passed hours under the trees by the river, scrubbing my one remaining shirt for future use, and working hide, &c. As writing in the toldo was made almost impossible by the curiosity of the children, crowding round me and asking questions, I generally used to take my note-book to my retreat; here, however, I was often interrupted by the girls, who came on the pretence of bathing, and evinced great playful curiosity as to the contents of my book—for here, too, I used to peruse and reperuse my library, namely, half of the delightful 'Elsie Venner,' which Crimè had picked up on board some ship to serve as wadding for his guns, and sold to me for a little powder. To enable the reader to follow our somewhat devious course and the intricacies of these hills and frequent rivers, the sketch map at page 128 will be found useful; it does not pretend to be exact, but gives a very fair idea of the line of country traversed and of our migrations between Henno and Teckel.

On the 23rd, Indians having been seen to the north and guanaco hunting proving a failure, Orkeke to my great delight, proposed a visit to the wild cattle country. The camp was accordingly struck, and following more or less the valley of the river, which flowed after one turn nearly due east, we shortly came out into an open plain running up between the mountains, at the head of which we encamped by some tall beeches on the banks of the stream. The whole of the latter part of the plain traversed was literally carpeted with strawberry plants all in blossom, the soil being of a dark peaty nature. Young ostriches were now numerous, and every hunt some were captured and formed a welcome addition to our dinner. The children had several alive as pets, which they used to let loose and then catch with miniature bolas, generally ending in killing them. Our programme was to leave all the women, toldos, and other encumbrances in this spot, named 'Weekel,' or Chaykash—a regular station, and which Hinchel's party had occupied a few weeks previously—and proceed ourselves into the interior in search of cattle. The following morning at daylight horses were caught and saddled, and, after receiving the good wishes of the women, who adjured us to bring back plenty of fat beef, we started off just as the sun was rising behind the hills to the eastward. The air was most invigorating, and we trotted along for some distance up a slightly irregular and sandy slope, halting after an hour or two by the side of a deliciously clear brook, flowing east, where we smoked. We had previously passed guanaco and ostrich, but no notice was taken of them, the Indians having larger game in view. After passing this brook, the head water of the river near which we had left the toldos, we skirted a large basin-like plain of beautiful green pasture, and after galloping for some time entered the forest, travelling along a path which only permitted us to proceed in Indian file. The trees were in many places dead, not blackened by fire, but standing up like ghostly bleached and bare skeletons. It is a remarkable fact that all the forests on the eastern side are skirted by a belt of dead trees. At length, however, just as we came in sight of a curiously pointed rock which in the distance resembled the spire of a church, we entered the forest of live trees; the undergrowth was composed of currant, bay, and other bushes, whilst here and there were beds of yellow violets, and the inevitable strawberry plants everywhere. After crossing a stream which, flowing from the north, afterwards took a westerly course, thus proving that we had passed the watershed, we proceeded, under cover of a huge rock, to reconnoitre the hunting ground. The scenery was beautiful: a valley, about a mile wide, stretched directly under us; on the southern verge a silver line marked the easterly river, and another on the northern the one debouching in the Pacific; whilst above, on both sides, rose high mountains covered with vegetation and almost impenetrable forests. On the western side of the valley a solitary bull was leisurely taking his breakfast, and above our look-out rock a huge condor lazily flapped his wings. These were the only specimens of animal life in view. Pursuing our way in perfect silence, as from the first entrance into the forests speaking had been prohibited, we followed the leader along the narrow cattle path, passing here and there the remains of a dead bull or cow that had met their fate by the Indians' lazo, and at length descended to the plain. It was about mid-day, and the day was warm, so we halted, changed horses, looked to our girths, got lazos ready for use, and then started on. As we were proceeding we observed two or three animals amongst the woods on the opposite side, but knowing that it would be useless to follow, pursued our course up the valley. Having crossed the western stream, we at once entered a thicket where the path was scarcely distinguishable from the cover, but our leader never faltered, and led the way through open glades alternating with thick woods, on every side of which were cattle marks, many being holes stamped out by the bulls, or wallowing places. The glades soon terminated in forests, which seemed to stretch unbroken on either side. We had expected before reaching this point to have found cattle in considerable numbers, but the warmth of the day had probably driven them into the thickets to seek shelter. We now commenced to ascend over a dangerous path, encumbered here and there with loose boulders and entangled in dense thickets, whilst we could hear and catch occasional glimpses of the river foaming down a ravine on our left, and presently arrived at the top of a ridge where the forests became more uniformly dense, and we could with great difficulty pursue our way. It was a mystery to me how Orkeke, who acted as guide, knew where we were, as on one occasion the slightly-marked paths diverged in different directions, and on another we literally found ourselves amongst fallen trees in a forest so dense that the light of day scarcely penetrated its shades. Our leader, however, never hesitated, but led us onwards in all confidence. Whilst brushing along, if I may be allowed the term, trying to keep the leader in sight, I heard something tapping on a tree, and looking up, saw close above me a most beautifully marked red crested woodpecker. We at length commenced to descend, and, after passing many channels of rivulets issuing from springs, where a slip of the horse's foot on the wet and mossy stones would have occasioned something worse than broken bones, as they were situated on the edge of a deep ravine, finally emerged from the woods and found ourselves on a hill of some three hundred feet in height, whence we looked down on a broad plain in the form of a triangle, bounded by the river flowing through the ravine on the north side, and on the southern by another coming from the south, which two streams united in one large river at the western apex, at a distance of about perhaps a league. Above and around, on all sides excepting to the west and the ravines through which the rivers flowed, rose the unbroken wall of the lofty mountains of the Cordillera, many of their peaks snow-clad. No sound was to be heard except the rushing of the river in the ravine, and no animal life to be seen except a condor or two floating high above us in the clear sky. The scene was sublime, and I viewed it in silence for some minutes, till the pipe, being handed to me, dispelled all nascent poetic tendencies. The Indians remained silent and looked disgusted, as a herd of cattle had been expected to be viewed on the plain below. We descended to the flats, and crossed the river, on the banks of which 'Paja' or Pampa grass grew in abundance, as well as the bamboo-like canes from which

Araucanian Indians make their lance shafts, and a plant called by the Chilians 'Talka,' the stalk of which, resembling rhubarb, is refreshing and juicy. On the northern edges and slope of the ravine behind us towered graceful pines 60 feet high, which, though an impassable barrier of rock prevented close inspection, appeared to be a species of Araucaria: the bark was imbricated, and the stems rose bare of branches for two-thirds of their height, like those figured by M. Gay. Many had been carried down by landslips, and lay tossed and entangled on the sides of the ravine. The increase of temperature after passing the watershed was sensibly great, amounting to from 7 to 10 degrees, and the vegetation far more luxuriant, the plants presenting many new forms unknown at the eastern side. After leaving the plain and crossing the shallow stream, we left our mantles, and girthed up near a tree in a thicket festooned with a beautiful creeper, having a bell-shaped flower of violet radiated with brown. The variety of flowers made an Eden of this lovely spot: climbing clusters of sweet peas, vetches, and rich golden flowers resembling gorgeous marigolds, and many another blossom, filled the air with perfume and delighted the eye with their beauty. Proceeding still westward we entered a valley with alternate clumps of trees and green pastures, and after riding about a mile I espied from a ridge on one side of the valley two bulls on the other side, just clear of the thick woods bordering the ascent of the mountains. The word was passed in whispers to the cacique, and a halt being called under cover of some bushes, a plan of attack was arranged in the following manner. Two men were sent round to endeavour to drive the animals to a clearing, where it would be possible to use the lazo, the remainder of the party proceeding down towards the open ground with lazos, ready to chase if the bulls should come that way. For a few minutes we remained stationary, picking the strawberries, which in this spot were ripe, although the plants previously met with were only in flower. At the end of five minutes spent in anxiously hoping that our plan would prove successful, a yell from the other side put us on the alert, and we had the gratification to see one of the animals coming straight towards our cover. Alas! just as we were preparing to dash out, he turned on the edge of the plain, and after charging furiously at his pursuer dashed into a thicket, where he stood at bay. We immediately closed round him, and dismounting, I advanced on foot to try and bring him down with the revolver; just as I had got within half-a-dozen paces of him and behind a bush was quietly taking aim at his shoulder, the Indians, eager for beef, and safe on their horses at a considerable distance off shouted, 'Nearer! Nearer!' I accordingly stepped from my cover, but had hardly moved a pace forward when my spur caught in a root: at the same moment 'El Toro' charged. Entangled with the root, I could not jump on one side as he came on; so when within a yard I fired a shot in his face, hoping to turn him, and wheeled my body at the same instant to prevent his horns from catching me, as the sailors say, 'broadside on.' The shot

A WILD BULL IN THE CORDILLERA

did not stop him, so I was knocked down, and, galloping over me, he passed on with my handkerchief, which fell from my head, triumphantly borne on his horns, and stopped a few yards off under another bush. Having picked myself up and found my arms and legs all right; I gave him another shot, which, as my hand was rather unsteady, only took effect in the flank. My cartridges being exhausted, I returned to my horse and found that, besides being considerably shaken, two of my ribs had been broken by the encounter.

The Indians closed round me, and evinced great anxiety to know whether I was much hurt. One more courageous than the rest, despite the warnings of the cacique, swore that he would try and lazo the brute, and accordingly approached the infuriated animal, who for a moment or two showed no signs of stirring: just, however, as the Indian was about to throw his lazo it caught in a branch, and before he could extricate it the bull was on him. We saw the horse give two or three vicious kicks as the bull gored him: at length he was lifted clean up, the fore legs alone remaining on the ground, and overthrown, the rider alighting on his head in a bush. We closed up and attracted the bull in another direction, then went to look for the corpse of our comrade, who, however, to our surprise, issued safe from the bush, where he had lain quiet and unhurt, though the horse was killed. This little incident cast a gloom over our day's pleasure, and lost us our Christmas dinner, as Orkeke ordered a retreat to the spot where we had left our mantles, although we tried to persuade him to attack the beast again, or, at any rate, remain and eat some of the dead horse, and try our luck next day, but he was inflexible. So having regained our spare horses we prepared to return home, hoping to be able to pass through the forests before nightfall. On our way across the plain previously described; wild cattle were seen and one chased; but he, although balled by Orkeke, contrived to slip the bolas, and escaping to cover stood to bay, where he was left master of the field. This bull would have been taken had the other Indians showed any degree of alacrity when Orkeke balled him; but, they were dispirited by the previous failure. As evening was coming on I noticed a cormorant on the river: this and the increase of temperature led me to believe that had we penetrated a few miles farther west we should have reached the shores of the Pacific. Pursuing our track homewards, after the second unsuccessful engagement, we managed to pass the thick forest before dark, and descending to the eastern valley saw numerous cows and bulls at intervals. A short time after dark we encamped for the night under the shelter of some trees near to the head waters of the western river, and after a pipe—by way of supper—wrapping ourselves in our mantles were soon fast asleep. At daylight we mounted and continued our journey, arriving about 2 P.M. pretty considerably hungry, having eaten nothing barring strawberries and talka, and a few unripe currants, since our last evening in the toldos. The women were naturally disappointed at our ill-luck, but uttered no complaints or reproaches, and hastened to pound some charqui for our refreshment. Next day, all except myself and my companion in the overthrow, who complained of headache, went out hunting and returned at night with young guanaco, and an ostrich or two. Some of the women had seen cattle near the encampment, and Orkeke informed me that in former years they used to occupy the plains below us in large herds, but that the Indians had driven them into the interior by excessive hunting: he also stated that on one occasion he spent some months in this spot, and caught and tamed a considerable number. His accurate knowledge of the country made his statement credible, and he also showed me a sort of corral that had been made to enclose the wild animals. For my own part the name of the Cordillera recalls the most hungry Christmas time of my life: to parody the 'Ancient Mariner,' it was 'Cattle, cattle everywhere, and never a bit of beef.' The following day was spent in the toldos, and some of the Indians were desirous, or pretended to be, of going once more in search of cattle. Orkeke would not hear of it, so on the 28th we marched, following the course of the river in a more or less north-east direction. The weather was beautiful, and after leaving the plain we rode along the winding valley, now and then starting a herd of guanaco or a solitary ostrich. Towards evening we encamped on the banks of the river, and the women, after pitching the toldos, employed themselves in grubbing up potatoes. This day we saw smoke to the north, caused by the hunting parties of the other Indians, and also some at a greater distance, which Orkeke said was that of the Araucanian Indians, whom it was expected that we should shortly meet with.

On the 29th we were preparing to march, and while the women were engaged in lading the horses some of us were picking the berries of the 'Califata,' or barberry (Berberis buccifolia), or looking for strawberries, when a boy, from a party of other Indians occupying the toldos near at hand, rode up as if despatched as a chasqui, and stated that his party had communicated with the Araucanians, amongst whom there had been a row in a drinking bout, resulting in the death of the cacique. This story was fully believed, and Orkeke was rather perplexed, as perhaps the new cacique might not be friendly disposed towards the Tehuelches. Without hunting, we rode quietly down to the next encampment, where the two strange toldos had already arrived. On our near approach one of the Indians came to meet us, and whilst discussing a pipe, after the observance of the usual ceremonial prescribed by etiquette (as we had not seen the man before), we asked him about the row amongst the Araucanos, which turned out to be all a hoax on the part of the promising youth who had visited us. After a while we adjourned to the toldos, situated on a bend of the river near a ford or pass. We had now arrived at the camp agreed on as a general rendezvous at Henno, previous to the dispersion of the Indians. This valley is called Teckel, and is a favourite resting place after the young guanaco season, both for the purpose of refreshing the horses and manufacturing the young guanaco skins into mantles, previous to proceeding to trade either at the Rio Negro or with the Indians of Las Manzanas. The encampment is usually situated on the ground occupied at this time, viz., on the west side of the river, about a mile from a large barren hill which shuts out the view of the Cordillera. On the east side the valley extends some three miles, and continues open to the north for perhaps six miles. It is all fertile, but the best grazing ground is at the north-east end. The banks of the river, which are destitute of trees, are in many places high, and formed under the surface earth of various stratified clays—blue, white, and red. In the bottom of the stream, which is singularly free from stones, thick beds of clay are of frequent occurrence; almost approaching to the tufa found in the Parana and other confluents of La Plata, and in some spots there are beds of black sand, probably auriferous; fish are procurable in any eddy or pool, and crayfish abound and form the most tempting bait for the others. Out of some of the finest clay I was enabled to manufacture a pipe by the simple process of shaping it in the hand and then baking it in the ashes, but it did not last long. Shortly after our arrival one of the small children, whilst playing with bolas formed out of the foot and sinews of an ostrich, hurt himself; and in consequence a slaughter of mares took place, which opportunely enabled us to dispense with hunting and rest our horses, which by this time stood in sore need of some bye days; though, as there was a good race-course, we frequently indulged in a race just to keep the horses in exercise. After we had been about a week settled here, the women being all hard at work making up mantles—which will be described in the next chapter—the Indians began to arrive, and the hunting was resumed; only, however, when absolutely necessary. Some of the new arrivals proceeded to the wild cattle district, and managed to kill a bull, although—as before—an accident occurred. As my lazo was used to capture the bull, I came in for a share of the meat, which was divided amongst the people in our toldo; but it proved very tough, and rather nasty. Perhaps the palate, having been so long accustomed to guanaco, ostrich, or horse, could not relish meat of a coarser description; but the hide was invaluable for making maneos and other horse-gear. On January 7 a messenger arrived from Casimiro requesting me to send him some information, and stating that he was distant some three marches, and wished to wait some time to refresh his horses, &c. After consulting with Orkeke and Jackechan, we sent back a messenger to say that, 'As game was scarce now in the vicinity of Teckel, and all were more or less desirous of pushing forward, he had better make haste and join us, otherwise we should continue our march towards Las Manzanas.' This message had the desired effect, as on the 11th he made his appearance, with several other toldos, a few only remaining in the rear with Crimè, who was reported to be unwell.

On Casimiro's arrival, as he now possessed a good toldo, I changed my quarters to his residence, as agreed on at the outset of the journey. I was sorry to leave Orkeke, and the old man was very much grieved, a present of a revolver

Teckel

Yattn

Weekel

Gogomenykaik

Wooded Ranges

Gisk

Hoshel

Large open Plains

Churik

Henno

Cápel

Applekaik

Telwecken

Yowlel

Yasaik

R. Sengel

Rocks resembling a Town

Supposed course of River Sengel

Alternate Hills & Valleys

C o r d i l l e r a

P A C I F I C   O C E A N

ROUTE
between 8th Oct. & 29th Dec. 1870
Showing Supposed Course
OF SENGEL RIVER.

only troubling him the more, as he informed me that he had nothing to offer in exchange; however, my assurance that I did not give him a present expecting an exchange, as is customary with Indians, appeared to console him. The usual consultation of the chiefs took place, in which all the preceding arrangements were agreed to, and we remained stationary in Teckel until January 20. As I had by this time become well acquainted with the mode of life and usages of the Tehuelches, and was looked upon as one of themselves—and in fact had acquired a position and influence among them—it may be as well to call a halt, and devote a chapter to a description of the manners and customs of the Tsonecas, as Tehuelches or Patagonians call themselves.

1. Fte. S. Espiritu.
2. The skull of a guanaco is well figured in Mr. Cunningham's work.

V

MANNERS AND CUSTOMS OF THE TEHUELCHES

THE first question asked about the Patagonians by curious English friends has invariably had reference to their traditionary stature. Are they giants or not? Whether the ancestors of the Tehuelches—to whom alone, by the way, the name Patagonians properly applies—were taller than the present race is uncertain; though tales of gigantic skeletons found in Tehuelche graves are current in Punta Arenas and Santa Cruz. The average height of the Tehuelche male members of the party with which I travelled was rather over than under 5 feet 10 inches.[1] Of course no other means of measurement besides comparing my own height were available; but this result, noted at the time, coincides with that independently arrived at by Mr. Cunningham. Two others, who were measured carefully by Mr. Clarke, stood 6 feet 4 inches each. After joining the Northern Tehuelches, although the Southerners proved generally to be the tallest, I found no reason to alter this average, as any smaller men that were met with in their company were not pure Tehuelches, but half-bred Pampas. The extraordinary muscular development of the arms and chest is in all particularly striking, and as a rule they are well-proportioned throughout. This fact calls for especial mention, as others have stated that the development and strength of the legs is inferior to that of the arms. Even Mr. Cunningham alleges this to be the case, but I cannot at all agree with him. Besides the frequent opportunities afforded me of scrutinising the young men engaged in the game of ball, in which great strength and activity are displayed, or when enjoying the almost daily bath and swimming or diving, I judged of the muscular size of their legs by trying on their boots, which, in nearly all cases, were far too large for me, although the feet, on the other hand, were frequently smaller than mine. The height of their insteps is also worthy of remark, one example of which may suffice. Having negotiated an exchange of an excellent pair of high boots, manufactured by Messrs. Thomas, for some necessary article, with a Tehuelche, the bargain fell through because he was unable to get his foot into the boot, the high arched instep proving an insuperable obstacle to further progress.

An instance of the walking powers of the Tehuelches came under my particular notice. On my first arrival at Santa Cruz, it will be remembered that the schooner was lying in the mouth of the river waiting for a fair wind. Two Tehuelches, named Tchang and Getchkook, had embarked in order to proceed to the Rio Negro, but their patience becoming exhausted by the delay, they asked to be put ashore, and walked back to the settlement—a distance of over forty miles—in about twelve hours, without food. I saw them on their arrival, and they did not appear in any way distressed, merely remarking that it had been 'a long walk.'

Their powers of abstaining from food are also very remarkable. When the disturbances and fighting were going on they rarely ate anything: also when travelling as 'chasquis,' or messengers, they will not unfrequently go for two, and even three, days without tasting food. In our expedition into the Cordillera we remained over forty-eight hours without food, except wild fruit, and, although I at first suffered from hunger, my companions did not appear to be in any way inconvenienced. As a Chilian deserter remarked on one occasion, it was all very well for them to go on without eating; 'but we can't—we've not so much fat.' Their strength of arm is very great, and the distance to which they can throw the ostrich bola is truly astonishing: thus I have seen Crimè and some others ball an ostrich over seventy yards distant. When cutting wood in the Cordillera with Hinchel, a Chilian deserter and myself had cut a tree through, and, having fastened a lazo to the top branch, were endeavouring to drag it down, but its branches became entangled in another tree and we could not stir it. Hinchel, seeing our difficulty, came up, and with one well-directed, vigorous tug cleared it from the branches and brought it to the ground.

Mr. Clarke also informed me that when he was ill with fever, and had to be removed from the Almacen to the lower house on the island, on account of the noise made by the drunken Indians, Wáki mounted, and, taking him in his arms, rode down seemingly unencumbered by the burden. Their faces, of course, vary in expression, but are ordinarily bright and good-humoured, though when in the settlements they assume a sober, and even sullen, demeanour. Wáki and Cayuke, two friends of mine, are particularly present to my recollection as having always had a smile on their faces. Their ever ready laughter displays universally good teeth, which they keep white and clean by chewing 'maki,' a gum which exudes from the incense bush, and is carefully gathered by the women and children. It has a rather pleasant taste and is a most excellent dentifrice, worthy to rival Odonto or Floriline, and it is used simply as such, and not, as Monsr. Guinnard says,[2] because their greediness is so great that they must chew something. Their eyes are bright and intelligent, and their noses—though, of course, presenting different types—are as a rule aquiline and well-formed, and devoid of the breadth of nostril proper to the ordinary ideal of savage tribes. The peculiar prominence over the eyebrows has been noticed by all observers, and retreating foreheads, though observable, are exceptional. The thick masses of hair, and the obvious risk, which would deter the most zealous craniologist from endeavouring to measure their heads, must be deemed sufficient excuse for my not being able to state whether they are dolichokephalic or brachykephalic; a point, however, which I confess did not particularly attract my observation; but, for the partial comfort of anthropologists, be it noted that both Chilians and myself interchanged hats with some Tehuelches, especially Orkeke and Hinchel, without finding misfits. The complexion of the men is reddish brown, that is to say when cleansed from paint, and, like an old picture, restored to their pristine tint, which is not quite so deep as to warrant Fitzroy's comparison of it to the colour of a Devon cow.

The scanty natural growth of beard, moustaches, and even eyebrows, is carefully eradicated by means of a pair of silver tweezers, and I was often urged to part with my beard, and undergo this painful operation, but I naturally objected to comply with the request. The men's heads are covered with thick, flowing masses of long hair, of which they take great care, making their wives, or other female relatives, brush it out carefully at least once a day. Very few appeared to have grey hair; though there were a few exceptions, one very old man's hair being of a snowy whiteness, which contrasted strangely with his tawny face. The women have, as far as I could judge, an average height of about 5 feet 6: they are very strong in the arms, but seldom walk beyond fetching the supplies of wood and water, all their journeys being performed on horseback. Their hair, which is of no great length, scarcely indeed equalling that of the men, and very coarse, is worn in two plaited tails, which on gala days are artificially lengthened, probably with horse-hair interwoven with blue beads, the ends being garnished with silver pendants. This practice, however, is confined, I think, to the unmarried ladies.

Being an admirer of long hair, on my first joining the Indians I greatly admired Tchang's daughter for her 'head of hair,' two immensely long tails beautifully embellished, which I naturally thought was all her own. But, meeting her by chance on the following morning returning to the toldo with water, to my great disappointment I found that she had taken her spare hair off and her natural locks were the reverse of long. The young women are frequently good-looking, displaying healthy, ruddy cheeks when not disguised with paint. They are modest in behaviour, though very coquettish, and as skilled in flirtation as if they had been taught in more civilised society. The fair widow who so nearly *hooked* the Englishman could on occasions appeal as prettily for help as a young lady in imaginary difficulties over a country stile. Thus, when at Orkeke's request I led the way through a river—half way across the channel suddenly deepened, with muddy bottom, and an abrupt bank to land on—I heard a plaintive appeal, 'Muster, help me! my horse is too small.' Exposure and work do not age them as soon as might be expected, but when old they become most hideous beldames, and the most weird-like witches imagined by Doré would be surpassed by a trio of Tehuelche grandames. The dress of the men consists of a chiripa, or under garment round the loins, made of a poncho, a piece of cloth, or even of a guanaco mantle: but, whatever the material, this article of dress is indispensable and scrupulously worn, their sense of decency being very strong. All other garments are supplied by the capacious and warm skin mantle, which, worn with the fur inside and the painted side out, will keep the wearer dry for a considerable time in the wettest weather. This is often dispensed with in the chase, but, if worn when riding, is secured at the waist by a belt of hide or leather if it can be obtained. When in camp the belt is not used, and the garment is worn loose, something after the fashion of the 'melodramatic assassin's' cloak. When sitting by the fireside, or even when walking about, the furred part of the mantle is generally kept up over the mouth—as the Tehuelches aver that the cold wind causes sore gums—a habit which assists in rendering their guttural, and at all times rather unintelligible, language more difficult of comprehension to the novice.

Their potro boots (p.138, fig. 5) or buskins are made from the skin of horse's hock, and occasionally from the leg of a large puma; drawn on up to the knee and fastened round the foot. It is thus worn for a day or two until the boot has taken the shape of the foot, when the leather is cut at the toes and sewn up to fit. When the sole is worn, or in very wet or snowy weather, hide overshoes are worn besides, and the footprints thus made are really large enough to convey the idea of giants' feet, and partly explain the term 'Patagon,' or large feet, applied to these Indians by the Spanish discoverers. The boots are rarely put on in camp for economical reasons, though turning out barefoot in the frozen grass at daylight is unpleasant even to a Tehuelche. But the material of the boot would soon wear out if used for walking. In riding they are secured by garters, either gay coloured woven bands, or, which is *de rigueur* for chiefs, of hide, with massive silver buckles. Although the usual head-dress of the men is simply a coloured fillet to confine the hair, yet sometimes, and especially on state occasions, hats, if procurable, are indulged in. Old Orkeke frequently wore a felt widewake, which was, on returning from hunting, carefully put up by his thoughtful spouse.

The women's dress consists of a mantle similar to that worn by the men, but secured at the throat by a large silver pin with a broad disc, or a nail, or thorn, according to the wealth or poverty of the wearer; and under this is a loose calico or stuff sacque, extending from the shoulders to the ankle. When travelling the mantle is secured at the waist by a broad belt ornamented with blue beads, and silver or brass studs. The boots worn by the women are similar to those described, with the exception that in their preparation the hair is left on the hide, while it is carefully removed from those of the men. The children are dressed in small mantles, but are more frequently allowed to run about naked up to the age of six or eight; their little boots are made from the skin taken from the fore-legs of the guanaco, softened in the hand. The small children generally remonstrated strongly and effectually against wearing this article of clothing; and whatever the severity of the weather, preferred running about barefoot. The cradles for the babies are formed of strips of wicker-work interlaced with hide thongs, fitted with a cover to keep sun and rain off, and made of a convenient shape to rest on the saddle gear of the mother when on the march. They are ornamented, if the parents are wealthy, with little bells, brass or even silver plates. The women are fond of ornaments, wearing huge earrings of square shape, suspended to small rings passing through the lobe of the ear; also silver or blue bead necklaces. The men also wear these necklaces, and adorn their belts, pipes, knives, sheaths, and horse-gear with silver. Those who can afford it also indulge in silver spurs and stirrups; most of their ornaments, except the beads, are home-made, being beaten out of dollars obtained by commerce in the settlements. Both sexes smear their faces, and occasionally their bodies, with paint, the Indians alleging as the reason for using this cosmetic, that it is a protection against the effect of the winds; and I found from personal experience that it proved a complete preservative from excoriation or chapped skin. It proved equally effective against the sun, which in Henno peeled my face completely until I resumed the paint—which I had left off—not wishing to appear as a noble savage to the newcomers. The paint for the face is composed of either red ochre or black earth mixed with grease obtained from the marrow bones of the game killed in the chase, all of which are carefully husbanded by the women, and when opportunity offers pounded and boiled in the large pots; the grease and gelatine being carefully skimmed off and secured. On state occasions, such as a birth feast, and for a dance, the men further adorn themselves with white paint, or powdered gypsum, which they moisten and rub on their hands, and make five white finger marks over their chests, arms, and legs. The usual morning toilette is simple, after the plunge in the river, which is almost always the first thing, except of course when circumstances prevent it, indulged in by both sexes, who bathe scrupulously apart, and generally before daylight. The men's hair is dressed by their wives, daughters, or sweethearts, who take the greatest care to burn any hairs that may be brushed out, as they fully believe that spells may be wrought by evil-intentioned persons who can obtain a piece of their hair. From the same idea, after cutting their nails, the parings are carefully committed to the flames. After the hairbrushing, which is performed by means of a rude hand brush, the women adorn the men's faces with paint; if in mourning they put on black paint, and if going to fight, sometimes put a little white paint under the eyes, which assists in contrast to the other in giving a savage expression. The women paint each other's faces, or if possessed, as sometimes occurs, of a fragment of looking-glass, paint their own. Both sexes tattoo on the forearm, by the simple process of puncturing the skin with a bodkin, and inserting a mixture of blue earth with a piece of dry glass: the usual patterns consist of a series of parallel lines, and sometimes a single triangle, or a double triangle, the upper one resting on the apex of the lower. I myself had one line tattooed by a fair enslaver, and confess that the process was rather painful.

Indians have a good deal of regard for personal cleanliness, and besides the morning ablutions enjoy bathing when encamped near a river, swimming and diving for hours together. They also are scrupulously careful as to the cleanliness of their toldos and utensils, and will, if they can obtain soap, wash up every thing they may be possessed of. Notwithstanding these precautions they are very much afflicted by vermin, which effect a firm lodgment in the wool of their mantles. This may be attributed to their mode of life, and their food, as well as to the materials of their clothing; and any traveller who wishes to sojourn with the Indians must make up his mind to subject himself to these inflictions, to which, however (*experto crede*), he will soon become inured. Their method of hunting and of cooking the meat obtained by the chase has been fully described in a previous chapter. Among the arms and implements figured in the illustration will be found (p.138, figs. 9 and 10) the weapons chiefly employed in the pursuit of game, namely, the bolas fitted with two balls called 'Chumè,' for capturing the ostrich, and those with three called 'yachiko,' for guanaco hunting, which are similar to those used by the Gauchos in the Argentine Provinces. The balls are generally of stone, but sometimes white metal or copper balls are employed, procured in the settlements, which require no covering, and are more and more coming into fashion of late years; iron balls also, or iron ore, obtained and hammered into the requisite shape by the Tehuelches themselves, are common; these are for the round striking ball or balls: but the oval shaped hand ball, which is grasped in the hand, and is necessarily lighter by at least one-third than the other, is generally made of the soft vesicular lava which abounds in so many districts. The tough light thong for swinging balls round the head is generally made, as previously described, of ostrich or guanaco sinews plaited in four plaits, the length of which should be between seven and eight feet. It is always best to ball a quarry when galloping in an exact line, as the necks of guanaco and ostrich are always aimed at; entangling the hind legs of the quadruped being useless, though cattle and horses are always balled round the hind legs. A shot at a bird or beast bounding or running across is almost sure to miss; of course misses are frequent, as fifty to seventy yards is often the distance of a shot delivered from a horse's back at full gallop; and the balls whirr through the air with their peculiar sound, only perhaps to fall into a tangled bush. Then it is that the advantage of the bright material becomes evident, for the horseman does not stop, but gallops on and throws another pair, returning afterwards to pick up the dropped weapons, frequently very hard to find on the pebble-strewn, grass-grown, or shrub-covered surface. I generally threw down a handkerchief or some such thing, easily seen, to mark the spot; but the metal bolas are so much preferred on account of being easily seen, that a pair are worth a horse. In addition to the bolas, a lazo is used when hunting cattle or horses, and sometimes for the pumas, although the ordinary method is to kill them by first stunning them with a blow on the head. The arms of the Tehuelches consist of gun or revolver, sword or dagger, a long heavy lance, used only by dismounted Indians, and altogether different to the light lance of Araucanian and Pampa horsemen, and the bola perdida or single ball, so called because once thrown it is not picked up again: this weapon is quickly constructed; a sharp-pointed stone is taken, covered with hide except the point, which is left out, and a thong of raw hide about a yard long is attached, with a knot made in the end to prevent it slipping from the hand whilst whirling it round previous to throwing it at an enemy. Before the introduction of firearms the bola perdida was the original weapon of the Tehuelches, and is even at the present day a most deadly missile in their hands. (p.138, fig. 11.)

I am aware that Pigafetta, the historian of Magellan's voyage, describes the ancestors of these Indians as using bows and arrows, but I am inclined to think that this must have applied either to a tribe of Fuegians or a party of Pampas living in the valley of the Rio Negro. It is certain that no ancient flint arrowheads are met with south of the Rio Negro, where they abound; also that there is but little, if any, wood nearer than the Cordillera suitable for bows, and it is reasonable to suppose that previous to the introduction of horses the Indian migrations were confined to a smaller area; besides, although no arrowheads are found in the interior of Patagonia proper, ancient bolas are not unfrequently met with. These are highly valued by the Indians, and differ from those in present use by having grooves cut round them, and by their larger size and greater weight. The introduction and diffusion of firearms has almost superseded the use of defensive armour; but chain suits, and hide surcoats studded thickly with silver, are still—as instances before given show—possessed and employed: and before going into battle the warriors are often padded like cricketers, corconillas or saddle-cloths, and ponchos being employed to form a covering, the folds of which will turn a sword cut or lance thrust.

During our long sojourn at Teckel, as hunting was avoided as much as possible, in order to rest the horses, the men occupied themselves in Indian arts and manufactures, some account of which may be deemed interesting.

As the horse is the mainstay of the Indian, let the saddle-gear take precedence. (p.138, figs. 1, 2, 3, 4.)

The saddles are constructed in the following manner. A piece of timber is split in two, and reduced, by means of a small hand-adze, to the requisite

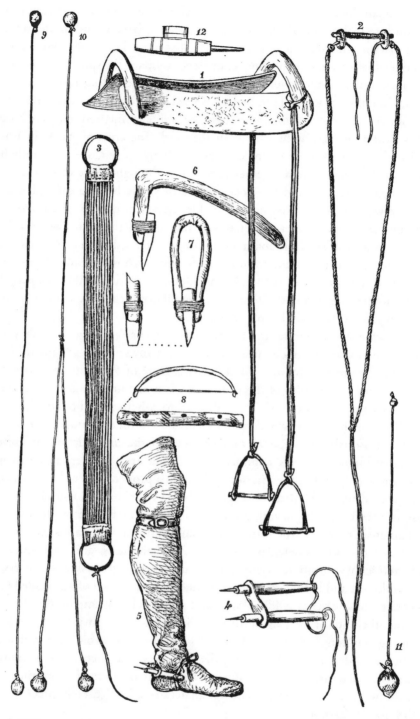

1. Saddle.   2. Bridle.   3. Girth.   4. Spurs.   5. Boot.   6. Adze.   7. Scraper.
8. Musical instrument.   9. Ostrich bola.   10. Guanaco bola.   11. Bola perdida.   12. Pipe.

size and thickness to form the side boards or flaps, skilfully adapted to the shape of the horse's back; in these boards holes are bored at each end, and the saddle-trees, which are chosen from angular limbs of trees, like knees for boat building, and reduced to the requisite size, are lashed on by hide. Over this fresh guanaco hide, divested of its woolly coat and carefully cut to the proper shape, is sewn with sinew, serving, as it dries, to bind the whole securely together. Casimiro was the most skilful workman of the party, and made a saddle for me which, although through having to start in a hurry it was not smoothed down or covered with hide, I used for about five weeks without any chafing of the horse's back. Underneath the saddle a thick mandil, or poncho, is placed; and over the saddle a corconilla, or housing, of puma or yearling guanaco skin, or, which is always preferred if obtainable, a black sheepskin. The Araucanians weave corconillas of most beautiful texture and brilliant blue colour, which are sold for as much as 5*l.* in the settlements. The girths are made of thirteen or fourteen ties of twisted hide from the neck of the guanaco, and fitted with two rings connected by a leather thong. The stirrups are suspended by strips of hide from the holes bored in the foremost saddle-trees. They are generally made of a piece of hard wood fixed into a raw hide thong, or sometimes of wood bent into a triangular shape. The swells, of course, sport silver stirrups, but they are frequently not used at all. The saddle is also taken off when the hunting circle is being closed and the horses ridden bare-backed, but it is replaced to carry the meat back to the toldos. Sometimes it occurs that an Indian loses his saddle at play, when he is perforce obliged to ride bare-backed, and it never appears to inconvenience them. The bridles are made of either plaited or twisted hide. The bits used vary, but the more general is a simple bar of either wood or iron, covered at either end with two flaps of stout hide, from which two thongs extend under the horse's jaw, forming an effectual curb, the reins being also secured to the hide-flaps. The bar is frequently omitted, and a simple thong is placed in the horse's mouth and rove through the piece of hide, which is secured to the bridle and tied under the jaw. I used this simple bit the whole of the journey, and never had reason to find fault with it. The spurs are made of two pieces of hard wood, with nails filed to a sharp point fixed in the ends, for which I once tried to substitute bone spikes, but they required constant sharpening and broke quickly. The spurs are secured to the feet by thongs. Head stalls for breaking horses are made either of plain or plaited hide, with a ring underneath for the Maneador.

Lazos are made either of twisted or plaited hide, similar to those in use among the Gauchos. The only other articles of horse-gear worthy of mention are the 'manèos,' called by the Indians 'caligi,' or straps for securing the horse's legs, in order to teach him to stand when the rider has dismounted; but the horses soon learn to await the return of the rider. Since my return a hunting friend, hearing the chase described, eagerly inquired, 'But who held your horse?' The well-trained Tehuelche hunters hold themselves, and no boy or man is available to render this service to anyone unlucky enough to be mounted on an uneducated steed. Our breakers might take a useful lesson from the 'savages.'

Another branch of general industry is the manufacture of pipe-bowls, which are peculiar in shape, as may be seen in the plate (p.138, fig. 12). They are made of either wood or stone, fitted with a silver or metal tube, and frequently ornamented with silver. The greatest pains is taken to keep them free from tobacco juice by constant cleaning with an ostrich feather.

Wooden platters are sometimes made, for containing meat or grease; and I have seen wooden or horn spoons constructed, but these articles are rare. Casimiro's toldo rejoiced in one of the latter, and it rather resembled a shoe horn. The men are many of them skilful workers in silver, made from dollars obtained in the settlements, and tempered until they become sufficiently malleable to be beaten out into the requisite shapes, either for buckles, garters, plates, beads, or studs for embossing belts or armour with. These 'cups,' or studs, are generally hollowed out in a suitable cavity, worked in a stone; they are then pierced at the edges with a bodkin, and sewn on to the hide with sinew. The anvils and hammers for working silver are generally stone implements; flints, however, are only used by the men for procuring fire. The Tehuelches are also very handy workers in iron, and will fashion a knife, or even an adze, out of any piece of metal procured by theft, commerce in the colonies, or from wrecks on the coast. One of the knives frequently used in the latter part of my journey was formed out of one blade of an old pair of scissors forged for me by Hinchel.

Their tools for working silver, iron, wood, &c., consist of files, known by the expressive name of 'Khikerikikh,' or perhaps a rasp, an occasional saw, an axe, the inevitable small adze (p.138, fig. 6), a pair of scissors, or an old chisel. Many of these have been obtained from shipwrecks on the coast, others by barter in the settlements.

The women's most important occupation in camp was the making up of skin mantles, which merits a full description.

The skins are first dried in the sun, being pegged down with thorns of the algarroba tree. When dry they are taken up, and scraped with pieces of flint, agate, obsidian, or some times glass, fixed into a branch naturally bent so as to form a handle (p.138, fig. 7). They are then smeared over with grease and liver kneaded into pulp, after which they are softened in the hand until quite pliable, when they are placed on the ground and cut with a small, very sharp knife into pieces, dovetailed so as to fit one into the other, in order to secure strength of seam, and parcelled out amongst a party of four or six women, with a corresponding quantity of needles and thread, consisting of bodkins formed out of sharpened nails, and dried sinews from the back of the adult guanaco. A whole mantle is never sewn together at once, but when one half is finished it is pegged out and the paint applied to it thus. The surface is slightly damped, and each woman takes a cake or piece of red ochre, if the ground is to be red, and, keeping it damp, lays the paint on with great care. When the ground is finished, the pattern of small black spots and blue and yellow lines is painted with the greatest exactness, the women working all day with the most assiduous industry. When completed it is left for a night to dry, and the other half and wings, which serve in lieu of sleeves, are duly completed, and subsequently all are joined together, presenting, when finished, an unbroken surface of fur. The most favourite pattern (except when the wearer is in mourning) is a red ground with small black crosses and blue and yellow longitudinal lines for borders, or with a zigzag of white, blue, and red. The untiring energy with which the women work, and the rapidity with which they sew, are astonishing. When a man is married, his wife, or wives, of course manufacture his mantles, assisted by their friends, whom they help in their turn; but should he be a bachelor, as in my unfortunate case, he gives out his skins to a fair lady, who works like other people I have heard of—on half-profits, and the hunter generally loses by the bargain; at least such was my experience, some thirty or forty skins only producing a mantle containing about one-third their number. Besides the guanaco mantles which are most generally worn, others are made from the skins of the fox, puma, wild cat, cavy, and skunk; the fur of the latter and of the wild cat are the most valuable, but, like the others, are generally intended only for barter. The women, besides making mantles, weave the fillets for the head previously mentioned, from threads of unravelled stuff obtained in barter at the settlements, or from their Araucanian neighbours. They work on the same principle as that on which a sailor constructs a sword mat. Besides these fillets, they occasionally weave scarves for the waist, and garters. Many of them also work in the minor details of silver ornaments, such as hollowing out or bending the studs, boring the holes, and stitching them on to the belts or armour, as the case may be. They also sew the skins together for the coverings of the toldos, which is very laborious work. They scrape and dress horse-hides for the furniture of the bed places, painting them in various patterns; make the bolsters of reeds (often also ornamented with silver) to place as a protection for their high saddles, cook the food, smash the marrow-bones and extract the grease; take care of the children, and fetch wood, water, and do all the 'chores,' as the Americans say. As may be seen, they are pretty nearly always occupied; nevertheless, they occasionally find time to play cards, and sometimes to squabble and talk scandal.

The children generally employ themselves in imitating their elders. The boys play with miniature bolas, and catch the dogs with small lazos, and the girls construct miniature toldos and sit in them; for this purpose they carry off unchecked anything that may seem suitable. Frequently when about to join the chase I had to interfere with these latter games, and recover my saddle gear, which had been appropriated by the juveniles.

The musical instruments of the Tehuelches have been previously described. In Teckel, besides the native orchestra (p.138, fig. 8) and harmonies, to which one had become accustomed, we furthermore rejoiced in a cornet, with music from which Jackechan's brother frequently enlivened our evenings. Many amongst the Tehuelches could blow the ordinary bugle calls which they had been accustomed to hear when in the Rio Negro or at Punta Arenas; and most of them appeared to possess a good ear for music. Their songs, however, are not melodious, and are mere repetitions of words devoid of all sense or meaning. Casimiro informed me that formerly the old men were in the habit of singing the traditions of the tribe and also some sort of prayer. It is much to be regretted that these customs have fallen into disuse. I tried on various occasions to obtain information about their ancestors, but all my efforts were fruitless. When I asked them how their people travelled before horses came into the country, they could not realise the fact that such was ever the case.

There is little to add to the details already given of the cookery and diet of the Tehuelches, which is necessarily almost confined to meat, which, however, they *do not* devour raw, as so constantly asserted. Fat is largely consumed, both fresh and preserved; the need of this being, as before said, attributable to the want of farinaceous food. Still they are very fond of all sorts of wild fruits and vegetables, when procurable; and besides the indigenous tuberous roots, and the ever-present dandelion plants, which the girls gather for their friends and relations, and which are eaten in a crude state, they will when in the settlements barter their wares for potatoes, turnips, and other vegetables. They are also extremely fond of biscuit and flour, which they mix with water into dampers, and bake them in the ashes. Previous to my sojourn amongst them, pepper was, I believe, unknown, but having a small store in my possession, I induced old Orkeke and his dame to try it, and they and others soon acquired a taste for it. Sugar, or anything sweet, they are especially fond of. Salt is a very necessary commodity with them, and when passing one of the numerous salinas that occur in the country the stores are replenished. It sometimes happens, however, if making a long stay in one place, or travelling in parts where salinas are scarce, they have to go without it; and this is probably the cause of a skin disease that at times occurs amongst them. Salt is carried as a rule by the men when hunting, both to mix with the blood, which is seldom eaten without it, and to season the guanaco or ostrich meat.

I think that as a rule the Indians, far from being gluttonous gormandisers, eat less than civilised people. They never eat at stated times, but when their appetite warns them; and on this point an Indian once made the remark to me: 'The Chilians eat at regular hours, which is foolish; we don't eat unless we are hungry.' I believe that I, as a single individual, generally consumed more victuals than any Indian, with the exception of my friend Cayuke, who was certainly a great gourmand. He was also a great smoker; and whenever I met him invariably said the few English words I had taught him, 'Load and light the pipe—smoke.' The general manner of smoking is as follows. The smoker lights his pipe, and then lies prone on the ground, and after puffing a portion of smoke to each cardinal point and muttering a prayer, he swallows several mouthfuls of tobacco smoke, which produces intoxication and partial insensibility, lasting perhaps for the space of two minutes. During this time his companions carefully avoid disturbing him in any way. When it has passed off, he gets up, takes a drink of water, and resumes his conversation or occupation. I have sometimes observed this intoxication accompanied by convulsions, but only in rare cases. The tobacco used for smoking (for they never chew) is generally obtained from the settlements, but failing this a herb substitute is procured from the Araucanians. This is never smoked pure, being invariably mixed with either wood chopped up small or 'yerba' (Paraguay tea) stalks, if obtainable. The mixture with dung mentioned by M. Guinnard is unknown among the Tehuelches.

The women sometimes are smokers, but the custom is not universal, being generally confined to the old ladies. Most of the men smoke, but there are exceptions. I was very much astonished, however, by seeing El Sourdo on more than one occasion give his pipe to his boy—a precocious three-year-old—who whiffed his 'bacca' with apparently great satisfaction to himself and his fond father.

The chief amusements amongst the Indians (for hunting is a matter of business and not pleasure) consist in horse-racing, card-playing, gambling with dice made by themselves with mathematical exactness from bones, and thrown from the hand, or with small stones, and playing a game of ball. The horse-racing has been already described. The cards used are sometimes the Spanish pack, obtained in the settlements, but very frequently constructed by the Indians themselves of hide. These, like the ordinary Spanish cards, are marked with the Spanish numerals up to seven; but the court cards are entirely different, having, instead of figures or pictures, monograms of native origin, the original significance of which, if any, was undiscoverable. The ace, however, is marked somewhat similarly to our own. The usual games played are 'Panturga,' 'Primero,' 'Siete,' and 'Yaik,' or fire, a sort of 'beggar my neighbour.' The players sit down in a circle, with a poncho or saddle-cloth to represent the board of green cloth; their markers consist of pieces of sticks or grass, and their system of marking is complicated. I generally—if I did indulge in the luxury of a gamble—played in partnership with another who took charge of the marking, but my invariable good luck rendered me unwilling to respond to the invitation to take a hand. When stakes are lost, whether a horse, troop of mares, saddle, lazo, or what not, the winner simply sends a friend for them, or goes himself and takes them; all debts of honour being scrupulously paid at once. Frequently large stakes are lost and won.

THE "PRETTY HOUSE" AND DANCE

On one occasion I had negotiated the purchase of a horse from an Indian possessed of a goodly troop, and having given earnest, had started hunting on the animal to test his staying powers. My friend the owner, who remained in camp playing, came to me on my return, and implored me to consider the bargain as nil, as during my absence he had lost nearly all his horses, and some of the articles of his wife's dowry. I of course gave up the bargain, duly receiving back the earnest, and he subsequently won back his horses and riches. The game played with small stones is similar to that in vogue among schoolboys, and known by the name of 'knucklebones.' It is generally played by the boys, but their elders will not unfrequently join. The women play at cards, and also at this game amongst themselves, staking their mandils, hides, and saddle-gear on the results. Mrs. Orkeke was very fond of play, and on one occasion I have reason to believe that she lost some of her husband's tobacco, and laid the blame on one of the Chilians, who she averred had stolen it. The man nearly lost his life in consequence, and his tears and abject supplications showed the terror he was in, but happily he on this occasion escaped. Strange to say, I was in no way suspected, although I knew where the tobacco was kept, which I doubt if the deserter did.

The game of ball is confined to the young men, and is played as follows: A lazo is laid on the ground so as to form a ring about four yards in diameter; the players, generally eight in number, step into the circle naked, with the exception of the waistcloth. A ball composed of hide stuffed with feathers, about the size of or larger than a tennis-ball, is used by each party, who throw it up from under the thigh, and strike it with the hand at the adversaries', each hit counting a point. Great dexterity and activity are shown by the young men, and although I never joined in any of their regular matches I frequently watched the parties occupied in the game, in which their splendid muscular development was brought out conspicuously. Besides these amusements, the Indians, when ammunition is plentiful, occasionally fire at a mark; but as their bullets are frequently hammered round with stones, the practice is at times erratic, and the guns are also sometimes more dangerous to the marksman than the mark.

The daily routine of occupations and amusements is varied sometimes by a fight, and more pleasantly by some one or other of the ceremonials which mark—as in all nations—the principal epochs of Tsoneca life, from the cradle to the grave. On the birth of a child, if the parents are rich, i.e. own plenty of mares and horses, and silver ornaments, notice is immediately given to the doctor or wizard of the tribe, and to the cacique and relations. The doctor, after bleeding himself with bodkins in the temple, fore-arm, or leg, gives the order for the erection of a mandil tent, or pretty house as the Indians call it, and mares are slaughtered, and a feast and dance follow, such as described in Chapter III, as having taken place in the valley of the Rio Chico. The child, shortly after birth, is smeared over with damp gypsum. The mothers are able to travel on horseback the same, or, certainly, the subsequent day, with the infant carried in a wicker cradle, and most tenderly cared for by both parents.

To every child in its infancy horses and gear are allotted, which are considered thenceforth as the personal property of the boy or girl, and cannot be resumed or disposed of by the parents. No ceremonial attends the naming a child, nor, as far as I could see, is there any fixed time for doing so. The names most commonly used are taken, I think, from places—from the place of birth. Patronymics or hereditary names—except in rare instances, which appeared to be imitations of Spanish usage—are unknown, but nicknames are universal, and parents are frequently known by the name of a child, which usurps the place of their own.

The boys soon learn the use of the weapons, and both boys and girls ride almost before they can walk: the sons rarely accompany the father to the chase before ten or twelve years of age, and do not join in fights till they are about sixteen years old, but there is no fixed period and no ceremonial to mark their admission to the state of manhood. The attainment of puberty by the girls is celebrated as described in Chapter III. From the age of nine or ten they are accustomed to help in household duties and manufactures, and about sixteen are eligible for the married life, though they often remain for several years spinsters. Marriages are always those of inclination, and if the damsel does not like the suitor for her hand, her parents never force her to comply with their wishes, although the match may be an advantageous one.

The usual custom is for the bridegroom, after he has secured the consent of his damsel, to send either a brother or an intimate friend to the parents, offering so many mares, horses, or silver ornaments for the bride. If the parents consider the match desirable, as soon after as circumstances will permit, the bridegroom, dressed in his best, and mounted on his belt horse, decorated with silver ornaments—if he possesses any—proceeds to the toldo of his intended, and hands over the gifts. The parents of the bride then return gifts of an equal value, which, however, in the event of a separation (a rare event), become the property of the bride. After this the bride is escorted by the bridegroom to his toldo, amidst the cheers of his friends and the singing of the women. Mares are usually then slaughtered and eaten on the spot; great care being taken that the dogs do not touch any of the meat or offal, as it is considered unlucky. The head, backbone, tail, together with the heart and liver, are taken up to the top of a neighbouring hill, as an offering to the Gualichu, or evil spirit. An Indian is allowed to have as many wives as he can support, but it is rare to find a man with more than two, and they generally only have one.

On the death of a Tehuelche all his horses, dogs, and other animals are killed, his ponchos, ornaments, bolas, and all other personal belongings are placed in a heap and burned, the widow and other womankind keeping up a dismal wailing, and crying out loud in the most melancholy manner. The meat of the horses is distributed amongst the relations on both sides; and the widow, who cuts her hair short in front and assumes black paint, repairs, bag and baggage, to the toldo of her relations, or if she has none in the party, to the toldo of the chief.

The body is sewn up in a mantle, poncho, or coat of mail, if the deceased possessed one, and is taken away by some of the relations and buried in a sitting posture, its face to the east, a cairn of stones being erected over the place, varying in size according to the wealth and influence of the deceased. I have never seen any of the graves described in Mr. Wood's work, but as my travels as a rule were confined to the interior, they may exist in some part of the sea-coast; nor did the exhumation and removal of the body ever come under my notice, and I should be inclined to doubt its being ever practised by the Tehuelches, inasmuch as it is a rule amongst them never to mention the name of, and to avoid all allusion to, the deceased, their idea being that the dead should be utterly forgotten, though they will add a stone in passing to the cairn of a distinguished chief or hero. The death of a child is marked by a display of sincere grief on the part of the parents. The horse it has been accustomed to travel on during the march is brought up, the gear placed on it, even to the cradle, and the horse, thus fully caparisoned, is strangled by means of lazos, whereas in all other ceremonies where horses are killed they are knocked on the head with bolas. The saddle gear, cradle, and all belonging to the child are burned, the women crying and singing. The parents moreover throw their own valuables into the fire to express their grief. These things some of the women who cry are allowed to snatch out, as a recompense for their services, but they seldom benefit much. On the occasion of the death of an only child of rich parents, fourteen horses and mares were slaughtered in addition to the one it had been accustomed to travel on. Towards evening of the day of the event, previous to the burial of the corpse, a select party of old women marched in procession round and round the camp, crying and wailing. Gifts were also sent to the bereaved parents by the chiefs and relations, as a well-meant effort to divert their minds from dwelling on their loss.

The religion of the Tehuelches is distinguished from that of the Pampas and Araucanians by an absence of any trace of sun-worship, although the new moon is saluted, the respectful gesture being accompanied by some low muttered words which I never could manage to hear. They believe in a great and good Spirit, who, according to the tradition related by Casimiro at the place, created the Indians and animals, and dispersed them from 'God's-hill,' as he explained the Indian name of the down. I am not at all certain that this was not a confused combination of the story of the Creation, as told by the missionaries, with his own ideas. There is a great tendency in the Indian mind thus to combine the marvels told them, or even to cap what they consider one legend with another; but there is no doubt that they do believe in a good Spirit, though they think he lives 'careless of mankind.' They have no idols or objects of worship, nor—if a year's experience can enable one to judge—do they observe any periodical religious festival, on which either the good or evil Spirit is adored. The mention of this by other travellers can only be explained by confused accounts which have attributed Araucanian customs to the totally distinct Patagonians. The belief which prompts all their religious acts is that in the existence of many active and malicious evil spirits or demons, of whom the principal one is always on the watch to cause mischief. To propitiate or drive away this spirit is the function of the wizard, or doctor, or medicine man, who combines the medical and magical arts, though not possessed of an exclusive faculty for either. All sacrifices of mares and horses, not at stated times, but as occasion requires, such as a birth, death, &c., are intended to propitiate the Gualichu. When a child hurts itself, the slaughter of mares seems to partake at once of the nature of a thank-offering that the hurt was no worse, and a propitiation to avert further harm.

In camp the Gualichu takes up his position outside the back of the toldo, watching for an opportunity to molest the inmates, and is supposed to be kept quiet by the spells of the doctor, who is not only gifted with the power of laying the devil, but can even detect him by sight. I inquired of one of the doctors what he was like, but received an evasive answer; on which I informed him that my devil took all sorts of shapes—sometimes appearing as a guanaco, ostrich, puma, skunk, or vulture, at which the medical man was intensely amused. This household devil is, as far as I could ascertain, supposed to enter into the different parts of the bodies of people, and cause sickness which the doctor is appealed to to cure. The treatment in the case of headache, for instance, is very simple: the doctor takes the patient's head between his knees, and performing a short ceremony of incantation, shouts in his ear; exhorting the devil to come out. Mr. Clarke, when travelling with the Indians south of Santa Cruz, was treated in this fashion when suffering from feverish headache, and said that at the time it relieved him.

Besides this Gualichu there are many others which are supposed to inhabit subterranean dwellings, underneath certain woods and rivers and peculiarly-shaped rocks. I was very much surprised at seeing the Indians salute these objects by placing the hand to the head and muttering an incantation; and for a long time held to the belief that they were only expressing admiration for the Creator's handiwork; but subsequently I learned that they sought thus to conciliate the spirits of these places, reputed to be the spirits of deceased members of the faculty. These devils' powers, however, are confined to the districts contiguous to their habitations.

On one occasion, a horse about to run a match was taken up to a neighbouring hill before daylight by the owner, and some secret ceremony was performed by the wizard. Previous to the race the owner (Wáki) came to me and advised me to put my stakes on his horse, as he had been made safe to win by mysterious incantations which had secured the favour of the local Gualichu; and, strange to say, the horse, which by his appearance was much inferior to the other, did win, thereby establishing a reputation for the wizard and the Gualichu.

I remember on one occasion when riding with Hinchel we came in sight of a peculiarly-pointed rock, which he saluted. I did the same, at which he appeared much pleased; and on our subsequently arriving at a salina, where we found good salt, much needed at the time, he explained to me that the spirit of the place had led us in that direction. In the meeting of Indians the devils are supposed to be driven away by the horsemen chasing at full speed round and round, and firing off their guns.

The office of wizard is not hereditary; indeed those I met with were unmarried. A boy or a girl, if what we should call odd, as in the case of Cayuke's daughter, an old-fashioned and eccentric girl of thirteen, is considered to be marked out as a wizard; but the functions, so far as directing ceremonies, are sometimes performed by an ordinary member of the party. The stock in trade of the regular wizard consists of a few fetishes, or charms, carried in a bag, carefully concealed from public gaze, and exhibited to his colleagues alone. In addition to these they seem to possess a real knowledge of simples, although this is not confined to them. Their professional operations are never accompanied by epileptic seizures and real or simulated convulsions. They, of course, are expected to prognosticate the success or failure of undertakings, and the issue of sickness, and foretell the future generally; and their position in this respect is a dangerous one, as a failure of their predictions is frequently punished with death; but, to make up for this risk, they are universally received with honour and hospitably entertained, and are usually enriched by the accumulation of presents. The power of witchcraft is by no means believed to be confined to them; any person may be suspected of this crime, and it is not an uncommon occurrence for people when dying to lay their death to the charge of some person by name. All the missionaries' instructions did not prevent Casimiro, after the death of either his mother or one of his wives, from sending an agent to kill a woman who, as the deceased averred, had bewitched her. Certain signs and omens are superstitiously regarded; one particularly dreaded is the cry of the nightjar, common on the slopes of the Cordillera, which, if uttered over a camp or toldo, betokens sickness or death to some of the inmates. They hold this bird in great veneration, and object to its being injured in any manner. Another animal supposed to be possessed of magical powers is a flat toad-like lizard, which is believed to lame horses by mysterious agency, and is killed whenever met with. Another superstition is that a two-headed guanaco exists in the south, the appearance of which is a forerunner of sickness. According to my informant, after its last appearance measles, or a similar disease, decimated the Southern tribe, the disease having been propagated by communication with Punta Arenas, where it was at that time rife. Any unfamiliar object that they do not comprehend, as for instance, a compass or a watch, is regarded with suspicion as being tenanted by an evil spirit. Sometimes these objects are supposed to bring luck at play, and are eagerly sought for. One of my companions was possessed of a watch, obtained in Punta Arenas, and, before playing cards, he would often ask me to set it going, the ticking being regarded as the voice of the hidden Gualichu. My compass was also in constant demand, but the privilege of temporary possession was necessarily restricted to a few favoured friends. I explained, to the best of my power, the use of this instrument, which was comprehended by many of them; and they became very fond of asking me to point out the precise direction of various points known to them, and were greatly delighted at the correctness with which their inquiries were generally satisfied. A locket, worn by me round my neck, was also regarded as a talisman, securing the wearer from death.

With all this superstition, regard for omens, and belief in demons, they by no means accord implicit faith and respect to the wizards. Nor do they trust to their spells alone in case of disease; many possess an acquaintance with medicinal herbs, and apply them with good effect. Besides being good farriers, they practise blood-letting, not only on the sick, but, like our grandfathers, at regular seasons have themselves blooded, believing it to be beneficial. Casimiro declared that the superior health of the Tehuelches, compared with that of the colonists or Christians, was attributable to this practice. They also understand and sometimes employ poisons, not to envenom their weapons, but for secretly taking off an enemy. Such cases are rare, but in one, which came under my own observation, beyond all doubt, death was caused by poisoning the inside of a potro boot, the wearer of which had a slight wound on the leg.

Inquirers into the Tsoneca language are referred to the vocabulary in the Appendix; but it is needful to state most distinctly that it is altogether different from either Pampa or Araucanian. Though able to converse in Tehuelche, I could not at all understand the Pampas; and this is noted with reference to statements made in M. Guinnard's work, which, coupled with other internal evidences already alluded to, compel me to doubt that the author was ever in the hands of the real Patagonians, his captors and masters being Pampas or Araucanos, whose customs are well described by him.

As distinguished from these Indians, the number of the pure Tehuelches, both northern and southern, in Patagonia does not exceed 1,500 men, women, and children, according to the returns of effective warriors given at the time when the union of all the various parties, combined during my journey for political purposes, enabled me to compute them with exactness. Beyond the two great divisions into northern and southern, the subdivisions of tribes, so frequently given, are imaginary, or arise out of names of temporary leaders. Nor is the term clan very appropriate to the nomad parties, combined by custom or often by chance. The population is steadily and rapidly decreasing, and the inroads of disease and ill effects of liquor are, as usual, doing the work of extirpation of this race.

As to their organisation, it must be distinctly understood that these Indians owe no manner of allegiance to any head cacique, such as Calficura, or any other, though they may agree to obey one chief, as, for instance, Casimiro; nor are they, except by intermarriage or voluntary association, politically united with either Pampas or Araucanians. Their natural bias is to independence, and rather insubordinate ideas of 'one man being as good as another.' Cuastro's dying words, 'I die as I have lived—no cacique orders me,' aptly express the prevalent feeling on this subject. Nevertheless, all 'parties,' however small, are, when travelling, under the command of a cacique or 'gownok,' who is sometimes also designated by the more endearing epithet of 'yank,' or father; but his influence is very frequently confined to ordering the march and chase. Some of the chiefs are hereditary, but it is not invariably the rule; and amongst the northern Indians there are many petty chiefs, who are men that, having become possessed of a few mares and horses, assume the title of cacique. Great etiquette is observed between them; one chief being prohibited by custom from entering the toldo of another unless presents have previously been interchanged. Another curious point of etiquette is, that a man is not allowed to look towards his father-in-law when in conversation with him; this is, however, not confined to the aristocracy, but also applies to the common herd. When two parties of Indians are approaching one another, and sufficiently near to distinguish the smoke of the hunting-fires, a signal-fire is lighted, and a chasqui— called by the Tehuelches coêto—generally some relative of the chiefs, is despatched from either side. On meeting they repair to the camp of the most powerful, and, on arriving near, more horsemen sally out and escort them to the toldo of the chief. On arrival the newcomer dismounts, his horses and gear are taken charge of, and he is shown, with great formality, to a seat, where he patiently remains, sometimes for an hour, answering, with grave face, all questions; and then delivers any message he may be entrusted with. Although he may be wearied, tired, and hungry, he never moves until the formalities are concluded; he is then provided with the best food and accommodation his host is possessed of.

It is to be hoped that the narrated actual life in the toldos will have enabled the reader to form an idea of the character of the Tehuelches more favourable than that which—except by the missionaries, Messrs. Hunziker and Schmid—has usually been assigned to them. They certainly do not deserve the epithets of ferocious savages, brigands of the desert, &c. They are kindly, good tempered, impulsive children of nature, taking great likes or dislikes, becoming firm friends or equally confirmed enemies. They are very naturally suspicious of strangers, but especially those of Spanish origin, or, as they term them, Cristianos. Nor, considering the treatment, treacherous cruelty and knavish robbery, experienced by them at the hands of the invaders and colonists alternately, is this to be wondered at.

In the southern part of the country, their frequent intercourse with sealers on the coast has rendered them favourably disposed towards Englishmen. This remark, of course, does not extend to the northern Tehuelches, who have not the same opportunities.

In my dealings with them I was always treated with fairness and consideration, and my few belongings—although borrowed at times, according to their mutual way of acting towards one another—were taken the greatest care of; thus an Indian would frequently ask to look at my arms, and, after examining them, would carefully return them to me. During my whole stay amongst them I only lost two articles: the first, a flint and steel, was, I have reason to believe, stolen by one of the Chilians; the second was a pair of ostrich balls, which were abstracted from the toldo. The Indians, although honest enough as regards each other, will, nevertheless, not scruple to steal from any one not belonging to their party. Thus, when they enter the colonies for trade, they will pick up a stray horse in the most natural manner; and in Santa Cruz, Graviel and others constantly pilfered iron nails and small articles. With regard to their truthfulness, my experience was as follows. In minor affairs they nearly always lie, and will invent stories for sheer amusement; thus, Mrs. Orkeke came to me whilst in Teckel with the news that Casimiro's wife was dead. My remark was, 'And a good riddance too!' which was received with a burst of laughter, and the information that she was as alive as ever, only her eyes were bad. I could cite many other similar instances of romancing on the part of the Indians. Old Orkeke I never caught out in a direct lie, and he always, when informing me about any subject, added; 'I do not lie.' In anything of importance, however, such as guaranteeing the safety of a person, they were very truthful, as long as faith was kept with them. After a time, when they ascertained that I invariably avoided deviating in any way from the truth, they left off lying to me even in minor matters. This will serve to show that they are not of the treacherous nature assigned to them by some ignorant writers. Nor are they habitually cruel, even to slaves or captives. The Chilian deserters were always well housed and fed, and lent horses to ride; and nothing but their incurably bad dispositions and constant plots brought on them a fate which, in truth, could hardly be thought ill-deserved, whereas the few good ones of the party rose into high favour.

For my own part, I felt far safer amongst the Tehuelches, as long as they had no drink or no fights, than I subsequently did in the Rio Negro. Of course when they are drunk their passions become unbridled; they remember old feuds, and at times will fight for mere fighting's sake. It is not necessary, however, to go so far as Patagonia to observe this. The finest trait, perhaps, in their character is their love for their wives and children; matrimonial disputes are rare, and wife-beating unknown; and the intense grief with which the loss of a wife is mourned is certainly not 'civilised,' for the widower will destroy all his stock and burn all his possessions: thus Paliki, before the death of his wife, was a wealthy Indian; but when I knew him he was poor and reckless, having destroyed all his property, and taken to gambling and drinking in despair at his loss. Casimiro even declared that his son Sam—whom I certainly should not have suspected of disinterested affection for any human being—had ruined himself, and become careless of his life, after his wife's death.

The children are indulged in every way, ride the best horses, and are not corrected for any misbehaviour. I was always astonished that the youths and young men did not grow up more headstrong and wilful, as a result of want of training. People who have no children of their own sometimes adopt a little dog, on which they lavish their affections, and bestow horses and other valuables, which are destroyed in case of the owner's death.

It has always been a matter of surprise to me that the missionaries should have been so unsuccessful in their efforts to teach these children of nature to read and write, for they are naturally very intelligent (though of course there are exceptions). As a proof of their quickness in imitations, with very little trouble I taught Hinchel's son to write his father's name and those of two other Indians in a very short time. I also used to draw ships on a board with a piece of charcoal for the children's amusement, and they readily copied them. Hinchel himself, wishing to explain a part of the course of the Rio Negro, drew out a rough chart on the board, showing the bends of the river, which I afterwards found to be perfectly correct.

Whilst in their native wilds, I observed little immorality amongst the Indians; in the settlements, however, when debased by intoxication, they are, no doubt, depraved and loose in their ideas. But it must be recorded that, on the entry of the Indians into the settlements of the Rio Negro, at a subsequent period, most of the young women and girls were left with the toldos in Valchita, outside the Travesia, to be out of the way of temptations. There are many Tehuelche youths now growing up who have the greatest abhorrence of liquor; and I hope that in time this abstinence will spread further among them, for they possess no intoxicants of their own, and the rum is an import from the Christians, the ill effects of which they are well able to discern.

One word of advice to the future traveller may conclude this imperfect sketch. Never show distrust of the Indians; be as free with your goods and chattels as they are to each other. Don't ever want anything done for you; always catch and saddle your own horse. Don't give yourself airs of superiority, as they do not understand it—unless you can prove yourself better in some distinct way. Always be first, as you are not likely to be encumbered by a wife or gear, in crossing rivers, or any other difficulties; they will learn by degrees to respect you; in a word, as you treat them so they will treat you.

1. *Vide* Appendix B.
2. *Three Years' Slavery*, p.233.

VI

TECKEL TO GEYLUM

ON January 21 the word was given to march, and all the united forces of the Tehuelches, numbering 200 men, with the usual allowance of women and children, prepared to advance to join the Araucanos. Ten toldos, forming Crimĕ's party, lingered behind, in consequence of the continued sickness of this caciquillo, who, however, sent word that he would follow in our rear.

All the horses were in excellent condition, and it was with great delight that I saw the immense cavalcade set out. Our family party in Casimiro's toldo included, besides the chief and his wife, sons, and little daughter Chingook, an old brother-in-law, Kai, nicknamed Chileno, and his wife and son Macho; and an old deaf and dumb woman of most repulsive aspect. The only good feature in Casimiro's character was his charity. He was always ready to afford an asylum to any destitute or infirm people, and his toldo was never without some such object of his pity. My honourable position as secretary and general referee next in rank to the cacique, scarcely reconciled me to the exchange of the orderly comfort of Mrs. Orkeke's household for the dignified discomfort of my present quarters. They were also shared by Meña, whose good qualities had raised him above his fellow Chilians. Their number had been reduced to four, Arica having disappeared whilst hunting near Teckel: without doubt his quarrelsome disposition had occasioned his death at the hands of some one whom he had insulted or offended. The route followed led northwards through a valley on both sides of which we hunted, and arrived in the afternoon at an encampment called Carge-kaik, or Four Hills. There was nothing remarkable in the scenery: the hill-sides on either hand were covered with scrub, and the summits presented masses of rocks, and in some places loose boulders, amongst which numerous armadilloes were basking in the sun. They are easily captured, as they are very slow; but if they once get into their burrow it is difficult to extract them, owing to the tenacity with which they hold fast to the soil. They are very good eating, and are usually cooked in the shell on the fire, the entrails, &c., being taken out, and the cavity filled with heated stones. When they are in their best condition, one leg is sufficient for a man, as there is about an inch of yellow fat on them. Of the shells the women make work-baskets, to contain their bodkins, sinews, &c., when sewing, or to serve as colour-boxes for the different colours when painting.

The day following our arrival, Tankelow and another Indian were despatched as messengers to the party of Araucanian Indians, or Manzaneros, supposed to be encamped a few marches distant. During that night a child was born, the parents of which were rich, and accordingly a great slaughter of mares took place, the mandil tent was erected, and a feast and dance announced.

Meanwhile, about 4 P.M., the chasquis returned, bringing with them an Araucanian Indian, who was escorted to our toldo in due form amidst a curious crowd, all eager to look at him, while he preserved a grave and stolid demeanour. After the usual ceremonious formalities he sat down, and by means of an interpreter stated himself to be a son of Quintuhual, a chief residing at present about four marches to the north. His father had with much pleasure received the courteous message sent by Casimiro, and it would give him equal gratification to welcome the Tehuelches; but he signified a desire first to meet Casimiro alone. This the latter monarch did not appear to see in the same light—if I may be allowed the expression—as it seemed to forebode no good intentions; but he replied evasively, and thus the colloquy terminated.

This Indian was about the middle height, dressed in coloured ponchos, with a silk handkerchief round his head. His features were regular, with restless sparkling black eyes, and complexion about the same as that of the Gauchos of the Rio de la Plata. He wore his hair cut short, and his general cleanly appearance afforded a strong contrast to the flowing locks and paint-bedaubed bodies of the Tehuelches.

Giving up my sleeping place to him, we soon made him at home, and after he had had some dinner we proceeded in company to watch the dancers, who were vigorously stepping out round the fire in front of the mandil tent. Here we were joined by Jackechan, whose knowledge of the Araucanian language enabled us to maintain a conversation. Presently, by particular request, I joined Golwin (White) and two others in the dance, coming out in full costume of ostrich feathers and girdle of bells, and properly painted, to the great delight of the Indians. My performance elicited general applause; and at last all retired for the night, myself taking my saddle-gear and sleeping under a bush near the toldo.

After a delicious breakfast of fried fish, cooked most skilfully by Meña, we prepared to march again, the chasqui bidding us farewell for the present, and by 9 A.M. the whole cavalcade of women and children were in motion, and the circle formed for the hunt.

Several shallow streams, fringed with dwarf beeches, were crossed, flowing into lagoons or into the Teckel River, the course of which lay north east of our line, and the cavalcade of women struck the valley occasionally in the march. Of the hills dividing these streams, the southern side consisted of gradual slopes covered with coarse grass, while the northern counterslopes were precipitous, and covered with loose rocks and stones. Orkeke, in the previous marches, had often informed me that the Araucanos' country was very stony, and that there were a great many armadilloes, but little other game; and this day guanaco were rarely seen, but ostriches were numerous and armadillo abounded.

After crossing several ridges and glens, we at length traversed a hillocky plain, of the usual scrub-covered aspect, and strewn with flint, agate, and other pebbles, and encamped for the night in a place called 'Woolkein,' situated by the side of a water-course which was now nearly dry, the water only remaining in the deep holes. We had left the cañon or valley of the river Teckel a few miles east, from which point it appeared to give a sharp turn in an easterly direction.

To the west the mountains of the Cordillera were visible about twenty miles distant, while on the south were the rocky abrupt hills already passed over, and on the north a range of rather peaked hills running west, and appearing to slope at their western extremity towards the plains beneath the Cordillera. Next morning, before the rime was off the pasture, we were again *en route*, and after a rocky descent of perhaps fifty feet reached a second plain, everywhere strewn with stones, which rendered galloping very difficult; nevertheless a large herd of guanaco were enclosed and numbers killed, while ostrich, on the contrary, appeared to be very scarce. To my great surprise, whilst running some guanaco, two large partridges got up from close to my horse's feet, and flying a short distance settled again. Partridges had been described to me in the neighbourhood of Santa Cruz, but I had never seen one, and these were the first met with in the country. Towards three in the afternoon we emerged from the stony district to a plain covered with sand and scrub, and after refreshing ourselves at a rivulet, travelled westward, with the Cordillera in full front, till we turned a high cliff which jutted out from the grassy slopes in which the hills fell gradually down to the plains, and beyond it, turning again northward, entered a level plain, at the far extremity of which we observed with great contentment the answering smoke from the toldos of the Araucanian Indians. On the south-west edge of this valley the high beetling cliff obscured the view of the wooded mountains, which, however, showed out between the hills shutting in the valley we had traversed up to this point. On the eastern side rose a range of hills, barren and desolate, with here and there a single guanaco in solitary majesty, cropping the stunted grass. In front of us, directly to the north, lay a large lagoon, in which numerous swans and flamingoes were wading and swimming about. Beyond it were visible the toldos of the Araucanians, ten in number.

We halted near the head of the lagoon, under shelter of some thick bushes, to collect our forces, don our best ponchos and silver ornaments, and change our horses, and then proceeded slowly to within about a quarter of a mile of the toldos. To our great surprise nobody appeared to receive us; but at length a woman arrived with the intelligence that all the men were away hunting, but had been sent for, and would arrive shortly.

Our women meanwhile erected the toldos on a green sward, carpeted with strawberry plants, near to a small stream which divided our camp from that of the Araucanos. All dismounted and rested after the long journey of fully forty miles from the previous station; and in about half an hour the Araucanos appeared, galloping like demons. Their women having previously brought up their fresh horses, they were, in almost less time than it takes to write it, in the saddle, and formed into excellent line, lances in hand, waiting for us to go through the ceremony of welcome. In about five minutes our ranks were dressed, and the usual galloping, shouting, and ceremonious greetings gone through. I was particularly struck with the bold, honest bearing of the young men of this party, who, dressed in gay-coloured ponchos, with clean linen drawers and white flannel vests underneath, presented a most civilised appearance. More noticeable than the remainder, who numbered but twenty-seven in all, were four brothers, particularly handsome, robust men, with florid complexions, who at a distance, where the colour of their eyes could not be distinguished, looked almost like Europeans; which remark made to El Sourdo, who was my right-hand man during the performance, called forth the reply in a low voice, 'Very much devil these Indians; perhaps fight.' That he could have entertained the idea when we were at least ten times their number, speaks volumes for the Araucanian character for bravery.

However, all passed off quietly, and a council was fixed for the following day. As we were returning to the toldos we observed some of the Araucanians bringing up a flock of sheep, and others a herd of cattle, from some woods bordering the stream, which flowed to the northward. On the eastern side of the valley some four or five hundred horses and mares were grazing on the green pasture; and Hinchel pointed out to me with great glee the horses and mares—about a hundred head—owned by his eldest son, who had married an Araucanian woman, and resided with them; and the proud father declared that we should not want for food, as he likewise owned cattle and sheep.

Casimiro informed me that many years ago whilst travelling northwards he met these same Indians on foot. Their custom was to hunt with large dogs that they kept expressly for the chase, and dividing the meat equally, carry it back on their shoulders to the toldos. They also when on the march loaded themselves with their household gear, leaving bags of grease hung up in the trees for future use. He left them a couple of mares, from which part of their present stock is sprung. This story, however, should be taken with reservation, although it is perfectly possible that in some fight their horses were taken from them, and that subsequently, when all the Indians were joined together under the Cacique Lenketrou to invade the settlements, they received a share of the spoils, and have since added to their stock by trade.

The day following our arrival a council was held, and an interchange of presents took place. Here I made the acquaintance of the old chief Quintuhual, and presented him with a dagger. He was a short, heavily-built man, with a grave and indeed solemn expression; but he had a bad name for getting intoxicated and using knife or revolver freely—in fact, running a-muck. He was of course a relation—nephew, it was said—of Casimiro; but notwithstanding, he at first received me with great suspicion, and when, in answer to his inquiries as to what I was and why I came, he was informed that I was in the service of the Cacique of England, who wished the Indians well, but that I had visited these parts for my own pleasure, he replied that he was not a boy to be humbugged easily; but having instituted private inquiries, he soon changed his tone, showing me the greatest civility, and was never tired of asking questions about England and Englishmen.

Here the letters forwarded some time previously, which we had thought were by this time arrived at Patagones, were handed back to us. They had been forwarded to Foyel's[1] people, but owing to those sent by me for England being written on pink note-paper they were returned, the Indians considering the colour of the paper to denote war.

Quintuhual had with him a Valdivian or Chilote named Juan Antonio, who acted as interpreter. This little man, who had originally come from what he called his 'Pago,' somewhere in the vicinity of Porto Montt, bringing liquor to trade with the Indians, had concluded to remain with them, esteeming himself to be better off as a poor man in the Pampas in company with Indians, than in the like station in the settlements. He of course spoke the Araucanian language, which is generally used in Valdivia, but was conversant with the Spanish tongue. Off his horse he was a miserable little specimen of a man, and though tolerated by Quintuhual, was looked upon as what Spaniards term 'Infeliz,' or unfortunate one.

After a while the council broke up, but Crimè arriving with the ten expected toldos, was resumed the following day; Quintuhual finally agreeing to unite his party with the Tehuelches, and proceed under Casimiro's banner to Las Manzanas.

The Chilote Juan Antonio paid us a visit in the evening, and informed us that the toldos had been several months in this place, which was named Esgel-kaik; the men having been absent hunting, first the young guanaco, and afterwards catching and taming cattle in the Cordillera.

By his account these Indians were great adepts with the lazo, and would gallop through the forests in chase of animals in the most wonderful manner; one man only being required to catch and secure an animal, and then proceeding to capture another. How different from our dreadful failure, where seven men could not lazo one animal!

He further stated that with Foyel's Indians, who were distant a few marches to the north, eight Valdivians had for the last two years been employed catching cattle, and having now succeeded in getting together a herd of about eighty head, intended shortly to return to Valdivia.

The third day after our arrival I visited the toldos of our new allies; and while talking to one of the principal Indians, named Malakou, who could speak a little Spanish, was asked if I could repair firearms, and one or two very antique specimens of flint pistols and blunderbusses were produced, the locks of which were wood-bound. Half an hour served to set these to rights, at which the owners were much delighted, and offered me tobacco, &c., which however I refused, taking instead a hide to make a small lazo.

After bidding, not adieu, but *au revoir*, to my new friends, whilst strolling back I was called into a toldo where four women were sitting sewing mantles. One, who appeared to be of the Pampa tribe, old and ugly, spoke Spanish, and stated that she was formerly in the Rio Negro with the cacique Chingoli. She acted as spokeswoman for the others, three tall, buxom lasses, daughters of a brother of Quintuhual, who was Capitanejo of the party. They were gaily dressed in variegated ponchos, with silk handkerchiefs bound round their fine glossy hair, which was plaited into two long tails, and set off their clear, fresh complexions charmingly. The first question they asked me was where I came from. On answering 'From the direction in which the sun rises,' they asked if it wasn't very hot there. They then asked if I had ever been above in the sky; if I had not been dead one time and come to life again; whether Casimiro had not been dead and come back again, and various other questions of the same description.

After satisfying their curiosity to the best of my ability, and smoking a pipe, I received a message by Juan Antonio that Quintuhual wanted to see me in his toldo. Proceeding thither, I was shown to a seat on a poncho, and discoursed with the old chief for half an hour; at the end of which he made me a present of a 'jurga,' or, as the Tehuelches term it, 'lechu,' a sort of blanket made by their women, similar to the poncho, except, instead of two parts with an opening for the head to pass through, it consists of an entire piece. It was perfectly new, having been just completed by his daughters.

After a good dinner we adjourned to see the races, a great match being on between the two tribes. The course was about four miles; and the race resulted in a victory for the Tehuelches. Both sides had backed their favourites heavily; and as on this occasion the ladies took a prominent share in the betting, the Tehuelches were in great glee, having won from the fair Araucanians many valuable mandils and lechus. In the evening a grand feast took place, with a mandil tent and dance.

Near this place grew a quantity of the wild potatoes, and the women used to start early in the morning and come back towards evening with their horses loaded. The tubers were the largest I had seen, and closely resembled the sweet potato in flavour. The usual way of cooking them was boiling in a pot, a sod of earth being placed over all to keep the steam in.

We made a stay of eight days in Esgel-kaik, amusing ourselves by racing, visiting the Araucanos, and passing a very pleasant time, the only drawback being the illness of Crimè, who grew gradually worse.

The day before our departure Jackechan and El Sourdo intimated that, as they feared a disturbance, and wished to keep clear of any fight, they would not accompany us to Las Manzanas, but purposed to proceed in the direction of Chupat, and send in a messenger to the Welsh colony. So I at once took the opportunity of forwarding a letter to Mr. Lewis Jones, requesting certain supplies of yerba, tobacco, and sugar.

On February 5th the whole camp broke up, Jackechan and two toldos marching to the north-east, and the remainder, who now formed an extensive train, marching almost due north. Before leaving Jackechan sent one of his wives and his youngest son, who was remarkably attached to me, to our toldo, to be under the charge of her father, Kai Chileno. El Sourdo had pressed me to go with their small party, and for some time I wavered, but thought it best to stick to Casimiro, and pay a visit to Cheoeque, and the much-praised Manzanas, where the Indians anticipated finding plenty of fruit and plenty of drink. After leaving Esgel the character of the country changed. We were no longer traversing Pampas, with their dreary monotony, but journeyed through level valleys of two or three miles in extent, watered by rivulets fringed with stunted trees, and abounding with game. The general line of the dividing hills—which were round downs and occasionally broken and waterworn cliffs—was from east to west, seeming as if they were thrown off as spurs from the Cordillera, from which, however, their western bases were divided by a valley often narrowing to a glen, down which flowed a stream in a northward course. Towards evening a halt was made at the side of a stream where there was sufficient pasture for the horses, and it was an amusing sight to watch the long line of women winding down the hills in the distance, like a flock of ants; the Araucanians driving their cattle and mares separate from our party, and their sheep bringing up the rear by slow marches under charge of some lads.

Early the following morning the camp was struck, and after crossing a hill directly above the encampment which was covered with rank high grass, we descended the northward slope to a wild, barren-looking plain, at the northern side of which, near to a low range of hills, some trees and a silver line marked the course of a river flowing from the Cordillera, the mountains of which rose to a height of 2,000 or 3,000 feet, wooded nearly to the summits, and their crests glittering with occasional patches of snow that had defied the power of the summer sun. Traversing this plain, which was dotted with barberry and other bushes, and varied here and there by small hummocky ridges, we closed the hunting circle by the banks of the stream, a few miles distant from the Cordillera. Here, in different parties, the usual fires were lit, and the hunting meal discussed, after which we proceeded to the toldos. The Araucanians had pitched theirs on the southern bank of the river, amongst some clumps of trees; whilst those of the Tehuelches were situated on the northern bank, the river dividing the two villages. Westward from our encampment the barren plain was succeeded by a wide level of grass, reaching to the base of the mountains, some two miles distant; but higher up the course of the river, which trended to the north, the plain appeared to resume its barren and stony aspect, with here and there a dry lagoon, until the slope of the mountains was reached, and detached belts of trees formed the commencement of the forest. On the southern side of the river the pasture was not very abundant; nevertheless there was sufficient for the horses, cattle, and sheep of our allies to graze upon.

After the usual stable drill most of us bathed in the stream, which, although nowhere of great depth, had pools at intervals suited for bathing; but the water was icy cold. The day following our arrival at this camp, which was named Diplaik, a birthday feast took place in the Araucanian toldos, to which most of us were invited, the usual tent being erected and a dance held in the evening, and the feast and dance were kept up for two days and nights, at the end of which a messenger arrived from Foyel to say that Calficura, the chief of the Indians encamped at the Salinas north of the Rio Negro, near Bahia Blanca, was going to make war on Buenos Ayres, the reason assigned being the murder of one of his relations by the Christians; he therefore desired the Araucanians and Tehuelches to join with him in the inroad. His literal message was as follows: 'My horse is ready, my foot is in the stirrup, my lance is in my hand, and I go to make war against these Christians, who tire us out with their falseness.'

A parlemento was called, and the chiefs deliberated for some time, but in the end determined to have nothing to do with the affair; so a message was sent to the effect that he might do as he pleased, but that they wished to maintain peace.

We remained some days in Diplaik, during which several races were run, resulting on this occasion in favour of the horses of the Araucanians, who won many horses and mares from their neighbours.

The international sports were diversified by a cock fight between Orkeke's bird and one belonging to an Araucanian. My assistance was requested to sharpen the spurs, and my friends were much astonished at my indignant refusal to have anything to do with such a proceeding. The Araucanian owner of the cock had also a hen which, during the march, sat upon a clutch of eggs and successfully reared her brood of six chickens, the hen, nest, and all being carefully transported on horseback, and Dame Partlet seeming quite as much at home in the saddle as any Indian mother with her nursling carried in the cradle behind her.

In the dry lagoons on the western side of the valley the women and, indeed, sometimes the men, were frequently engaged in grubbing up an edible root which grew in large quantities. The leaf of the plant is very minute, and the root, which is found about a foot below the surface, varies in length from 1 to 3 inches: it is quite white, and about a quarter of an inch in diameter; when raw its taste resembles that of a chestnut, but is rather sweeter. The Indians boil it and drink the water, which is very sweet. During the last two days of our stay we subsisted entirely on this food and fish caught in the stream, as meat was not obtainable. Some of the Tehuelches were here induced for the first time to taste the fish on which Casimiro, Meña, and myself were regaling, and some of them took a great liking to it, and borrowing my lines and hooks were soon sitting on the bank waiting patiently for a bite. They caught several, and towards evening returned with my lines and a share of the fish for us, which we did not require. As I had plenty of hooks, these ingenious savages soon made lines for themselves out of twisted ostrich sinews, and may, for all I know, at the present time be occupied in fishing. The fact that none of these Tehuelches would before this touch the fish caught by me, and even expressed great disgust at the idea, is worthy of note, as it has been stated that on the coast they catch and eat sea fish, which could only be alleged by persons ignorant of their real habits of life.[2]

On the 12th we marched; the cause of our detention for the two extra days being the continued sickness of Crimè, who, however, at length determined to make an effort and proceed, although barely able to sit on his horse. The women followed, more or less, the valley of the river, whilst the hunters ranged over the hills, which on the eastern side were in most parts free from rock and stones and abounded with ostriches. During the journey I came suddenly on two wild cats, one of which my dog attacked and killed, and the other fell a victim to my bolas. These were of the species common in the provinces of La Plata, and especially in the islands of the Parana. Towards evening we came on another small stream flowing into the main river, into the plain of which we subsequently descended and found the toldos already pitched, literally 'sub tegmine fagi.' During this day's ride, happening to be in the same part of the circle as the Araucanians, we cooked our dinners in company and rode home together. On the way Quintuhual's eldest son, with whom I had always had very friendly relations, said that he desired to recognise me as his brother. So we accordingly joined hands, and riding together formally declared that we were as brothers, and would always remember the duties of our relationship and assist each other, if needs be, in whatever part of the world we might be placed. All this was very satisfactory, and it may be interesting to the reader to know that my sisters and cousins were the good-looking girls who had asked such curious questions at Esgel, and with whom, though we could not understand each other's language, I had always kept up a laughing acquaintance, thereby arousing considerable jealousy in the bosoms of my Tehuelche friends. The gloriously warm weather which, for a wonder, continued during our stay at Lilly-haik, as this station was named, rendered our residence there most enjoyable, and we revelled in the simple pleasures of the woods; sometimes three or four of us would go away across the brook, and traversing a plain occupied by the horses and cattle, search for strawberries amongst the ravines of the neighbouring mountains, or climb the tall trees and gather the yellow insipid fungus adhering to the branches, or lie down amongst the wild violets and enjoy the *dolce far niente*. These Indian children of nature showed themselves as thoroughly able to appreciate the idleness of gathering fruit and flowers and roaming in the woods as school children on a holiday ramble. On one occasion Casimiro and several others proceeded in search of wood wherewith to construct saddles, and we felled several fine trees, selecting and cutting off suitable pieces of timber. It was hard work with blunt axes, but Indians are indefatigable when they once commence a task. After my spell at the axe I wandered off with a companion into the thicker forest in search of fungus to make tinder. Of this we found little, but thirst soon made us seek for water, and discover a delicious ice-cold rivulet, embowered with currant bushes bearing ripe fruit. Here we remained a short time smoking and picking currants, recumbent on the mossy turf, till a shout in the distance warned us that our companions were returning. On our way home we killed one of the flat toad-like lizards which the Indians regard as devilish; we also caught a young skunk, which Casimiro wished to keep as a pet for the children, but at my instance let it go and enjoy the delights of freedom. 'Fancy a tame skunk!' some may exclaim; but in Hinchel's toldo there were two skunks which, perfectly tame and as playful as kittens, ran about everywhere, never using their offensive powers, and sometimes getting lost for an hour or two caused a dreadful outcry to be raised by the children until they were found.

The hill slopes were a garden of calceolarias, alyssum, tiny wild geraniums, and other flowers unknown to me. Amongst them were two magnificent creepers, one resembling a vine, with rich violet trumpet-shaped flowers, and another displaying gorgeous circular orange blossoms, with black lines radiating, like the spokes of a wheel, from the centre. I looked in vain for seeds, but there were none mature, so contented myself with plucking a flower, which was subsequently lost with other specimens.

A disagreeable incident here gave me an opportunity of observing the disposition of the Araucanians to enslave and illtreat any unhappy 'Cristiano' that they can either kidnap or purchase. One of the Chilians, after more than once removing from one Tehuelche toldo to another, listened to the delusive promises of an Araucanian and deserted his old protectors rather than masters. He soon found that he had exchanged an easy berth for real slavery. One day he besought me to interfere to protect him from the cruelty of his master, who was urging him with his whip to continue his labour of wood felling. He complained that he was worked all day, and scantily fed, and obliged to sleep outside the toldo; very different from his life amongst the Patagonians, when food, shelter, and a horse to ride were always his lot. At my intercession Quintuhual took him into his service to protect him, for no Tehuelche would receive him; but he was afterwards reported to have been killed by his quondam master, as a punishment for his desertion.

During our stay great gambling with cards was carried on amongst some of the party; and Casimiro and Hinchel worked most assiduously constructing saddles, which when finished they were in as great haste to gamble away. A wedding also varied the proceedings in this place; and another little incident, in the shape of a separation by mutual consent of an Araucanian husband and Tehuelche wife, gave the old ladies subject for gossip; but a reconciliation was soon after effected.

On the 16th of February we left Lilly-haik, and bid adieu to the pleasant river and the sylvan delights of this Paradise, as it seemed to us, with its flowery shades. As we ascended the northern declivity of the high ground bounding the valley, I halted to take a farewell look; and nowhere has a more beautiful scene presented itself to my gaze. The valley narrowed as it curved to the west, and at its head, through a gigantic cleft, the perpendicular walls of which rose several hundred feet, the waters of the river issued from their mountain cradle. So deep was the gloom of this gorge, that it was impenetrable to even Indian eyes, and the river seemed to flow into the sunlight out of unknown darkness. Above, on either hand, the precipitous cliffs sloped upwards into high mountains clothed with a rich mantle of the dark green, cedarlike foliage of the beech forests; and between their summits might be discerned the dazzling peaks of far distant loftier mountains crowned with perpetual snow.

Turning our backs upon this lovely scene, we crossed a remarkable succession of barren and stony terraces or benches of curiously irregular formation, the terraces running in different directions, and presenting no parallel lines to indicate any uniform action of water; the regular slopes and level surfaces resembling a complication of gigantic steps. We at length descended to a plain bordering a river, which all the Indians agreed in declaring to be the main branch of the Chupat. The banks on the southern side were remarkable for being fringed with a species of Pampa grass, while on the northern side grew a few trees, near which the toldos were pitched.

The river was about forty yards in width, and easily fordable in most places, although there were deep reaches where a horse had to swim. The foremost party of the hunters crossed first, and some, either not knowing or careless of the fords, enjoyed a bathe, swimming alongside their horses. By eventide all our party, women and baggage, had arrived. A few days' halt was occasioned in this place, named Chupatcush, by the continued illness of the cacique Crimè. We hunted in all the surrounding country, which presented no very remarkable features. Down river, or to speak more correctly to the eastward, after passing a range of hills of the usual description, covered with short tufty grass, interspersed with shrubs, through which the river forces its way in a succession of narrow gorges, a large plain opened out, which extended for perhaps nine miles on each side, scantily covered with grass, excepting towards the banks of the river, where the pasture was luxuriant.

A subsequent comparison of the observations made by Welsh settlers as to its lower course with my own, aided by Indian accounts, enables me to state that the Chupat river is characterised throughout its course by the narrow gorge-like cuttings alternating with similar wide plains, all of which are suitable for cultivation. Besides the Sengel, which is doubtless one of its main feeders, other streams occurring in our journey had also been described as tributaries of the Chupat, and by their direction of course it would appear that their waters, if they reach the sea, must flow into this river; but it seems to me difficult to understand how, if the Chupat receives the drainage of so large an area of country, its stream near the mouth, as described both by Indians and settlers, can be of such small dimensions. It is, therefore, probable that some, if not most, of the lesser rivers lose themselves in lagoons or swamps in the central districts, and the reader must be pleased to remember that the courses of these rivers, as indicated on the map, are not in all cases laid down from my own observation, but partly from Indian description and partly from an already existing map, probably compiled from similar data.

To the westward plains occur at intervals apparently until the river debouches from the ravines of the high mountains of the Andes, about twelve miles from the encampment. At this point the stream flows from the northward, and the Indians informed me has its source in a large lake, most probably Nahuel-huapi. The pasture in the immediate vicinity of the camp was scanty, having apparently been recently burned, but the soil was of a rich alluvial description. In the chase the most remarkable thing observed was the abundance of armadilloes, one hunter frequently bringing in two or three. Fish also were abundant in the river, and averaged a larger size than those previously caught.

On February 18th smoke was observed to the northward, not far distant, and towards evening a chasqui arrived, bringing with him a couple of bottles of liquor for Quintuhual, as well as news that things were going on well amongst Foyel's people; and on the 21st we again marched over a high plateau broken by numerous irregular ravines which appeared to have been swept by an inundation. High isolated cliffs stood up as though the waters had washed round them and swept away the intervening soil, leaving their waterworn faces marked with the indelible record of the floods, as plainly as the torn and blasted rocks in the southern districts bore the traces of volcanic fires. At last a more unbroken plain terminated suddenly in a shelving descent of 300 to 400 feet, the wall of a chasm covered with grass and shrubs interspersed with scattered boulders, down which we made our way, encamping near the base, where a beautiful spring gushed from the side. The bottom of the cañon, which was nearly half a mile in width, contained a watercourse, the bed of which was dry at this season, except a few pools of stagnant water unsuitable for drinking.

It was intended to despatch messengers from this place, which was called Cushamon, to Foyel, and also Cheoeque, the chief of Las Manzanas, warning him of our near approach; and accordingly, after our arrival in camp, I wrote a letter to the said chieftain at the dictation of Casimiro, which in well-rounded periods and with much complimentary verbiage explained the fact and reasons of our having united all the Indians and inviting their co-operation.

The following morning, after the letter had been read and explained to the assembled Caciques, the two messengers (sons of Caciques) appeared with two horses each, and after receiving some verbal injunctions, started on their journey, amidst the howl of a few old women and a blast from the cornet. The remainder of us, who had mounted, to add to the pomp and ceremony of the occasion, went out hunting, some following the ravine in an easterly direction, which, penetrating high pampas, opened into a plain containing a lagoon fed by the waters of the brook, whilst others encircled the high pampas above. Hinchel, whom I accompanied on this occasion, pointed out to me several small holes with little mounds of earth and rubbish at the mouth, which he asserted to be the abodes of snakes, but no occupants were visible outside. He described the snakes as dark in colour, about 2 feet 6 inches long, and perfectly harmless, adding that they would be good to eat, which facts were subsequently corroborated by Casimiro.

One of the troubles of pampa life is occasionally losing one's horses, as was my case in this place, and I spent one entire day in search before I recovered them, as they had strayed in company with a troop of mares far up the valley, which here divided into two branches, opening into watered grassy plains extending to the Cordillera. As there were horse tracks up both valleys, according to the usual law of contrariety I took the wrong one at first and had a long gallop for nothing. At any time it is troublesome to have to look through about two thousand horses all unmarked and many of the same colour, and perhaps resembling those belonging to the perplexed searcher. An Indian, however, with his natural quickness of sight, will distinguish his own horses at a great distance amongst a hundred others. It has been already said that in this roving life all must look after their own horses, for Indians do not understand another person doing it for them, unless he be a son or relation, and in all cases when preparing for the march everyone is expected to find and bring up his own.

During our stay (until the 28th) in this encampment, the cold winds again set in, and snow fell on one occasion, but not in great quantity, and we were all very glad at length to get the order to march, and proceeded in joyous expectation of shortly meeting the chasquis with news from the other Indians. By this time the young guanaco had grown to considerable size and afforded a lengthened chase, but their skins were useless for mantles, the fur having acquired more of the thick woolly nature of that of the full-grown animal. The next halt was made in a place called Telck, a valley of considerable width, on one edge of which the burrow of a Patagonian hare or cavy was pointed out to me, but the owner was not visible. Here a messenger arrived with an answer to our letter from Foyel, indited by a Valdivian Indian named Antonio Guaitu, educated by the missionaries, who filled the post of secretary to the chief. The Caciques having formed a circle, in which my place was next the president, Casimiro, the chasquis were introduced and ceremoniously handed me the letter, written in most peculiar Spanish, which, after some private study, I was able to decipher and expound to the attentive assembly. It contained many expressions of good will and hopes of a speedy meeting, winding up with an apology that, owing to having left his country north of the Rio Limay and come down into these parts in order to hunt the young guanaco, he regretted having so few warriors in his train wherewith to welcome 'the great chief of the south,' viz., Casimiro. After this function, with my deportment in which, be it modestly said, all the chiefs were much pleased, as well as gratified by the amicable contents of the despatch, one of the Araucanian caciques assuring me with many compliments that his horses were always at my disposal for a mount, all adjourned to a shooting match, or rather pistol practice, at which the performances were decidedly moderate, and the mark seemed to be the safest place. Starting thence on March 3, and travelling always northwards over the barren upper pampas with scarcely a shrub on them, the wall-like Cordillera rising on the west, and ranges of hills bounding the view to the east, about 2 P.M. we arrived at a marshy plain: there, as we were halting to make a fire, a cloud of smoke rose suddenly from the opposite side, indicating the near approach of the chasqui sent to Las Manzanas. Half a dozen of us were immediately despatched to verify the supposition, and, leaving our dinner for a future occasion, raced across the valley at full speed, the Indians firmly believing that the messengers would bring liquor with them, and every one being ambitious of the first drink. We at length made them out, and perceiving us in return they halted and dismounted by a small hillock, where we shortly joined them, Casimiro following sedately, as became so grand a personage. The Indians were disappointed as to the advent of liquor, the messengers having brought nothing with them except a few apples, some of which, distributed to us proved to be very juicy and refreshing, equalling any European apple. The only answer to our letter was a verbal message to the effect that we should be welcome at Las Manzanas, and that Cheoeque would collect a force to meet us, all his people being at present busy in the mountains gathering the harvest of apples and piñones; he also stated that he had received late news from Patagones, one Mariano Linares, brother of the head chief of the tame Indians in that settlement, being at present a visitor at Las Manzanas. Casimiro was rather irritated at not receiving a written answer, but on my pointing out that it was just possible Cheoeque did not own a secretary in his suite, the chief was somewhat pacified, although his dignity was rather hurt, and he recurred again and again to the subject.

On our way to the toldos, which, during the interval of our hearing the news, roasting apples, &c., had been pitched, Casimiro pointed out to me the scene of a former fight in which a chief and several Indians had been killed. It was a very desirable place for encampment, but, owing to these antecedents, was carefully avoided, and instead of it our party occupied a damp and even sloppy site on the borders of a small stream that lost itself in a large marsh farther to the east, while the Araucanians had selected a better spot a little higher up the valley. The following day we hunted over some hills in the vicinity of the mountains, and killed a great quantity of ostriches, scarcely a man coming home without a good supply of meat.

On March 5, early in the morning, whilst most of us were rounding up our horses, others smoking at the fireside, some men appeared in the distance with several horses, one of which appeared to be loaded. In a moment many Indians were away to meet the newcomers, and one came back at speed to inform us that they were Manzanero Indians bringing liquor to trade with. They proceeded to Quintuhual's toldo, one of them being a connection of the chief and there dismounted, unloading their horse of two sheepskins filled with rum. Great was the rejoicing amongst the Indians, and large the crowd that soon collected round Quintuhual's toldo, carefully keeping at a respectful distance. Casimiro and myself were shortly sent for, and on riding over were invited to preside at the commencement of the festival. On our dismounting, in company with several of the other caciques, four lances were planted in the ground (one having a white weft or poncho placed on it), and the chiefs, each taking a horn or pannikin containing a very little rum, marched round the lances muttering an incantation and sprinkling a little liquor on the ground, also on the lances as they passed. This ceremony was repeated twice, a select body of old women attending to sing and cry, to assist in frightening away the evil spirit. After this my brother, who appeared to be master of the ceremonies, handed pannikins of grog round, and all were soon very convivial. After taking a glass or two I retired in company with Orkeke and Hinchel, neither of whom was inclined to drink much, owing to the possibility of a disturbance. The rest of the party then began to buy drink, as the first free allowance was stopped, and in a short time many were in an advanced stage of intoxication, amongst whom was our head chief. The terms of barter were mantle or unbroken colt for two bottles of villainous Valdivian rum, which was, as the Tehuelches agreed, a very exorbitant price; but inasmuch as the dealers left it free for them either to go without or pay up, the liquor was soon finished and the merchants possessed of some eighteen new mantles and a good number of mares and colts. The artful Tehuelches, however, during the ensuing night, stole back a portion of the mantles and humbugged the Araucanians about the horses, professing not to be able to catch them. Everything went on quietly until about 3 P.M., when a fight took place, but the combatants were disarmed. From this up to 8 P.M. Quintuhual, Orkeke, and many of the people who had kept sober, were occupied in quelling disturbances, Casimiro being as bad as any, and sending for his gun wherewith to shoot some imagined enemy, which I fortunately intercepted, and after plugging up the nipples hid it behind the toldo. There was little sleep to be obtained till nearly morning, when the inebriated ones laid down anywhere and everywhere to sleep off their potations. The following morning Casimiro awoke with a bad headache and bad temper, and commenced talking about something that had been said to him the previous day, on which I informed him that he must have no shame left in him to get so intoxicated, and that no Indians could respect a chief who was the first to set an evil example by wishing to create a disturbance, while Quintuhual had remained sober, taking care of his people as became a chief, and that he (Casimiro) should have done the same. This raised the ire of the ancient monarch, who answered in a most impolite manner, so much so, that to avoid a row I left him to his bad head and quitted the toldo till he should be in a better frame of mind. Shortly after this little episode we broke up the camp and marched a few miles to the north. Having been detained by a missing horse, I did not start with the hunting party, but overtook the people who had arrived with the grog, returning with their remaining mantles, horses, colts, &c., and loudly abusing the Tehuelches for a set of thieving rascals. One of this party was a Valdivian boy who spoke fluent Spanish, and invited me to accompany him to Los Llanos, whither he now intended returning. He stated that in seven or eight days he hoped to reach his destination, and that from thence to the port of Valdivia was but a day and a half's journey. On arriving at the next encampment I bade adieu to these people, who continued their march farther to the north, not liking to trust their property again in the neighbourhood of our camp.

Only halting for the night we resumed our journey shortly after daylight, mounting a rather steep ascent to a high plateau strewn with sharp stones and crossed by ridges of rocks at intervals.

Ostriches and guanaco were numerous, and although chasing them almost involved the certainty of laming one's horse, many were killed. In this hunt a male guanaco came racing towards me from the Indians on the western side of the circle, and on my galloping to intercept him, he turned and descended a ridge of rocks. I was about to throw the bolas, being within distance, when he suddenly tripped and, falling on his head, lay stunned at the bottom of the cliff, where I soon despatched him with my knife.

These barren pampas terminated suddenly in a line of cliffs, gradually but steeply shelving in some places, and in others presenting a perpendicular descent of 200 feet; at the base lay a large plain watered by a brook, and enclosed on the southern, eastern, and partially on the western sides by these cliffs, while the northern and north-western boundary was formed by hills rising in gentle slopes. In about the centre of this plain, close to the brook side, were to be distinguished the toldos of Foyel, to which the women were wending their ways having descended by a ravine to the east, while some distance to the north-east on the upper plains were to be distinguished the hunting fires of the proprietors of the toldos. In due course of time we arrived, but as the hunting party did not return till late, we saw nothing of Foyel's people that evening, though letters were exchanged between the chiefs, felicitating each other on the meeting, and appointing next day for the ceremony of welcome.

The following morning, however, day broke with a furious south-west gale, with passing squalls of snow and sleet, and so bitterly cold and miserable that Foyel sent a note to state that, 'as the day was rather frozen,' perhaps it would be better to postpone the ceremony till finer weather, inasmuch as after it a parlemento would have to be held to consider matters in general. Casimiro answered, through me, that he was of the same opinion, but would do himself the honour of paying a personal visit. Presently we sallied out in the storm, taking the presents and the necessary number of women to cry, and proceeded to Foyel's toldo, where we handed over the gifts, the women melodiously howling during the operation. A short parley then ensued between the two caciques, neither of whom, be it remembered, could understand the language of the other. After this ceremonial was concluded, which took place outside the toldo during a blinding snow storm, we returned to our home, and shortly after the day cleared up a little, and Foyel's people were visible bringing up cattle and sheep from distant parts of the valley to which they had been driven to seek shelter from the storm. Some headed in our direction, and were driven close to the toldo, over which the Buenos Ayrean colours proudly waved to designate the dwelling of the chief. Foyel then arrived and had an interview with Casimiro, presenting him with cattle which were lazoed by some of the Valdivian Indians, and a light-haired man dressed in Christian clothes, but with rather a wild appearance. My first idea was that he was either Scotch or English, but as he approached me whilst despatching one of the cows, I asked him in Spanish where he came from, and whether he was not English; he answered that he was from Chili, but had lived nearly all his life in Valdivia working cattle, and had for the last two years been in company with the Valdivians catching cattle in the Cordillera, and making his head-quarters at Foyel's camp. His name was Ventura Delgado, and he had visited Patagones the previous year in company with the secretary, Antonio Guaitu, who took an application for rations for Foyel. As we were both busy we arranged to meet and have a talk later in the day. A good deal of eating took place in the forenoon, and to escape the crowd, and also the persecution of having continually to write some nonsensical message from Casimiro to Foyel, who about every half hour used to interchange written messages, although the toldos were not above two hundred yards apart, I quitted the chief's quarters for a stroll. While roaming about the camp looking for the toldo in which my new Valdivian acquaintance put up, I was called into another, where Casimiro's aunt, one of our domestic circle, and my 'companion of the pipe,' was sitting by the fire drinking grog, in which she invited me to assist her; nothing loth, I sat down and we had two or three cheerers together, after which the owner of the toldo, a brother-in-law of Foyel's, a Pampa Indian, arrived. He spoke fluent Spanish, having formerly been for a considerable time near the settlements, and was an intellectual, fine-looking man; he was very civil and escorted me to Foyel's toldo, where I spent the afternoon in company with Antonio Guaitu and Ventura Delgado, the Valdivian.

On March 8, the day being fine and suitable for the ceremony of welcome, Casimiro gave orders at an early hour for all to mount and hold themselves in readiness to go through the necessary evolutions. About an hour after the orders had been given, most of the Patagonians were mounted and ready, so all proceeded to the part of the valley where the united Araucanian Indians, under Quintuhual and Foyel, were already formed in line, lances in hand, waiting for our motley crowd, who gave considerable trouble to the chiefs, owing to their loose ideas of formation: the caciques and adjutant no sooner had got one part of the line into something like order, than the people at the other extremity would break up into knots and converse or smoke. Foyel sent several messages to Casimiro to keep his line properly formed, and at length the Tehuelches were arrayed in something like order and the ceremony commenced. After it was concluded a great Parlemento was held, which lasted until the afternoon; all the previous resolutions were confirmed, viz., that Casimiro should be recognised the chief of the South, his jurisdiction extending over all Indians south of the Rio Limay; that with his people he should guarantee the safety of Patagones, and hold in check the Pampa Indians of Las Salinas, under the chief Calficura, in the improbable event of his endeavouring to cross the Rio Limay for the purpose of making raids into the settlements; 2ndly, that we should, all united, march to Las Manzanas to visit Cheoeque, and propose to him to guarantee with his forces the safety of the north bank of the river, which would effectually bridle Calficura and secure Patagones. After the Parlemento I proceeded to visit Foyel, and was received by him with every expression of friendship and regard. During the course of our interview he asked me to show him my compass, the fame of which had gone before it. I at once took it off my neck, where I was in the habit of carrying it, and endeavoured to explain its uses to him. Unlike the other Indians, although at first regarding it rather with superstitious awe, Foyel soon understood its uses, though he also hinted that it might not only be useful for finding the way at night, but perhaps would bring luck at play as well. I accordingly begged him to accept it, which, after a little demur, he did with evident delight, wrapping it carefully up and giving it in charge of his daughter.

He then commenced a conversation on the subject of Indians and their relations with white people. He stated that he was in favour of friendly intercourse both with the Valdivian people on the western side and the Argentines on the eastern shores. I quote some of his exact words: 'God has given to us these plains and hills wherein to dwell; he has provided us with the guanaco, from the skins of which to form our toldos, and from the young of which we make mantles to clothe ourselves with; also the ostrich and armadillo for food. Our contact with the Christians of late years has given us a taste for yerba, sugar, biscuit, flour, and other luxuries formerly unknown, but which now have become almost necessary to us. If we have war with the Spaniards, we shall have no market for our skins, ponchos, feathers, &c., therefore it is for our own interests to be on good terms with them; besides, there is plenty of room for all.' He then went on to state that he was endeavouring to find a route to Valdivia, avoiding Las Manzanas and the Picunche tribe of Indians, who are against all foreigners; and that if possible he would get families of Valdivian Indians and endeavour to cultivate some of the valleys in the neighbourhood of the Rio Limay.

I was not at that time aware of Mr. Cox's descent from Lake Nahuel-huapi, or could at once have informed him of that means of communication with the settlements on the western side; still I doubt the practicability of that route for women and children carrying with them household goods and agricultural implements. After some more conversation, and receiving a general invitation to visit his toldo whenever I felt inclined, and a hospitable assurance that there would always be food for me if I was hungry, I retired to Casimiro's, whilst Foyel went away to play cards, taking with him my compass for luck, and curiously enough he won several horses, silver stirrups, and other valuables from the Tehuelches.

The following day a race took place, the Tehuelches first taking their horse up to the top of a neighbouring hill, where the doctor performed some magical ceremony to ensure his winning, which he did, though apparently inferior to his competitor. In this plain, called by the Indians Gatchen-kaik or Rocky Hills, Crimè's illness caused us to remain encamped until March 21, during the greater part of which time I and several others were suffering from neuralgia and ulcerations in the mouth, caused, I think, by the bad water we had to drink, perhaps also by the want of salt, which had become a very scarce commodity.

Friendly rivalry was kept up between the tribes in play, hunting, and other sports, in which fortune varied from one side to the other. Every other day I visited poor Crimè, whose groans might be heard at night accompanied by the chaunt of some old hag. The sick man always asked me how long he would live. I at first tried to persuade him that he would get well, but after a time, as he was really fast sinking, gave him to understand that he might live a month if he was lucky. I offered to open his leg and endeavour to cure him, but this he would not allow, stating that if he died under the operation it would go hard with the doctor, which was indeed true, so I gave up my intentions of performing a surgical operation.

Before we broke up the camp a Valdivian and other Indians arrived from Cheoeque's, but brought little news, stating that the Manzaneros were still dispersed amongst the valleys of the Cordillera engaged in gathering the yearly harvest of apples and piñones: of these we had already received plenty from Foyel's people, who kept up a constant communication with their relations near the Rio Limay.

On the 21st all left the valley and travelled a few leagues through a diversified country. On the line of march cliffs, which stood out in the glens in irregular, picturesque manner, were of yellow and red sandstone, but to the westwards black basaltic heights could be seen abutting on the plains, while in hunting over the higher ground masses of ironstone and igneous rock were met with scattered over the surface. We remained for the night in a valley called Changi, and, proceeding next day, arrived about noon at a large plain shut in by sandstone cliffs on the eastern side, at the northern side of which towered a peculiar pointed rock, perhaps 300 feet in height, standing out alone on the sloping descent; viewed from the western side it appeared like a natural column composed of stratified yellow and red and black layers of sand, and, on the summit a condor had his eyry.

The plain extended for several miles to the west, where it was again closed in by cliffs, differing from those to the eastward in being composed of basalt. In this plain, called Geylum, situated, according to Indian accounts, a few leagues to the eastward of Lake Nahuel-huapi, and distant sixty miles from the Rio Limay, and seventy-five miles from Las Manzanas, it was determined to spend the time required for sending chasquis to give notice of our near approach, prior to all marching in company for Cheoeque's headquarters.

1. Also called Poyel.
2. Cf. Guinnard, *Three Years Slavery*, p.73

VII

LAS MANZANAS

THE day after our arrival at Geylum, Manzaneros or Araucanians arrived from the north with cider of their own manufacture stored in sheepskins, apples, and piñones, to trade; and a scene of debauchery ensued, as usual. At night an attempt, nearly successful, was made to rob our toldo: one of the women, however, was awake, and heard the thief endeavouring to get into the back of the sleeping places where some newly-finished mantles were stored; she gave the alarm to two of the men, and they endeavoured to catch the would-be intruder, who, hearing the alarm raised, started off at speed, not without receiving a cut from a knife which marked him deeply on his shoulder; and, what was worse, being recognised as he ran off.

Foyel invited me to drink at his expense, but I merely stayed in his toldo long enough for the observance of etiquette; then retired to keep Hinchel, who would not drink, company by his fireside. Whilst chatting together he related how, many years ago, this place had been the scene of a great battle between the Tehuelches and Manzaneros, in which he, though only a boy, was struck down by a bola perdida and wounded with a lance whilst on the ground; the battle resulting in a victory to the Tehuelches.

The day following the drink, meat being scarce, I dined in Foyel's toldo off a little cornmeal and a dessert of apples and piñones, of which the honours were done by his daughter, a pretty girl of eighteen, with long black silky hair, which it was the special duty of her handmaid—a captive Tehuelche girl—to dress daily. This young lady never condescended to any menial labour, though she occasionally busied her delicate fingers with the needle; her dowry of about eighty mares and the influence of her father made her of course a most desirable match; but she, up to the time of my departure, had exercised the privilege of an heiress and refused all offers. This evening she was in great trouble, having lost a new mantle and some other valuables, stolen no doubt by the Tehuelches. I promised to set inquiries on foot through Casimiro, which resulted in the stolen property being given up, and the thief proved to be the same individual who had endeavoured to rob our toldo.

Shortly after this two messengers were despatched to Cheoeque, who returned on March 25 with intelligence that the said chief would be ready to receive us on April 2, and 'that we were to bring our arms,' which latter message was rather ambiguous. I had been given the option of taking our chief's message to Cheoeque, but owing to one of my horses being lame, and for other reasons, preferred going with the mass later on. Meña, the Chilian, was therefore honoured with the despatches in my place, as he alone was competent to read the Spanish letters written by myself as secretary, and he returned with glowing accounts of the civility shown him at Las Manzanas, and the generally civilised appearance of those Indians. We passed several very hungry and disagreeable days in Geylum previous to starting; there was little game in the surrounding country, and the weather was cold and wet, with occasional snow. For two whole days Casimiro, Meña, and myself, who were usually messmates, had nothing to eat but an armadillo and a few fish which I caught in a pool of the stream. Near the Column Rock, whilst hunting, we discovered a 'cache,' belonging to Foyel's Indians, which contained something wrapped and lashed up in hides: although the temptation was great to overhaul its contents, the package was left unopened, and a quiet warning conveyed to Foyel that others were not likely to be so scrupulous. This confirmed what Casimiro had said as to these Indians providently leaving bags of fat and provisions in various places to which they expected to return at no very distant period.

On the day fixed in the council, held subsequent to the return of the chasquis, we all started, fully equipped, on our journey to Las Manzanas, mustering 250 men of the united Indians, without toldos or baggage, and in light marching order with a few spare horses. A few horses were loaded with coverings for toldos, mantles, &c., which the women hoped to sell to advantage to the Araucanians, and a few of the women accompanied the expedition to conduct their barter, while a guard of perhaps forty men remained behind to provide food for the women and children who were to await our return.

We crossed the gradually sloping irregular plains covered with stunted bushes, but scarcely deserving the name of high pampas, which bordered the northern side of the valley of Geylum, and after passing between two parallel walls of rocks, forming a sort of natural street, we emerged into a succession of grassy plains, separated by barren rocky hills covered with scrub, on attaining the summits of which the wooded Cordillera on the western side rose into view some few leagues distant. About 11 A.M., after we had been some four hours on our march, we met two men, bringing with them a pack horse with a couple of skins of grog for Foyel's people. They were soon surrounded by Tehuelches, who proposed to drink there and then, and were much inclined to help themselves; but a messenger from Foyel's people in the rear arriving, they were permitted to pass unmolested on their way to Geylum, and we proceeded on our journey and formed a circle to hunt. The country became more impracticable for riding as we left the lower plains and mounted some hills broken by deep gorges and bristling in every part with rocks sparkling with unusually large plates of mica, which glistened like glass in the sunshine; these hills were terminated by steep cliffs, over which the ostriches were driven, a party having previously descended to look out for them below. It was a curious sight to see the ostriches dropping down heights varying from 10 to 50 feet often two or three together, with outspread wings. They appeared generally to be stunned for a minute or two on reaching the bottom, and by the time they were on their legs found themselves hampered by a ball from the unerring hand of some stalwart Tehuelche, and running a yard or two fell with broken legs.

Descending from these cliffs we mounted a range of hills more than 2,000 feet high, by means of a tolerably practicable track for travelling, and on arriving at the summit halted for the remainder of the cavalcade. From this point a most magnificent view presented itself; right below us, looking quite close, but really some thirty miles distant, lay a dark line as of a deep cutting, marking the valley of the Rio Limay, which on the west side was terminated by high wooded mountains with steep precipitous sides. Away to the N.W. was a very high snowclad mountain, on which the rays of the setting sun were shedding a rose-coloured light. Between this and the line of the river rose wooded ranges of hills, the real apple groves we had heard so much about; below these again was a low peaked eminence, at the foot of which, invisible to our eyes, lay our destination, viz., the toldos of Cheoeque. For weeks Las Manzanas and Cheoeque had been almost the sole topic of conversation, and the general excitement, which had been intense at starting, now culminated at the sight of our distant bourne. As we halted the Indians all raised their hands to their foreheads, saluting the distant river, and inviting the Spirit of the locality to be propitious to our undertaking, as to the issue of which there was great uncertainty. The night before Casimiro had pointed out the redness of the setting sun, and declared it to be an omen of war; but without paying attention to the omen, which indeed was not perceptible to my eyes, the unprecedented visit of 250 Tehuelches ostensibly for peace might very possibly be otherwise understood by Cheoeque: indeed, it afterwards appeared that he, in reality, was by no means assured of our pacific intentions.

When all were collected and prepared to descend the mountain, it transpired that Casimiro, who had been missing since the hunt commenced, had, in company with several other Tehuelches and Foyel's Indians, returned to drink. This was very annoying, and all present united in abusing him for setting such

CROSSING THE RIO LIMAY

an example when about to enter a part of the country whither we were going on sufferance, amongst a not remarkably friendly-disposed set of people. We halted after nightfall in a valley at the side of a small rapid stream, the banks of which, for a short distance, were covered with high tussocks of broad-leaved pampa grass, amidst the shelter of which we bivouacked, although the night was cold and frosty. Firewood was plentiful, supplied by drift wood brought down by winter or spring floods, so with blazing fires and under the lee of the pampa grass we slept warmly enough. It was necessary, however, to keep a sharp look out on the horses, as pasturage was scanty. Before daylight, after a slight consultation, Guenalto was given chief command, and we again started; after following a winding valley for a short distance and scrambling up a steep slope, we continued to ascend a hill of considerable height and attained a more open country, the western side of which was bounded by the Cordillera. In one of the valleys bordering the mountains we came suddenly upon the Valdivians, driving their cattle *en route* to return to their own country, Cheoeque having sent orders to the Picunches occupying the country near, the only known passes through the Cordillera, to allow them to traverse their district unmolested; notwithstanding this precaution, they were by no means certain that the Picunches would not ease them of the trouble of taking care of their animals on their arrival in the neighbourhood of the passes. Clearing this open country we again ascended a slight rise, at the top of which grew a single apple tree in solitary majesty, but it had been stripped long since of its fruit. Descending this one-tree ridge we entered a cañon, and after half an hour's ride a sudden turn brought the valley of the Rio Limay into view immediately below. Having passed through the cañon, we halted on a slight eminence immediately underneath the barranca bordering the southern side of the valley of the river. From this cliff to the river bank, varying from about a mile to half a mile in width, extended a grassy plain cut up here and there by streams, and wooded at intervals. About a league to the west the barranca blended with the declivities of high precipitous mountains, and the river appeared to force its way from the south between steep precipices before trending into the valley. On the northern side the valley, though dotted here and there with clumps of trees, was more open, and the distance to the barranca greater than that on the southern side. Immediately opposite our post was situated the tolderia of some of Inacayal's Indians, and grazing on the surrounding pastures cattle, sheep, and numerous horses were visible. The river appeared to be of very considerable width, but very rapid through the whole course of this open valley. A mile west of the opening of the cañon three small islands were descried, which Hinchel pointed out as the pass, or ford if it deserves the name. We accordingly proceeded in that direction, and taking off all unnecessary gear, strapping our mantles close up, or wearing them like plaids over our shoulders, descended through the trees and soon plunged into the river.

The first part of the ford was deep, but the water then shallowed on nearing the shore, and the velocity of the noisy stream greatly increased. Still we arrived easily enough at the first island, but to pass from that to the smaller one appeared at first to rather daunt even the Tehuelches. The current was running like a millrace, and the waters foamed over the uneven bottom with a rush and roar that rendered all warnings inaudible. It was evident that only strong horses could cross at all; but one or two bolder spirits dashed in, and although unacquainted with the pass, reached the second island some distance down the river in safety, so the remainder shortly followed, the women crossing behind the men; here and there were places in the ford which necessitated swimming, and in others were huge boulders, over which the water swirled in large waves. At last we all reached the bank in safety, and were met by some of Inacayal's Indians. Being among the lucky first arrivals, I came in for some apples and other food that some of these people of Inacayal's had thoughtfully brought with them from the toldos.

When all were mustered and had resumed their clothes, we started for the toldos, where we were received by Inacayal, and as it was needful to await those who had remained behind drinking, we bivouacked by the bank of the river, and shortly some cattle and mares were brought up and slaughtered to satisfy the cravings of our hunger. After bathing in the river, I was sitting by the fireside watching our dinner cooking, when I received a message to say that I was required in one of the toldos. In that indicated I found an old Indian, a brother of Quintuhual, who spoke fluent Spanish; he invited me to sit down and then narrated that an Englishman named Cox had formerly descended the river from Lake Nahuel-huapi in a boat, but in trying to descend under cover of night, had been wrecked in the rapids at the bend, about a mile above the ford which we had recently crossed: he then took refuge among these Indians, by whom he was hospitably received, and subsequently returned to Valdivia across the mountains, being unable to proceed to Patagones. The old Indian entertained a most friendly feeling for Mr. Cox, whom he had known well, as he had remained several days in his toldo.

After talking some time about this, food was served, and he then proceeded to ask my opinion as to the treatment the Indians experienced from what he called the Spaniards, stating that the Chilians were encroaching on one side and the Argentines on the other, by which means the Indians must eventually be driven off the face of the earth, or else fight for their existence.

After some more conversation I returned to our fireside accompanied by a half-bred nephew of Inacayal, who had left Patagones some eight months previously, having been 'wanted' by the Juez de Paz on account of his having deserted from the army, and having further, in a quarrel, either killed or wounded a Frenchman. He was anxious to induce me to use my influence with Casimiro to allow him to join us, which I did not do for the best of reasons, viz., that he appeared to be a great scoundrel, but I volunteered to take a message to some of his friends in Patagones.

About midnight, bugle calls on the opposite side of the river indicated the approach of the rest of the party, who arrived next day, but Casimiro was in the bad temper customary with him after a debauch, and steadily refused to proceed and take advantage of the fine weather; so another day was spent in loitering about by the side of the river and eating a great deal of beef.

My first cousins, who were also nephews of the old man who had formerly been acquainted with Mr. Cox, started in company with him to procure some apples and piñones, promising me plenty when they returned. Meanwhile I made acquaintance with a Pampa Indian named Gravino, who must have originally been a Christian captive; he himself stated that his mother formerly resided near the settlements, and described her as a Pampa Indian; on her death he, being about fifteen years of age, left the settlements to join the Indians of her tribe, and had got but three days on his journey when he met the united party of Tehuelches, Pampas, and Araucanos, or, as he called them, Chilenos, under the cacique Lenketrou, proceeding to make a raid on the settlements; he had nothing for it but to turn back, and much against his will proceed to rob people under whose protection he had formerly been. In the foray he, with another youth of about his own age, succeeded in driving off a troop of mixed horses and mares, but being dreadfully tired he laid down to sleep in a retired place, having secured his riding horse by means of a lazo attached to his own ankle. At night he was awoke by a stampede of all the horses; and his own taking fright at the same time dragged him some yards, until disentangled by his companion, who cut the lazo: they then tried to secure their animals, but found that the Araucanians had taken off all the best, so he did not make much by the invasion. He had since been employed as a 'manso' or tame Indian in the service of the Argentine Government, but disliking the work had returned to the Pampas and married a relation of Inacayal's. He was a fine-looking young fellow, neatly dressed in ponchos made, as he informed me, by his wife.

On the following day, amidst a storm of wind and rain, we started for Las Manzanas. After ascending the northern barrancas of the river valley, we traversed a level plain where a hunting circle was made for form sake, as the ostriches were very scarce, and I only saw one killed; and passing below, or rather to the N.E. of the hill before mentioned, descended into a valley watered by a small stream; this we followed for some distance, until we arrived at a point where another valley opened into it, the two united forming one of considerable width. Here, under the shelter of some trees, we halted and lit fires to warm ourselves, for the drenching rain had by this time thoroughly forced its way through our mantles. Whilst conversing and making as merry as possible under the circumstances, a messenger dashed up, splashed with blood, and with the effects of drink or furious excitement visible in his face. All crowded round to hear the news, and he shortly informed us that the party who had started to obtain apples on the previous day had met another party of Indians with liquor. A drinking bout ensued, and a quarrel occurred in which a man was killed; but the rest went on drinking, leaving the body outside, where the dogs made a meal of it. This so exasperated one of his comrades that he galloped off to Cheoeque, to whose tribe the party belonged, and the chief at once sent twenty-five horsemen to surround my cousins and demand payment for the death. This they refused to give, so a fight took place, in which four out of the five brothers and another were left for dead, with lance thrusts all over them, the youngest escaping on his own or somebody else's horse, after dropping four of the enemy who tried to intercept him, with a revolver brought by me from Santa Cruz. This was bad news for us, as we were bound to protect these people, who belonged to our united Indians. A consultation took place, in the middle of which Inacayal dashed up with a party all well armed with lances, in addition to their other arms. Foyel's people came next, eager for the fray; the Tehuelches, however, having an eye to business, in the way of bartering the mantles they had brought with them for trade, overruled the warlike ideas of these people, saying 'it was better to wait a little.' Meanwhile guns were loaded and arms got ready, and a party were being told off to proceed to the scene of the *mêlée* and pick up the wounded, when a messenger arrived from Cheoeque with proposals of a peace. I and the rest of the relations of those who had been killed, as we then supposed, were placed under a guard of Tehuelches for a short time until the party started to find the wounded men. We then all proceeded a short distance down the valley, and bivouacked in the pampa grass about a mile and a half from, but out of sight of, the toldos of Cheoeque. Messengers passed two or three times between the latter's residence and our bivouac, and ultimately a very old woman came over and made a long oration on the benefits of peace. This was all very well, but as both parties were evidently suspicious of each other, a watch was kept in the event of a surprise; and as we thought it probable that the negotiations would fall through, we spent the night shivering round the fires and making bolas perdidas. I assured Quintuhual and Casimiro that there would be no fight, at which the latter grew very irate, saying he knew better, that the whole business was a trap to obtain the gear and firearms of our party, also stating that I did not understand these Indians, in which I differed from him. Later in the evening news came, that although fearfully cut about, none of 'my cousins' were dead; the opposite party, however, had fared worse, losing three killed outright. For six men to fight against twenty-five seems long odds, but I believe that Quintuhual's and Foyel's people are the bravest Indians to be met with in the southern part of America, fully deserving the proud title of 'the Warrior Indians.'

The following morning at daylight all mounted their best horses, and forming into column of six proceeded, with the lancers of the warriors at our

head, towards the toldos situated in a valley running at right angles to the
one we had rested in the previous night. On arriving in sight of Cheoeque's
ancestral halls, we observed the Araucanians or Manzaneros forming into line
and manœuvring about half a mile distant; we approached to within 300 yards,
and then forming into open line to display our whole force (my proposal of
hiding a reserve behind an eminence having been overruled), awaited the course
of events. Thus we remained about half an hour watching the Manzaneros,
who presented a fine appearance, dressed in bright-coloured ponchos and
armed with their long lances; they manœuvred in four squadrons, each with a
leader—from whose lance fluttered a small pennon—moving with disciplined
precision, and forming line, wheeling, and keeping their distances in a way that
would not have discredited regular cavalry.

   At the end of the half hour's suspense hostages were exchanged, and we
went through the ceremony of welcome. The Tehuelches were all very excited,
and being in the middle of the troop, when we formed column and raced
down towards the Manzaneros, I at first thought that we were in for a general
scrimmage. On arriving, however, at the line, our leaders wheeled sharp round,
and we went through the usual routine, with the unpleasant exception that both
sides had their guns and revolvers loaded with ball, and every now and then a
bullet would whistle past one's ears or close over our heads. After the usual hand-
shaking between the chiefs, the great Cheoeque, an intelligent-looking man of
some thirty-five years of age, well dressed in blue cloth ponchos, a hat, and
leather boots, rode down our line, shaking hands with everybody and making
some remark. When he arrived at my number I felt rather ashamed of my
dress, a simple mantle not in a very good state of repair. He, on his side, having
asked who I was, appeared rather astonished at hearing I was an Englishman,
and having been further informed that I had written the Spanish letters
previously sent to him, which had been translated by a Valdivian, stopped for
some minutes conversing with me. After this a parlemento took place, during
which all remained mounted, and the discussion lasted till sundown, by which
time every one was very hungry. The conclusions arrived at related chiefly to
effecting a firm and lasting peace amongst the Indians present, on which point
a happy unanimity prevailed. Another day was appointed for the discussion of
Casimiro's proposition for guarding Patagones, and the Chilian war with the
Indians farther north; also to consider Calficura's message concerning a raid on
Bahia Blanca, and the Buenos Ayrean frontier generally.

   One of the principal persons present at the parlemento was a chief subordinate
to Cheoeque, named Mafulko; a fine-looking old man, magnificently dressed in
ponchos which, as well as his arms, were profusely ornamented, indeed almost
covered, with silver; he was remarkable for a most stentorian voice, which
when raised in discussion became an absolute roar, as of a bull of Bashan.
He afterwards noticed me particularly and was very courteous, pressing me

to come and visit him in his own country, which lay to the northward of the Snowy Mountain.

In his train was a man who accosted me in pure Spanish, stating that he had read and translated my letter, and warning me that these Indians hated the name of Spaniard. Before I could make any inquiries he was called away; but, when in Patagones, questions were asked as to an unfortunate settler who was a captive and slave amongst the Araucanians, and the description tallied exactly with that of the poor Spaniard. His master was, doubtless, fearful of recognition and mediation on my part, so hastened to interrupt our colloquy.

We dispersed and bivouacked in the neighbourhood of Cheoeque's toldos, where animals were lazoed and slain for our immediate wants; and Manzaneros and Picunche Indians came round bartering piñones, apples, and now and then a little flour, for knives, bolas, &c. The piñones were some in husks and some ready husked, the white almond-like kernels, about the size of dates, being strung on threads; and, whether roasted like chestnuts in their husks or boiled, proved delicious. The apples also were deliciously fresh and juicy, and I considered a score of them fairly purchased for a pair of bolas, although my comrades declared I had been cheated by the Picunche thieves.

Towards evening Cheoeque sent over to say that, as it was late and disturbances might occur, he considered it would be better not to allow any liquor to be sold until the following day, when all arms might be stored in a safe place, and anybody who felt disposed to get drunk might do so with comfort. To this Casimiro agreed, further assuring me, in the most positive manner, that *he* would keep sober. Whilst we were sitting by the fireside, a bird, exactly resembling our well-known nightjar, flew over our heads, uttering its peculiar grating cry; the Indians all looked startled, asserting that it was a sign of ill luck, and that whenever this bird croaked in the vicinity of an assembly of people some one was sure to fall sick or die. Their superstitious belief in the ill-omened bird received a confirmation, for in the middle of the night, while asleep by the fire, I was roused by Graviel, who, shaking my arm and shouting 'Let us go, let us go!' rushed away from the fire-light into the dark night. His father and myself followed him, and after a long chase caught and, with difficulty, mastered him. He was raving mad, struggling violently, and vociferating incoherent nonsense. When the fit had passed off, his exhaustion and prostration were so great that all thought he would die; but he recovered for the time.

At break of day we were all on the alert; and, as the evening previously we had been too tired and hungry to observe the scenery, I proceeded to reconnoitre the locality generally. To my great surprise, the head-quarters of Cheoeque consisted but of four toldos, belonging to the chief and his brother-in-law, the men who had received us having come from distant residences unaccompanied by their wives, and bivouacking, like ourselves, in the open air. The scene of the encampment was a valley running east and west, the western end being apparently shut in by some high mountains, spurs of the Cordillera. A good stream watered this valley, which was everywhere more or less wooded: away to the north-west, about four miles distant, the apple-groves might be seen; these trees had, however, already been stripped of fruit, and it was necessary to proceed much farther to the north to procure any; but an expedition to visit that district and to get fruit, planned by Orkeke, Hinchel, myself, and others, proved impracticable. Beyond the apple-groves the place was also pointed out where the araucarias grow, from which the piñones are gathered, just below the snow-clad mountains we had viewed from the ridge above the Rio Limay, and about thirty miles distant.

In our valley the pasture was rather scanty, although there appeared to be sufficient for the three flocks of small sheep, each owned by one of Cheoeque's wives, to get into good condition; but sheep will feed anywhere. Immediately behind the toldos was situated a corral for enclosing cattle, none of which, however, were visible, having, probably, been driven off to some secluded valley near at hand, to avoid giving our people a chance of helping themselves. Round this corral were grouped the Indians of Cheoeque's tribe, and the Picunches with fruit, &c. to barter; and between the corral and the river lay the bivouac of the Tehuelches; our fireside being denoted by Casimiro's flag, the colours of the Argentine Confederation. Up and down the valley, and even about the neighbouring hills, were scattered our horses. Proceeding to inspect the toldos, at which I had given but a cursory glance the night before, I found that they were all fixed dwellings; that is to say, not put together so as to be moved in marches, like those of the Patagonians. They were, indeed, constructed in the same manner, but the poles were much stouter, and the whole edifice more resembled a house.

Cheoeque's toldo was quite sixteen feet high, and able to accommodate forty men; while three fires of huge billets of wood burned in the front part. It was closed in completely, except a doorway in the corner with a skin curtain by way of door; and along the front ran a species of verandah, composed of interwoven branches, forming a pleasant canopy, under the shade of which we sat and smoked. Inside, the bed-places were raised on timber; and altogether, what with the sheep, corral, &c., the place had such an air of civilisation about it that, with a small effort of imagination, one might have fancied oneself in a frontier estancia of the settlements. There were other toldos hidden amongst the trees on the northern side of the valley, but these I did not visit.

About eight o'clock several loaded horses came in sight, bringing the liquor which had been stowed away in the valley in which we had encamped the night after the disturbance. As soon as the jars and skins had been unloaded in Cheoeque's toldo, an order was passed round for all arms to be given up, and after some little difficulty they were nearly all collected and stowed in a safe place. The chiefs were then formally invited to drink, and subsequently all comers were asked, the liquor being provided in the most liberal manner by Cheoeque. This chief was fully conscious of his high position and power; his round, jolly face, the complexion of which, inherited from his Tehuelche mother, is darker than that of his subjects, exhibited a lurking cunning, and his frequent laughter was rather sardonic. He possessed a regally strong head, and was disposed to despise Casimiro for his inebriety; in fact it was plain that he regarded himself, and not without reason, as superior to all the caciques, even though they were not subject to him.

Hinchel, myself, and many of the Araucanians had remained away; and I was proceeding to look up the horses, when I was called to the corral by some of the Picunches. These men presented a cast of countenance decidedly differing from, and much inferior to, that of the Araucanians, from whom they were easily distinguished by their darker complexions; but they were very courteous, asking how I came to be with the Tehuelches, and what sort of a place my country was; and were pleased when I told them it was hilly and well wooded, and, referring to Devonshire, that apples abounded. Of course all our conversation was carried on by means of an interpreter (a Valdivian). After a few more questions some rum was produced, and having taken a glass I mounted and proceeded on my original quest. Hinchel rode a part of the way with me, as he was bound in search of a former acquaintance, whose toldo was pitched about four leagues distant, and who was, he said, the best worker in silver amongst the Indians. I afterwards saw specimens of his handiwork, in the shape of silver tubes for ornamenting stirrup-leathers, and the appearance of these and other silver ornaments made of solid metal in peculiar patterns, evidently of their own devising, left little doubt in my mind that these Indians or some of the neighbouring tribes possess the knowledge of the places whence the precious ore is to be obtained, and smelt it themselves.

On returning after having counted and driven the troop of horses belonging to our party down to the best pasture, I found that Cheoeque had sent several messengers in search of me, so I at once proceeded to his toldo, where I found him and Mariano Linares sitting on two real chairs, the latter playing a guitar, Casimiro slightly inebriated and vowing eternal friendship, and howling Indians, men and women, in various stages of intoxication, all round. Cheoeque shook hands, invited me to a seat, and provided me with a glass of grog out of his own bottle, which it is needless to say was not watered like the remainder. I then took advantage of a slight confusion occasioned by an Indian wishing to embrace Cheoeque, and retired, but was intercepted, and had to drink with various acquaintances before reaching the bivouac. As our fireside was soon occupied by noisy, half-drunken Indians, amongst others Hinchel's son, who, very drunk, had come to get his gun for the purpose of killing the master of the revels, but was fortunately overthrown and bound down by his father, who opportunely arrived, I retired to Foyel's bivouac, where Gravino and others were keeping guard, to be in readiness to look after their chief. He arrived soon after midnight, much to their relief.

The jealousy existing between Foyel and Cheoeque, which had broken out in the disturbance so nearly fatal to my cousins, had existed ever since the migration of this chief and Quintuhual to the south, and all the Araucanos of their following kept themselves on this occasion as much as possible aloof, and abstained from sharing in the jovialities, while the Tehuelches, who were unconcerned in the matter, enjoyed themselves freely.

The next day Foyel and Quintuhual marched off their followers in regular array, and proceeded homewards followed by many of the Tehuelches, the great races which it had been settled to hold being abandoned in consequence of the uneasy state of feeling and the consequent fears of a quarrel: the fight in that case would have been an obstinate one, as Cheoeque's forces would not have been much too strong for their opponents, although outnumbering them. We had been surprised on arriving not to find more Indians ready to receive us, as we only counted ninety lances, but it transpired that some were concealed in the woods by the side of the river, who did not appear; besides these seventy or a hundred men had gone to Patagones to obtain their chief's ration of cattle, but 200 more, friends and relations of Foyel, who were on their march to the rendezvous at Las Manzanas, had turned back on hearing of the attack made by Cheoeque's party on their friends, my cousins. Whether they remained away in order to be neutral or to come to the support of their kinsmen did not appear, but Foyel had frequently boasted that 200 of Cheoeque's followers would espouse his quarrel. The Picunches were the original cause of the feud. This tribe, asserted by Antonio Guaitu, who gave them the name of Chollo, to be a branch of the Araucanians, are under Cheoeque's dominion, though governed by local caciques. As already mentioned, they live near the passes of the Cordillera and plunder all travellers. They had not respected Foyel's messenger bringing him stores from Valdivia, and at last forcibly annexed two sheepskins of rum, on which occasion some fighting ensued. Thereupon Foyel sent Cheoeque a defiant message to the effect that if any more robberies by his subjects took place, he should make reprisals; that the latter chief must have imagined that he (Foyel) had forgotten how to ride and use his lance. All this was subsequently amicably settled, but in the end Foyel, who was by right under the rule of Cheoeque, preferred to throw off his allegiance and retire across the Rio Limay. The chief reason alleged by him was that although Cheoeque received large rations of cattle from the Buenos Ayrean Government, he never thought fit to share them with his subordinate chiefs. How far these stories were true I cannot say; as to the Picunches and their subjection to Cheoeque, the Valdivians had been detained over a year waiting for a safe conduct, which was at length obtained on the eve of our arrival, and as far as could be afterwards ascertained, they passed unmolested, although probably suffering loss of cattle from the weather, as it was full late in the year to cross the passes, which during the winter are obstructed by snow and swollen rivers.

Antonio and Ventura Delgado assured me they would have to cross one river seven times owing to its tortuous windings, and on every occasion be obliged to swim their animals. This I at first fancied to be a branch of the Rio Limay, but in answer to other inquiries the Valdivians stated that it flowed to the westward. *Apropos* of this route, an enterprising German had some short time previously crossed from Valdivia to trade with the Indians; he was allowed to pass unmolested with all his merchandise, and drove a profitable trade, and at last started on his return journey with a goodly stock of horses and gear, but near the passes he was stripped of everything and left to make his way homewards on foot if possible. It was very tantalising to be so near Valdivia and not to be able to explore the route thither and visit the Picunches, and indeed Casimiro and myself had planned a trip from Las Manzanas, but it was abandoned, owing to the lateness of the season and other circumstances, combined with my own conviction that if the Cacique got into Valdivia he would not be able to tear himself away from civilised pleasures for too long a period.

After the drinking bout and the departure of Foyel's party, a day devoted to trading intervened, political discussions being postponed in consequence of the indisposition of Casimiro, who required twenty-four hours to recover from the effects of Cheoeque's hospitality. Our Tehuelches, thanks to the profuse generosity of Cheoeque, disposed of all their wares to advantage, and became the happy possessors of numerous horses, silver ornaments, and mandils. Had it been necessary for them to purchase liquor, they would have returned empty-handed and in bad tempers. The Manzaneros appeared to depend on the Tehuelches for their supply of toldo coverings, just as the latter in their turn must procure from them the woven mandils and ponchos. I noticed that the horses brought up for sale by the Manzaneros more resembled those used in the Argentine States than the breed common amongst the Tehuelches, showing finer points and greater speed for racing on flats, but being inferior in the staying powers requisite for hunting.

The second parlemento or council, attended by numerous chiefs, was duly held, in which Mariano Linares, brother of the chief of the Indians in pay of the Government, participated. He was a connection by marriage of Cheoeque's, and had been despatched from Patagones to induce him to keep the peace. The speeches of the Araucanos were made in a peculiar chant, intoned in fact, in a manner closely resembling that I have since heard in some churches at home. Cheoeque thus intoned an harangue setting forth how chiefs had come to him from Araucania proper, soliciting his aid in the war with Chili. He had at first refused to receive them, but at last had heard what they had to say, and it was probable that he might send a small force to assist his countrymen.

Calficura's message relating to the foray on the settlements had been forwarded to us already. Many speeches were made, and Linares and Casimiro pointed out that it was to the Cacique's interest not to interfere, as he would inevitably lose the valuable supplies of horses and cattle given him by the Buenos Ayrean Government, and that it was more profitable to receive the annual rations than plunder and break up the Rio Negro settlements. Finally, it was unanimously resolved that a message should be sent to Calficura, desiring him to confine his hostilities to Bahia Blanca, and that Cheoeque should protect the north bank of the Rio Negro and guard Patagones on that side, while Casimiro guaranteed the southern, which arrangement was duly adhered to on both sides. Accordingly Calficura revenged his real or supposed injuries on the 'Cristianos' by two destructive inroads into Bahia Blanca, carrying off plunder and captives. But letters from the Rio Negro have informed me that peace had been restored, and an exchange or ransom of prisoners effected. This will be more fully dwelt upon, but it is mentioned here in order to show that the Indians are fully aware of the advantages of peace, though they are undoubtedly, the Araucanians especially, jealous of the encroachments of foreigners, and the traditions of their past history have caused them to hold the very name of Spaniard or 'Cristiano' in abhorrence. It is also difficult for the superior caciques in all cases to restrain the petty caciquillos from small depredations; but a fair and well-arranged system of 'rations' will prevent them from making forays, and it is much to be regretted that the well-intentioned and liberal plans of the Buenos Ayrean Government for the protection of the frontiers are too often thwarted by the unscrupulous agents who enrich themselves by appropriating the supplies intended for the Indians. Some may consider the method of keeping the chiefs quiet by pensions undignified; but it is certainly a more humane and economical policy than continual wars of reprisals, which in the end would lead to the extermination either of the Indians or the settlers, most probably the latter, and the certain impoverishing of the country.

After the parlemento a grand banquet was given by Cheoeque to all the assembled caciques and their sons. Over three huge fires in his spacious toldo, large iron pots were supported on tripods, containing beef, mutton, and horse flesh. The guests sat down as they could, while Cheoeque sat, as the Spaniards say, 'on horseback' on a chair in the middle of the toldo, dressed in a magnificent cat skin mantle, and holding a 'revengue' or hide whip in his hand, with which he ever and anon chastised an intrusive dog, or even one of his numerous sons if they came too near, or made too much noise.

The small boys were evidently used to it, and showed great agility in avoiding a blow, and equal unconcern if they received it. The chief's three wives presided at the fires, and wooden platters loaded with large portions of meat and a due allowance of fat were handed round for the first course. Each guest was expected to consume all that was in the platter, and when cleared it was carried off washed, and re-filled for another. The second course consisted of apples and piñones, raw or cooked according to taste, and it was strict etiquette to eat or pocket all the fruit supplied. Water was handed round after the feed, no other drink being produced save a private bottle, from which the chief helped two or three of his most favoured guests. There must have been at least thirty present at once, and there were ample room and abundant supplies. And subsequently a succession of guests of less distinction were fed; all the Tehuelches as well as Araucanos and Picunches being maintained during their stay by the chief.

I was very much struck with the obedience and respect evinced by these people towards their Cacique. His authority extends as far north as Mendoza, over hundreds of Indians, residing in fixed tolderias, some few in the valley near Manzanas, but the chief part more to the northward, near the groves of araucarias. But the power of the chief is absolute, and his word is law to his most distant subjects. At an order from him they leave their toldos, wives, and children, and repair mounted, and ready for any service, to his head-quarters. His wealth is considerable: besides the numerous flocks and herds, one of the toldos was used simply as a treasury, where his stores of silver ornaments, ponchos, mantles, &c., were safely stowed away.

I was present in his toldo at the arrival of a messenger. The Indian, who had evidently come from a long distance, did not venture to enter until commanded to do so, when, with the utmost respect, he took his seat at a distance from the chief, communicated his message, received his orders, and retired; when again ready for the road he appeared to receive final instructions, after which he mounted his horse and rode off without more ado.

The subordinate caciques, whose office and rank are hereditary, appeared to be finer and more intelligent men than the rank and file. Whether this was owing to a difference of race, or merely to their aristocratic descent and hereditary refinement of features and bearing, I cannot say; but their superiority was very marked; whereas among the Tehuelches no such difference between the caciques and their clansmen is observable. The superiority of these semi-civilised Araucanos to their southern neighbours was evident in every way, save only bodily strength. Their residence in a more fertile country, near the apple and araucaria groves, gives them great advantages over the nomad Patagonians. They cultivate wheat, small quantities of which were brought to us for sale; besides storing the natural harvest of piñones and apples, from which, as before stated, they brew cider of unusual strength, and also distil 'pulco,' an intoxicating liquor, from the algarroba bean. My intercourse with both Foyel's people and those at Manzanas was not sufficiently long to enable me to become conversant with their language and customs, which have been described by others. The language, of which I learnt a few words, seemed softer and more melodious, as well as possessing a more copious vocabulary, than the guttural Tehuelche, and appeared to me closely akin to the Pampa tongue; but Jackechan, who could speak both, and Gravino, strongly insisted on the distinction between the two dialects. Their personal habits were excessively neat and cleanly, the morning bath never being omitted by men, women, and children, who all regularly trooped down to the water just before dawn; and their dress was much more carefully attended to than that of the Patagonians. I had no opportunity of witnessing their religions ceremonies, but was assured that they are worshippers of the sun, and there was no vestige of idols of any sort possessed by them. Their ceremonials on occasions of births, &c., were very similar to those of the Tehuelches, save that the 'doctor' appeared on such occasions more elaborately adorned with various colours.

When Quintuhual's niece was sick, her brother enacted the part of 'wizard,' duly painted and adorned with a headdress of feathers. Instead of a mandil tent, a screen of ponchos hung over posts was erected, and all the finery of the family displayed. I was a guest at the feast of slaughtered mares, but was not present at the previous proceedings, as by this time the restraints of dignity as a caciquillo forbade my wandering about as an idle spectator.

They were invariably scrupulous not to commence a meal without first throwing broth or a small piece of meat on the ground, at the same time muttering a charm to propitiate the Gualichu, and they are generally more superstitious and more fearful of witchcraft than even the other Indians. They have some knowledge of precious stones, and seem to attribute certain virtues to them. Thus Foyel possessed what seemed to be a magnificent rough turquoise, which he was on the point of bestowing on me, when his wife and brother-in-law interposed some remark, upon which he apologised, saying that he did not like to part with it, as it had been long in the family. They object strongly, however, to any strangers picking up stones as specimens, or appearing to 'prospect' in any way, which, being forewarned by Ventura Delgado, I was especially careful to avoid. Mons. Guinnard has given a description of some of their games, differing from those in vogue among the Tehuelches, as for instance gambling with black and white beans. Casimiro is my authority for stating that this people preserve the singular custom of abduction in marriage. The intending bridegroom does not trouble himself to obtain the consent of the bride, but having paid the fixed dowry or price to her parents, he gallops up, and forcibly seizing the girl carries her off before him to the bush, whence, after an enforced honeymoon of two days, they return as man and wife to his dwelling. This, however, is not the practice in the case of the marriage of a cacique's daughters. Polygamy is allowable: thus the great Cheoeque possessed three wives, the chief favourite, whose amiable good-humour deserved the honour, occupying the central place in the toldo; but all three lived in perfect harmony and took care of each other's children with impartial affection.

These Araucanos are, as I have said, apt to kidnap or buy captives, and I am inclined to suspect that there is a scarcity of women amongst them, of which the exterminating cruelties practised towards women and children by the frontier 'Cristianos' is a probable cause. They are certainly more dangerous to strangers than the Southern Indians, and it is unsafe to venture amongst them without proper safe conducts from the cacique.

To myself Cheoeque offered permission to travel directly north through the interior of the country as far as the Argentine Provinces, guaranteeing my safety; and the temptation was only resisted by reflecting on the necessity of keeping faith with my Tehuelche friends by proceeding to Patagones. He also gave me a cordial invitation to return, and an assurance that I should be always welcomed as a friend. All our business, both commercial and political, being concluded, and the farewell banquet over, Cheoeque distributed gifts of horses, &c., among the Tehuelches in return for the numerous presents he had received from them. As a set-off to a set of gold studs, he presented me with one of the peculiar lances always used by his people, about fifteen to eighteen feet long and very light, the shaft being made of a cane, which grows in the Cordillera forests, strongly resembling a bamboo, and of the thickness of the butt of a stout pike rod. This present, by the way, caused me to commit a breach of etiquette. I placed it leaning against the toldo, and was at once requested to remove it, as it was a sign of war, though whether it was regarded as a challenge or an omen was not clear; but I was instructed that the lance must either be laid down on, or planted upright in the ground. Another lance was also bestowed on Casimiro, besides numerous horses and other valuables. We took leave of the powerful Cheoeque, and of Linares, with whom, as it had been settled that I should proceed as chasqui, I made an agreement to meet in Patagones, and on the 11th started on our return to the toldos, all in high satisfaction at the success of our visit. The natural exultation of Casimiro was much lessened by the continual illness of his son Graviel, on whom a careful watch had to be kept to restrain him, in the event of his being attacked by another paroxysm of madness.

Riding up the valley where we had slept the night previous to arriving at Cheoeque's, we observed some cattle in the thicket on the borders of the stream; part of the herd belonging to the chief, which had been stowed away in various secluded parts of the neighbourhood. We crossed the barren high pampa, and descended, about one o'clock, to the banks of the Rio Limay, bivouacking in the same spot as on our journey to Las Manzanas, close to Inacayal's toldos. Here we found Orkeke and a good many other Tehuelches; also the four wounded men, two of whom were already on the high road to recovery.

We proceeded to Inacayal's toldo at his personal request, where we remained until evening was drawing on, when cattle were brought up, caught, and slain, and divided amongst the chiefs. Whilst busy shaving a piece of hide wherewith to make some gear, I received a message from Orkeke, whose fire was situated at perhaps a hundred paces from ours, that he wished to see me when disengaged, and after supper I strolled down, and found the veteran sitting loading his pipe. After a smoke, he invited me to accompany him to inspect his newly-acquired troop of horses, and show him which I considered to be the best. I picked out a young white animal that had belonged to Cheoeque's own stud. 'Very well,' he replied; 'take him; he is yours; I never made you any return for the revolver you gave me in Teckel.' Although I did not require the horse, it would have been insulting to refuse it, so I walked off with my racer in tow. This little incident is mentioned to correct the notion entered by some that the greed of gain is a predominant feature in the Indian character.

The following morning we bid adieu to Inacayal and his people, and turned our horses' heads for the pass of the river Limay, which was if possible more swollen and rapid than on the previous occasion; but we all crossed in safety, although Casimiro's and my horse fell once, fortunately where the water was shallow. Everybody, however, got thoroughly wet, and a continual downfall of rain coming on, prevented all chance of drying our mantles. We marched back by a route lying to the westward of that we had before followed, passing under and amongst the high wooded mountains, on the heights of which every now and then we could perceive a condor sitting in majestic solitude, looking down on us like a priest from a pulpit.

About 4 P.M. the rain cleared off, and we bivouacked in a grassy valley, with incense and other bushes growing on the sides. Here, owing to the sickness of Graviel and another of our party, we passed a miserable time, not even being able to get dry; and in addition to our previous discomfort, towards evening a frost set in, and when I woke up about midnight to look round for the horses my mantle was like a board.

I kindled a fire, as the weather was now clear, and soon all the party were huddled round it to warm their half-frozen limbs before lying down again.

The next morning at daylight, thoroughly chilled and hungry, two of us started to fetch the horses, some of the new ones having, as we expected, found their way back to within a few miles of the Rio Limay. However, by the time the sun had risen to sufficient height to give some warmth, we had caught up the others of our party, and not sparing our horses, by two o'clock had passed through the street of rocks and come in sight of the toldos, where we shortly arrived.

Before sunset all the Tehuelches had returned to the bosoms of their families, and all were glad to sleep under the shelter of a toldo once more, after having passed twelve days and nights in stormy weather without any covering save our mantles.

The 14th of April, the morning after our return, a complaint was made by Foyel's people that the Tehuelche Indians left behind, thinking it useless to proceed to the plains, some miles distant, to hunt for the supply of the toldos whilst cattle and sheep were grazing in the immediate vicinity, had helped themselves in the obscurity of the night. Meña corroborated the fact; and although he had been away hunting with the greatest assiduity, he had met with but little success, and complained bitterly of the hungry times they had endured.

Soon after our arrival Kai Chileno was seized with illness, and in a few days several of the more aged and children sickened with headache and fever, showing all the symptoms of severe influenza. Alarmed lest the sickness should spread, on the 16th of April most of the Tehuelches struck toldos and took the road leading to Patagones; but our toldo and another remained behind on account of the continued illness of Graviel and the others. Towards evening of the same day we suddenly heard shouts and cries in the toldos of Foyel, and all except Casimiro, who sat quite still by the fireside, rushed to seize their arms, naturally thinking that a party had arrived to fight from Las Manzanas. After a little suspense we observed a line of men advancing towards our toldos on foot, shouting, firing, and brandishing their arms. Casimiro, who was having a quiet laugh at us, then explained that they were only fighting the sickness. The party advanced to our toldo, beating the back of it with their lances, to scare away the Gualichu, and then retired.

We all had a good laugh over this affair; and I was amused to hear Meña, who was an intelligent youth, arguing that the Indians were quite right, as sickness never attacked an armed man.

We lived chiefly on air the last four days of our stay in Geylum, as no hunting was done; but Foyel, after learning our wants, came to the rescue, presenting me with a couple of sheep, which I received with gratitude, and divided amongst the party.

It had been intended that his party should accompany the Tehuelches to Patagones, but as it would be necessary to leave their women and children in Geylum with only a few boys to take care of the flocks and herds, and they were not confident as to the pacific intentions of the Manzaneros, he and Quintuhual considered it more advisable to remain for the present in their camp, and afterwards, by riding in fast, to overtake our party *en route* previous to their arrival in the settlements.

I bid an affectionate adieu to Miss Foyel, who had always shown me the greatest kindness, and the natural grace of whose manners would have adorned a civilised drawing-room. Her parting words were an invitation to return if possible and pay another visit to the toldo, where I had been made to feel myself at home.

Her father asked me to procure him a grinding organ, as Casimiro had informed him that he had seen music made by turning a handle. I promised to get one if I could, and after a cordial farewell returned to our toldo, as we intended going away at daylight on the 17th.

Accordingly we prepared for a start; and a boy came over from the other toldos to join us. He was a Tehuelche, whose father had been killed on suspicion of witchcraft, and being a remote connexion of Casimiro's, had claimed his protection, which of course was granted, and he (Casimiro) had agreed to take him with us, informing him that he was to act as my page, look after my horses, &c., and make himself generally useful. This was a very fine idea, but one glance at the face and figure of this illustrious youth was sufficient to show me that I should probably spend my time in looking after him, and a more mischievous imp I never saw. When told that he might catch one of my horses to travel on, he immediately fixed on the wrong one, a horse that I had myself barely mounted for perhaps six weeks, in order to get it into condition for the journey into Patagones.

This horse he caught, and came down to the toldos at full gallop over rocks, stones, and bushes, with a grin of delight on his face. After being warned in mild terms that he was not to ride that horse, which I took from him and turned loose, he proceeded to catch one of Casimiro's, which he treated in the same manner, but at length got the right one, and then, without saying 'With your leave, or by your leave,' galloped off yelling at the top of his voice, to follow the road which the Indians had taken the previous day.

We were about to start ourselves when, at the last moment, Quintuhual sent to say that he wished to have a council. So Casimiro and myself remained in the pouring rain squatting on the grass listening to a repetition of what we had heard the previous day.

When the council was concluded a sheep was brought up and killed. The poor beast was lashed to a post with its head looking to the sky, and the throat being cut, salt was forced into the wound, the lip of which was compressed *secundum artem*, in order to flavour the blood and lungs, &c., which formed the repast. All the girls then crowded round, each preferring a request to us to bring a little yerba, flour, sugar, &c., from the settlements, till, our horses being ready, mine having been additionally burdened with the dead mutton by way of provisions for the road, we extricated ourselves from the crowd, and amidst repeated injunctions, charges, and affectionate farewells, got away, and towards 4 P.M. started to overtake the now distant cavalcade.

VIII

GEYLUM TO PATAGONES

WE were now fairly started on our journey eastward to the Rio Negro, on my part with contending feelings of regret at quitting my recently acquired and amiable relatives, and of joyful expectation of reaching Patagones and finding there that which travellers, amidst all the excitement of new countries and strange people, still so eagerly long for—news from home! We galloped forward casting longing looks behind at the forest-clad slopes and snowy peaks of the Cordillera, the never-to-be-forgotten beauty of which made the dismal prospect of the country before us still more dreary.

My friends had been unanimous in describing the district that intervened between Geylum and a place spoken of as Margensho nine marches distant, as both difficult to travel, and affording scanty pasture for the horses and little game for the people. The rain which had been falling when we left, had turned to sleet driven by a strong westerly gale, and my load of mutton sadly interfered with the management of the sheltering mantle. Fortunately, as the direction of our route was easterly, we thus escaped having to face the storm, while the gale in our backs stimulated both horses and riders to their utmost speed.

At the entrance of the rock-strewn gorge which formed the eastern gateway of the valley of Geylum, to the south of which towered the isolated column of rock, we were suddenly startled by the apparition of mounted Indians galloping towards us from the direction which our advanced party had taken. Conjectures as to possible calamity in the shape of a fight or accident were speedily dispelled, as they proved to be Tehuelches riding back in search of lost horses, which they averred had been stolen and craftily concealed by the Araucanians. So we continued our march through a succession of narrow rocky gorges winding amongst the hills, till, as the twilight was growing dark, we arrived, wet and weary, and feeling symptoms of illness, at the encampment situated in one of the usual grassy valleys. The toldo when reached proved to be in utter disorder, two of the women and a child having been attacked with the epidemic; so we set to work ourselves to light a fire, secure the skin covering of the toldo, and arrange the beds, and after a time the interior assumed a more ship-shape aspect, although the grass (our carpet) and everything else were wet. On every side one heard complaints of some child having fallen sick, and throughout the night the wailing cry of the women 'Ah gelay loo!' over their darlings rendered sleep all but impossible. Next morning broke fine and clear, so it was determined to march onwards in the hope that speedy change might get rid of the epidemic, but starting was almost as difficult as staying.

Of our party Meña had returned to look for a missing horse; Crimè was dying, and Casimiro was attending to him; and what with sick friends and children all were occupied or distracted, and the business of catching the horses devolved on myself, single-handed at first. Having secured the troop, the next task was to catch my newly-acquired steed; the sight of a lazo was sufficient to make him gallop a league, and as he was very swift, three hours were spent in ineffectual efforts, but at last, two or three of my comrades coming up to my assistance, he was caught. Giving my flibbertigibbet page charge of the remaining horses, I started, in company with one of my friends, to join the hunting circle, already in course of formation.

We rode up a valley in an easterly direction, on our way passing the invalid Crimè, who, groaning with pain, lay stretched out at full length on a sort of couch composed of blankets on the horse's back, his wife leading the horse and wailing out loud. But as condolences were of little use, we passed on in silence, and shortly emerged from the valley, which sloped up by gradual ascent to a wide plain of sandy soil and stunted bushes, bounded on the eastern horizon by a line of high jagged hills, which stretched to the southward as far as the eye could reach. While sitting under a bush by the fire, I was attacked with headache and sickness, the premonitory symptoms of the epidemic; however, I mounted and joined the hunting party, and at the end of the circle felt much better, although unable to eat.

The finish brought us to the entrance of a valley which wound among the precipitous rocky hills of the range seen from the farther verge of the plain. While watching the cavalcade of women and baggage, I looked long in vain for my own troop of four horses, but at last descried them trotting without a guide in the rear of the column, their natural sagacity or perhaps thirst having induced them to follow their comrades. The trusty page had left them to take care of themselves, and gone off hunting on his own account, which behaviour, repeated on a subsequent occasion, caused the loss of the stud. Towards evening we encamped in a valley enclosed by three hills, one of which, of decidedly volcanic aspect, was named 'Oerroè.' The side of this hill was thickly scattered with fragments of the vesicular lava which furnishes the favourite material for the hand bolas. As most of us had exchanged our weapons of the chase for apples, piñones, &c., in Las Manzanas, many were soon employed picking stones and fashioning bolas. I took very good care that my page should be unprovided with hunting implements, but, alas! here he fell sick, or pretended to be, and was just as useless as before. The day after our arrival Crimè's sufferings were terminated. I received a summons to his death-bed; the Cacique, though wandering, knew his friends, and called all to witness that his death had been caused by a Southern Tehuelche whom he named and described, and then, raising his arm, pointed to a vacant space and cried, 'Look at him, there he stands.' He then asked me to 'feel his arm,' and as, to please him, I laid my finger on his pulse it beat slower and slower, till, with a sudden gasp, he died. According to etiquette we silently retired, and the toldo resounded with the clamorous crying of the women and the wailing of his widow. The usual funeral rites were hurriedly gone through, but most were too absorbed in their own troubles to participate in them. During the night three children died, and more were at death's door; and, the supply of horseflesh from the funeral victims being abundant, all thoughts of marching were abandoned, and the camp resounded with the lamentations of the women. In our toldo all the inmates were sick, and the duty of looking after the horses devolved on myself and Casimiro, who was recovering from his attack.

We were joined in this place by Hinchel's son with his Araucanian wife, with whom another man came to look for a girl who had run away from Foyel's toldo, but his quest proved fruitless, as she remained invisible, stowed away in some of the toldos. This man brought further news that Cheoeque's people, renewing the old feud, were arming to fight now that we had gone; also that a man had been killed in a drunken brawl since our departure, and that a rumour was current that the Valdivians had had their cattle taken from them, and various other stories, most of which were declared to be lies by Orkeke, who, having lost a horse, had returned to look for it in Geylum; the budget of alarming news thus proving to be a fresh illustration of the Indians' proneness to invent if they have nothing of real importance wherewith to astonish their hearers. Crimè's widow took up her abode in our toldo; and as, by this chief's death, the post of Capitanejo, with the rank of Lieutenant in the Buenos Ayrean army, and the right of drawing rations, was vacant, Casimiro consulted me as to his successor. But successive proposals of those who seemed most fit, beginning with Wáki, were objected to by the Cacique, who at last declared that he should name his almost insane son Graviel as the chief to be placed by the Argentine Government upon the list of the Caciques to be conciliated by annual pay! On April 22 a start was made, but we remained to the last, as four of Casimiro's horses which I had brought down to the valley the previous evening were missing, so the chieftain returned to look for them, and the rest of the toldo pursued their journey.

After taking a farewell look at the Cordillera, which was presently shut out from view by the hills, the counterslope of which we descended, a hurried march led us through a very barren rocky country entangled in broken irregular hills, with scarcely a bush to shelter under, and little or no pasture. We encamped, or rather reached the camp after it was pitched, in a cañon containing a small spring and a very little green pasture, and went to bed supperless, as, not being in time for the hunt, and game being very scarce, what we could beg from our neighbours was naturally given to those recovering from sickness.

Jackechan's wife and child were still very unwell, and, as the child was supposed to be dying, the doctor was sent for. He proceeded to cure it by laying it on the ground, muttering a charm and patting it on the head; after which he put his mouth close to its chest and shouted to bring the devil out: he then turned it on its face and repeated the same process. The child's health mended next day, and it was shortly out of danger.

About ten o'clock at night Casimiro returned with his horses, which had strayed a considerable distance on the road back to Geylum. The next day a long march of twenty miles brought us to an encampment on the western verge of a broad plain, watered by a brooklet. During the hunt the first Patagonian hares, or cavies, were caught. These little animals live in burrows, but are generally out feeding or sleeping in the grass during the day. They are excessively swift for perhaps a mile, but, like the foxes of this country, soon get tired. The chase of these small deer afforded an agreeable relief to the monotony of the journey. As soon as we entered a plain or valley where they abounded, as they always were found in numbers where the pasture was good, all hurried off to 'stop the earths,' i.e. close up the burrows with bushes; but the cunning little beasts often evaded us by slipping into a burrow overlooked by the earth stoppers. It required considerable skill to bring them down with the bolas, as, if only caught round the legs or body, they disentangled themselves quickly, but a blow on the head proved at once fatal. They are good eating, though the flesh is somewhat dry when roasted. Their skins are made up into mantles, but are of little value, as the hair soon comes off.

About a mile below the encampment, where the sandy plain narrowed and sloped down to a low-lying grassy valley, a singular phenomenon presented itself. The morning after our arrival, when going out to look for the horses, a furious easterly gale whirled the dust aloft in dense clouds, and, to my great surprise, the sand, which was driven into our faces, was as hot as when the fire so nearly encircled us. Almost blinded in forcing our way through this curtain of driving sand, we rode right into a hollow, where the earth appeared to be on fire; as the horses plunged through the heated surface the hair was burnt off their fetlocks, and they were nearly maddened with fright, so that it was a difficult feat for the riders without saddles or stirrups to keep their seats. Once I was somewhere near my horse's ears, but, more by good luck than good management, just escaped being thrown as it were into the fire. After the gale had partially moderated, I proceeded to inspect this place, and found that, although not, as I at first thought, absolutely on fire, the ground was smoking as if from internal combustion, the surface presented a crust of baked yellow clay, which, yielding to the horses' feet, disclosed a black subsoil; there was no flame, but a thin white vapour issued from the ground. When I incautiously ventured a step on the treacherous crust it gave way, but I managed to extricate myself with no further damage than burning my potro boots. The Indians stated that the fire had been originally caused some years previously by their having kindled the pasture higher up the valley, and that the ground had been burning ever since. It was impossible to discover whether there was any subjacent bed of combustible matter which might thus have been ignited; but, as there are hot wells and springs in the same range not many miles distant to the south-east, it seems more probably due to volcanic agency. The principal hot spring was described as a circular basin of about six feet in diameter, the water, of a temperature not so hot as to scald the hand, bubbling up through numerous holes in a clay bottom. In many of the surrounding hills there are lava and pumice of not extremely ancient formation; some of the hills have also an appearance of having been at a recent period the outlets of eruptive forces, which have scattered large shattered masses of rock over the sides of the extinct craters.

In this encampment I had a serious misunderstanding with our chief, which all but ended in a downright quarrel; but after consideration we agreed to make it up, as although on two occasions of danger he had left me to my fate, I thought it better on the whole to keep friends for the present. The evening of this quarrel, as a party of three toldos were starting off to go to the Chupat, and Casimiro was desirous of extending his fame to the Welsh settlement, I wrote a letter to the authorities enquiring about some saddles, part of his Argentine rations sent thither by mistake, which the chief declared to have been intended for him, but which had been distributed amongst other Indians. The letter was forwarded by one of the Indians who was supposed to be of English parentage on one side, although he showed but little traces of English blood in his type, with the exception perhaps of his hair, which was of a lighter colour than that usually met with: he was a very good-natured fellow, and I regretted his departure, as he was one of my adherents, but being a man of very sober habits he did not wish to be mixed up in the universal orgie which would probably take place on arriving in the vicinity of Patagones. With this party the young widow who had made overtures of marriage to me also departed, after an affectionate farewell, and receiving a handkerchief as a remembrance. The following morning we also started, and one of the universal loafers who had gambled his property away, asking for a mount, was told to catch the 'white horse' presented by Orkeke: he accordingly borrowed a horse to catch him, and at the end of our day's journey had not succeeded in doing more than driving him in, to use a nautical term, in our wake; this was exactly what I had intended, as this Indian was a great rogue, and had cheated me at cards out of a set of metal bolas, equivalent to a horse.

Our march lay up the valley, and the circle was formed on the surrounding volcanic hills, the sides of which, besides the vesicular lava, presented large masses of the ironstone noted as having been observed at Santa Cruz. Shrubs were sparsely scattered on these hills, and game was exceedingly scarce. Towards evening we encamped on the borders of a stream in a place called by the Indians Telck. There the sickness broke out afresh in its worst form, and several children died, in consequence of which a quantity of mares and horses were slaughtered, and numbers of ponchos, ornaments, and other property burnt by the parents in their grief. It was most distressing to see and hear the melancholy manifestations of sorrow, and the sound alone of that dreadful crying aloud, and the dismal 'ullagoning,' to use the Irish expression, of the old women, haunted me even in my sleep. The night of our arrival a mock combat with the Gualichu took place, in which everybody joined. After dark, when many were sitting by the firesides conversing, and I myself was reclining on my bed smoking, the Doctor came into the toldo, and communicated with the chief, who told all to get their arms ready, and loaded his gun: on a shout being set up all fires were immediately extinguished, and all commenced firing off guns, clashing their swords, and beating the backs of the toldos, and yelling 'kow-w!' at each blow; firebrands being, at the same time, thrown into the air by the women, with clamorous shouts and cries. The scene was wild and striking, the darkness of the night being only illuminated by the flashes of the guns or the sparks from the brands whirled high into the air. At a given signal all stopped simultaneously, and for two or three minutes the camp remained in perfect darkness, after which the fires were relighted and things resumed their ordinary aspect.

The following day, strange to say, a real fight took place, in which one man was wounded, and for a few minutes a general mêlée or free fight appeared imminent. Parties were already forming to cancel old blood feuds, when further mischief was checked by the return of Hinchel, myself, and others. We had been absent trying new horses on the race course, which, as in almost all the camping-grounds since leaving the Rio Sengel, was a regular beaten level track of about a couple of miles in length, and my new horse had established his fame as a racer by winning a match over a distance of a mile-and-a-half; meanwhile the quarrel broke out—such are the uncertainties of Indian life.

We remained some days in this place, and whilst hunting in the surrounding country (where hares abounded), we observed a new description of spinous shrub with small ovate leaves and yellow flowers, resembling holly, and growing to about two feet in height. Casimiro and myself agreed to try whether the leaves might not be medicinal, so a quantity were bruised and boiled: the infusion proved exceedingly bitter, reminding me of quinine, and acted as an admirable sudorific, being administered to the invalids with great success. In one of our excursions we had crossed the hills and descended on a high elevated plain, concluding our hunt near a swelling eminence exactly resembling a huge 'barrow' thickly overgrown with shrubs, from which what appeared to be a salina was espied, to our great delight. Hinchel and myself being alone, and having a fat ostrich to discuss for dinner, determined to enjoy our meal by its shore, first testing the quality of the salt, a luxury which we had long been destitute of. Dismounting, we proceeded to investigate it; but to our great disappointment, after walking over every part of it, and digging down with knives a foot below the surface, the supposed salt proved to be bitter and nauseous nitrate of soda.

After quitting the vicinity of the Cordillera the weather had every day become warmer, and the frosts at night much lighter: indeed whilst in Telck some warm days were experienced, although the winter season was fast approaching. Near this encampment the small edible root previously described as growing in the dried-up lagoons was found in abundance, and was collected by the women and children. Cavies were plentiful in the hollows and valleys in the neighbouring hills, and even close to the encampment, but the chase of other game proved difficult, the hill sides being so strewn with stones as to render galloping a horse a certainty of laming him. In this neighbourhood Hinchel pointed out a detached pinnacle of rock, much resembling that noticed at Geylum, and according to custom invoked a blessing from the guardian spirit; and then he informed me that on the third next march we should pass a deposit of yellow ore, lying to the south of the route, and that during the hunt he would show it to me. Orkeke also corroborated this statement, and I have every reason to believe that there is in that locality a deposit of iron or more probably copper ore.

As the meat of the slain horses was nearly consumed we marched the following day across a most stony, rocky, and inhospitable country, and at length arrived at a range of hills, through which ran a steep, narrow gorge. Descending through its tortuous windings, we at length arrived at a spring, the waters of which, joining with another small rivulet, flowed out and formed a sort of marsh at the head of a large plain. From the slope of the hill bordering the ravine a fine panorama extended to the east, the entire face of the country appearing to be more uniformly undulating than the confused ranges of hills, through the intricacies of which we had been marching and hunting since leaving Geylum. In the foreground were visible distant black figures, moving with swiftness across the plain in pursuit of numerous ostriches; and away to the eastward rose a column of smoke, the cause of which was eagerly speculated on.

I am conscious that the description of this part of the journey is not likely
to give a very clear idea of the country traversed; and that the directions of the
successive ranges, and the general character of the ground, are left too much
to the reader's imagination; but, in deprecation of criticism and censure, it is
pleaded that I was under the impression that this district had been traversed,
and accurately surveyed and described, by a savant employed by the Argentine
Government; and that I was deprived of the assistance of my compass, which
had been presented to Foyel. The notes taken at the time were very scanty,
and my recollections were confused, inasmuch as I was labouring under a
constantly-recurring attack of sickness, which was only kept at bay by resolute
endeavours not to give way; but which rendered observation and record, in
addition to hunting and the usual toils of marching, impossible. It was the
more needful for me to endeavour to keep up, as all were more or less ill, and
becoming increasingly gloomy and dispirited. To add to the troubles which
weighed down the Indians' spirits at this place, the doctor's horse fell while
descending a precipitous rocky hill. The unfortunate physician was stunned,
and very nearly crushed to death by the horse falling on him; great grief was
universally expressed at this catastrophe, as no one was left to cure the invalids
and contend with the malignant Gualichu, who it was natural for the Indians
to imagine had laid a trap for his opponent, and upset the medicine man's steed
in order to have the field clear for himself.

We encamped in a sort of morass by the side of the hills overlooking the
plain, and were woke at daylight by the chattering of a flock of blue and orange
parroquets; these birds, which brought back old pleasant associations of the
banks of the Parana, and almost seemed to be harbingers of civilised life, were
numerous in this locality, though they were the first of the species that I had
observed in the country.

The distant signal smoke was concluded to indicate the presence of Jackechan
and the Pampa Indians under Teneforo, and all were in spirits at the prospect
of obtaining news, and perhaps luxuries in the shape of flour, yerba, &c., from
Patagones. The order was accordingly given to march and a large answering
signal fire kindled in some dry pasture bordering the hill side, a messenger being
at the same time despatched to ascertain the news. After a rather long march
over a barren plain strewn with angular masses of chalcedony and projecting
rocks resembling alabaster, we arrived at a dreary encampment, sheltered under
a bank, from which a spring gushed out, forming a refreshing rivulet.

The mutiny of my page had compelled me to enjoy the pleasure of driving
my own cattle, following the track in advance of the other people; besides this,
an attack of fever rendered me indisposed, and, indeed, incapable of hunting.
While languidly jogging on in the centre of the circle which was made on both
sides of the tracks, and anathematizing one of the horses who would every now
and then endeavour to join the hunt on his own account, I observed an ostrich

coming straight towards me: the sight was reviving, and leaving the horses to themselves, I galloped to the cover of a friendly bush, and when he was within a short distance dashed out, and discharging the bolas, had the satisfaction of seeing him turn a somersault and lie with outstretched wings stunned. An Indian riding up at the time claimed the customary division, and took charge of the bird, on which we regaled our friends at the close of the hunt. Many of the hunters came in empty-handed, or with only a skunk, of which there were numbers in this vicinity, hanging to their saddles. By this time the armadilloes had taken up their winter quarters underground, and only came out of their burrows on a remarkably sunny day.

At night we encamped under a barranca or steep rising to the eastward. On his arrival Hinchel informed me that we had passed the vein of ore previously spoken of, and the hot springs, the Indians having shortened the journey by deviating from the usual line of march.

The chasqui returned late at night with intelligence that the smoke had been caused by a party of Pampas Indians travelling to join Quintuhual, or, at any rate, in that direction, but whatever provisions or tobacco they had they kept to themselves, and had purposely avoided us. Jackechan and Teneforo had started for Valchita *en route* for Patagones, after waiting for our coming more than a month in Margensho, the place appointed as a rendezvous. Whilst there they had received liquor and other luxuries from Patagones, but no disturbances had ensued, the only casualty being that a woman had been severely burned by falling into a fire whilst in a state of intoxication. All was reported to be peaceable at Patagones, and a rumour was current that Commandante Murga was about to give up his governorship. Casimiro, on receiving all this intelligence, immediately wished a despatch to be indited, although I pointed out to him that it would be better to wait until we had arrived at a nearer point; he was so urgent that on the following morning I composed an elaborate letter, detailing the union of the tribes, the precautions taken for protecting Patagones, and requesting a hundred mares for Casimiro and his people: when finished it was carefully wrapped up and stowed away in my baggage till wanted.

The talk then naturally turned on the subject of the choice of messengers to be despatched to Patagones on our arrival at Margensho. It had been previously arranged that I should be sent fully commissioned, as being better able to represent to the authorities what had been resolved on, as well as to impress upon them the immediate requirements of the Indians, and several others now volunteered to accompany me, and got quite merry at the thoughts of a drink. But we were still three marches distant from Margensho. The following day we were again *en route*, traversing a succession of plains with rocky ridges cropping up at intervals, until we at length reached a grassy valley enclosed by steep walls of rocks sixty feet high; gravely perched on the summits of which several slate-coloured Chilian eagles were visible, their occupation being to prevent the excessive multiplication of little cavies. On the hill sides bordering this valley, our old friend the incense bush, which had for many marches back been very scarce, grew in luxuriant profusion. At this season it was covered with berries which, though uneatable, are used by the Indians mixed up with water as a drink; this infusion has a very sweet taste, but I should think must be very unwholesome. On arriving at the encampment, at the head of the valley, near some pools of standing water, we were apprised, by the lugubrious sounds of the women's monotonous chants, that the number of the children had been further diminished by several deaths. One of this day's victims to the epidemic being Algo, Tankelow's youngest daughter, the father was in great distress and anger, as he attributed the death not to the distemper, but to witchcraft.

The warm and tolerably fine weather experienced since our departure from Telck had been succeeded by a heavy, murky, still atmosphere, and the clouded sky promised a downfall of rain, which speedily came. The next day more children and the old deaf and dumb woman died; over her little moan was made, but the lamentations over the children were terrible to hear, and on all sides mares were slaughtered. The abundance of meat, and the general confusion, combined with the rain to defeat Casimiro's anxious desire to proceed. The accumulation of miseries had rendered all the Indians gloomy and ill-humoured; and since our departure from Geylum we had had ample experience of the wretched side of Pampa life.

This district is always dreaded by the Indians, who assert that they invariably are attacked by a similar sickness when in it, notwithstanding that some considered it to have been occasioned by poison or deleterious drugs administered by our late neighbours. The marches had therefore been forced and prolonged, and the increased fatigue had doubtless aided the distemper in its fatal effects. Nearly half the children and several of the elder people died during our progress to Margensho, and the utter misery and discomfort cannot be described. The rain had continually drenched us; the women, distracted with their endeavours to soothe the sick children and their grief over the dead, could not attend to their domestic duties; our mantles were unmended, and proved but a poor shelter from the rain, no small misery in this climate, and the arrangements of the toldos were utterly devoid of their customary care and comfort. The usual good temper and cheerfulness of all had fled, and grief, sickness, and angry suspicion cast a gloom over every countenance. One misery, starvation, had certainly been avoided by the abundance of horse-flesh, but it can easily be imagined that we could have borne hunger better. We had endured cold, and hunger, and fatigue, as well as danger, before, but nothing has left so indelible an impression of a thoroughly bad time as that march from Geylum to Margensho.

At last Casimiro issued orders to march, and with two or three more of us started in advance. While waiting under the shelter of a mass of rocks for the remainder to overtake us, I fell asleep, and on waking up found the rain pouring down in torrents, and the chief just directing Meña to return and see what the women were about. Our page arrived a little later to say that the Indians had refused to march, the occupants of our toldo alone being on their way to join us: these soon appeared, so we proceeded in the storm, having agreed that to return, after having once started, would be an ignominious proceeding.

We followed for some distance the valley, or rather the plain, into which it had opened out, and then ascended some abrupt rocky heights at its eastern extremity; crossing these hills, in the valleys or ravines of which incense bushes grew almost like a forest, we halted for a time by the side of a rivulet flowing from a spring on the hill side.

After kindling a fire to warm our bodies, wet as we were and chilled by the wind, which, originally west, now blew from the south with cutting violence, the sight of numerous guanaco on the heights above determined us to encircle a herd; we accordingly mounted the heights, and having completely failed in our attempt, descended to the other side. A large lagoon lay at our feet, and away to the east a succession of plains extended to the encampment called Margensho.

These plains were bounded for a short distance on the north side by a range of hills, which came to an abrupt termination at the end of the lagoon, on the south side by another range gradually sloping to the eastward, and on the western side by the rocky heights we were descending. The view would have been enjoyable on a fine day, but in such a Patagonian tempest of rain and wind, landscapes were by no means appreciated. Near the lagoon was another herd of guanaco, some three thousand strong, who tempted us to a vain endeavour to encircle them, but they descried us before we could approach within a mile, and were soon lost to sight on the plains leading towards Margensho. Whilst riding down the edge of the hills Casimiro pointed out some thyme, a little of which we gathered to flavour our soup with in the evening. We then descended and sheltered under the over-hanging bank of a dry watercourse leading to the lagoon. The women and remainder of the cavalcade shortly arrived, and loading my page with firewood, to his intense disgust and the extreme delight of every one else, we proceeded a little farther to the south, where the pasture was good, and established ourselves for the night.

The following morning early we all started to hunt, and were more successful than on the previous day, though the wind was blowing a fearful gale from the S.W., with occasional storms of sleet. Towards the afternoon, by which time, having finished our hunting, we were snug enough under the toldo, it rained hard, and with the rain the Indians commenced to arrive, till before dusk a town of toldos occupied the borders of the hills. Casimiro this evening sent for volunteers to go in with me as messengers or chasquis to Patagones, on our arrival at Margensho, now but one march distant. But of those previously so desirous to go on, not one appeared, nor would any one Indian consent to lend his horses for so long a journey. The chieftain was sadly put out, and cursed the caciquillos all round. He then tried to dissuade me from going myself, saying that it was a great distance, that the desert or travesia was a fearful place, that I should probably lose my horses, that many people had starved, at the same time wishing me to lend my horses to some other Indian. He narrated how he himself had occupied twelve days in crossing it, and had been obliged to abandon a horse and the saddle and gear of his remaining steed, and with difficulty, nearly starved, on foot, and driving his almost worn out horse before him, had made his way to a station.

At the same time a young Indian started to cross the desert, but lost his way, and, quoth the Cacique impressively, 'His bones are there now.'

One statement, that the chañals or white thorns grew higher than the horses' heads and tore the unlucky riders' mantles to pieces as they forced their way through them, my own after experience fully verified. I, however, adhered firmly to my original intention of going, as agreed to by him, and conveying, with my own hand, the letter I had written: and it was finally settled, that Meña, Nacho, and I should, on arriving at Margensho, start on our journey as chasquis. Casimiro's real motive for dissuading me was distrust, as we had on two or three occasions disagreed, and once nearly come to blows; he was therefore afraid that I should, on arriving at Patagones, work against his interests and give him a bad character. Meña, who had taken a great fancy to me, volunteered for the purpose of keeping an eye on Nacho, who was my 'bête noire' and not to be trusted.

These arrangements having been brought to a satisfactory conclusion, we proceeded to the toldo of a friend and assisted at the ceremony performed by the doctor of curing a sick child, more especially concerning the part of painting with red ochre, killing, and eating a white mare.

On this occasion the parents formally invited the principal chiefs and their relations and friends, and the ceremony commenced as follows:—All the men were either sitting or standing in a circle, in the centre of which sat the mother holding her infant in her arms. The doctor then came in, and under his direction the mother plastered the infant from head to foot with white clay, the wizard meanwhile muttering incantations; when this was completed the doctor disappeared for a minute or two, returning with an ornamented hide bag in his hand; this he opened, and produced from the bottom some charms carefully enveloped in rags, which he, after performing some mystic hocus-pocus, returned to the bag. He next took the baby from the mother, and patting it gently on the head, and muttering in a low tone, dipped its head into the bag two or three times, and then returned it to its mother. A white mare was brought up and, after being daubed all over with hand-marks of red ochre, was knocked on the head, cooked, and eaten on the spot, the heart, liver, and lungs being hung on a lance, to the top of which was suspended the bag containing the charms. Care was taken, as in other ceremonies, that no dogs approached to eat the offal, which was buried, the head and backbone being removed to a neighbouring hill.

On the 9th of May we started, arriving the same evening at Margensho, which was, as the Indians had previously described it to me, a large grassy plain lying below a step or barranca, and watered by a brook running N.E. and S.W. During the hunt over the previously described plains there was nothing remarkable except the extreme scarcity of game, skunks alone being numerous; fortunately I killed a male guanaco, and as I had the previous day corrected my page he brought up the horses most carefully, so that all was in readiness for an early start. Before sundown the chiefs were collected, and the contents of the letter read to them; they all appeared pleased, and after adding a postscript setting forth the names and number of the chiefs who required rations I closed the correspondence.

Hinchel came and provided me with tobacco, asking as a favour that if any of his friends in the settlement should enquire if he got drunk when occasion offered in the Pampas, I would bear witness to his sobriety; he also entreated that I would either return to the Indians or remain in Patagones until he arrived, which latter I promised to do.

At the risk of repetition it must be said this man was the best Tehuelche, excepting perhaps Wáki, I ever had anything to do with; he was frank, honest, generous, sober, and in every way fit for a chief; a ready and skilled workman in all Indian trades from breaking a colt to constructing a saddle or silver necklace; his only vice being gambling, but for which last habit he would have been the richest and most powerful chief; as he was universally respected.

Orkeke also sent for me, and put into my hand a packet of tobacco for the journey, which he assured me would be long, tedious, and dangerous. I promised to ask particularly for his ration, and if the Government would not grant it, to make him a present myself. He wished me to return, but I pointed out to him that for various reasons it would be better not, so we parted, agreeing to meet in Patagones.

It may be as well to mention that if the post of chasqui or herald, as he may be styled, be an honourable one, for which as a rule only the near relatives of chiefs are employed, the duties are sufficiently hard. The chasqui is expected to ride like 'young Lochinvar,' as fast and as far each day as the horse will carry him; he must not turn aside or halt even for the purpose of hunting, and unless an ostrich or other game cross his path may have to go without supper after his day's fifty or sixty miles' journey, while his bed and bedding are the ground and mantle. Of course endurance, sobriety, and reliable steadiness of purpose are essential qualifications, especially if the distance to be travelled over be great. And Nacho had always approved himself an excellent chasqui, and was an unerring guide even across the trackless travesia.

When the chasqui falls in with other Indians on the march, or an encampment, he is ceremoniously received and honourably entertained, and it is usually expected that in case of need he will be supplied with fresh horses to prosecute his mission.

The following morning at daylight another consultation took place, and the letter had to be again produced, and another postscriptum added. I then took down in my notebook the immediate requirements of Casimiro and other friends, which, according to agreement, were to be sent back by Meña and Nacho, myself remaining in the settlement until the arrival of Casimiro, when we were to proceed together to Buenos Ayres either by land *viâ* Bahia Blanca, or by steamer.

At about eight o'clock, when the rime of the frost was just cleared off the grass, we, after bidding adieu to all friends, caught our horses and started. I took with me only my suit of clothes in a bag, and the letters. Each of the party was provided with a piece of meat from the guanaco I had slain the previous day by way of provision, and with two horses apiece we were at length *en route*, the old women chanting melodiously to keep the devil out of our way. My page affected great distress at my departure, but as he had my remaining horses to take charge of, and a legacy of a mantle I had no particular use for, having worn it almost without interruption since leaving Santa Cruz, he was, in all probability, delighted to see, as he thought, the last of me as we disappeared over the ridge.

We travelled slowly for the first half hour, and had just released our spare horses from the lazos, which hitherto had restrained them from rejoining their fellows, when we heard a shout behind us, and an Indian appeared driving a troop of horses. He was from the encampment, and being a Pampa was *en route* to join his tribe, whom he expected to meet somewhere about Valchita, five days' journey on, and from whom we were to get fresh horses wherewith to cross the travesia to the settlements. This addition to our party was unexpected, but we considered the more the merrier, and three at any rate is an awkward number to travel sociably together. Putting our horses to a hand canter, we now regularly started, leaving care behind, and looking forward to bread, coffee, and other long untasted good things. We passed the time in talking over what we would get, how we should be received, and in smoking and singing. Our route lay along the barranca, which changed as we proceeded in a N.E. direction, to higher rugged hills interspersed with sandy valleys covered with scrub and incense bushes.

By nightfall we had arrived at a pointed hill, under the brow of which we encamped. We had seen plenty of ostrich and guanaco, but had not delayed to hunt, only pausing to pick up an armadillo that happened to be basking in our road.

On dismounting we secured all the horses with lazes or manéos, as they might probably be inclined to stray away. After gathering a little firewood, kindling a fire, and discussing the armadillo and a small piece of meat each, we wrapped ourselves in our mantles and lay down to sleep, every now and again during the night getting up to have a look at the horses. The morning star was shining brightly above the horizon when we saddled up, and crossing the brow of the hill mounted to an adjoining pampa, where the rocky nature of the ground obliged our unshod horses to go at a foot pace. Added to this a bitter cold wind and small driving rain were not improving to the temper, until after an hour or two of difficult and slow travelling, the sun rose magnificently and dispelled the mists and drizzle, and restored our cheerfulness. We at length descended into a ravine leading to a series of small valleys, containing here and there ponds covered with teal and other water birds. We travelled at a gallop through the same description of country till 5 P.M., when, after passing a high barren plateau, similar to that encountered at starting, we suddenly came to an abrupt declivity, at the bottom of which, in a plain extending for about five miles, lay a large salina.

We descended where it was feasible, and after stopping to get a little salt, proceeded to encamp near a small spring of fresh water. About a mile to the eastward large herds of guanaco and several ostrich were visible in the plain, and near our halting place we found the tracks of a puma, for which we searched diligently, but without success.

After securing our horses, as on the previous night, we dined, minus armadillo, off a piece of scraggy meat, and turned in. The salt from the salina was of excellent quality; it was necessary to remove a little of the upper surface, which had slightly deteriorated by exposure to the atmosphere, and then we cut out cakes of salt like pieces of ice, which served for plates. It is a strange fact that both into this and other salinas small rivulets of fresh water flowed, fed by springs in the neighbouring hills.

The next morning (if it could be so called) at the same hour we were in the saddle, and traversing the plain crossed some ridges of moderate height, and continued passing through a tract of country thickly wooded with incense and other bushes. About 2 P.M. we arrived at a rivulet of water, near which were marks of a recent encampment; after examining these we came to the conclusion that a week had perhaps elapsed since the occupants had left. We travelled forward at our utmost speed over ground of much the same description, diversified now and again by ranges of low hills, putting up occasionally a partridge, of which birds we observed two different species, one crested, and nearly as large as a hen pheasant, and the other smaller than an English bird, and which took only short flights and then cowered—and were fortunate enough to kill a couple.

The sun went down behind some hills, and still we found no suitable place to halt in; at last, however, we came to some ponds of water, where we all, being pretty well tired, dismounted, and tethering two of the horses allowed the remainder to go loose. We found the water brackish, though drinkable, but the animals would scarcely touch it, and wandered about, necessitating a watch on them all night; this was rather weary work, especially as a sharp frost came on, and with all our care, at starting time two horses were missing. After a search of an hour they were found, having wandered in search of better water, and, wiser than ourselves, found out a spring about two miles to the east.

The sun was up before we got away, after warming and eating the last of our food, which we had cooked overnight: it was dry and dusty, and all the washing in the world could not have got the grit out of it; however, we laughed over it, saying we would soon have a bottle of wine to wash away the dirt from our throats. One thing we congratulated ourselves on was being well provided with tobacco, and although we boasted no pipe, mine having been lost at a previous encampment, Casimiro's correspondence with Foyel and Cheoeque, which I had carefully kept, provided us with cigarette papers. We rode on accordingly, rejoicing, and passing out of this wooded country traversed a succession of high pampas, set with small blocks of granite exactly resembling paving stones, and placed as thickly and regularly as if paviors had been at work. The appearance of a London street undergoing repair brought this singular formation vividly to my mind. These pampas terminated in waterworn cliffs thickly strewn with stones, and as our horses scrambled like cats up the slopes, their hoofs sent the stones clattering down, and they found it hard to keep their footing. At the foot of the cliffs were watered valleys, and whilst descending into one of these valleys I noticed for the first time the algarroba thorn, which was in fruit. There were two sorts, one with black fruit, which Nacho warned me not to touch, as it was poisonous, the other bearing yellow pods, which though somewhat dry, as the season was so advanced, we plucked and ate as we rode along, the taste proving something between tamarinds and peach.

Near a lagoon in one of these valleys we halted for a few minutes, and on pursuing our journey espied a horseman with a troop of led horses approaching from the opposite side. I had halted for a moment and saw my companions rein up, and racing up to know the cause, observed him. When within 200 or 300 yards, all halted; and Nacho rode forward, and ceremonious explanations ensued, followed by formal introductions. He was a Pampa Indian outward bound to join those mentioned as having passed us eastward of Margensho; he gave us news that Jackechan's, Teneforo's, and other Indians were in a place called Trinita, some four hours' gallop only distant. When he found that I was 'Anglish,' he spoke in high praise of my countrymen whom he had met in Rio Negro.

This man was a perfect picture; he was splendidly mounted, and had a troop of horses all as good as the one he bestrode. He was well dressed in ponchos and white drawers, and wore a silk handkerchief round his head. Over his saddle was a poncho containing, as we supposed, a store of yerba, flour, or other luxuries, and he had a bold, careless, good-humoured face, with restless eyes; altogether he gave one an idea of the imaginary generous bandits one reads of in novels, and to make the character complete it turned out afterwards that he had almost certainly stolen the horses from Trinita.

After five minutes' conversation we started in opposite directions, and our party pressed on at speed. From the steep hill above the valley we saw, to our joy, the smoke of hunting parties, apparently not far off. However, it was four o'clock when we arrived in the vicinity of the fires in a green pastured valley. From one of the two toldos pitched there, a man emerged with a matè pot in his hand and a bombilia or reed used for imbibing matè, like straws for sherry cobblers, in his mouth. As these people proved not to be the Indians we wanted, after saluting him we galloped on, and crossing the valley, where we had to jump our horses over a brook, ascended the opposite hill. A new growth of bush growing 16 feet high, with long switches like osiers, forced itself unpleasantly on our attention, as, when riding fast, they sprang back into one's face in the most painfully annoying manner. On the hillside we overtook and passed a caravan of women travelling in the same direction as ourselves, and from the summit of the range saw in the valley below two different groups of thirty to forty toldos each, about half a mile apart. Galloping on we arrived, about 5 P.M., at the nearest tolderia; but on inquiring for Patricio, to whom we had been directed to go by Casimiro, found that he belonged to the others, to which we proceeded, and were duly received, our horses, &c., taken care of, and ourselves ushered with all ceremony into the presence of Patricio (a half-bred Pampa and Tehuelche). After the hour's etiquette of answering questions, we were each given one rib of a guanaco apiece to eat. I was so hungry that I could have eaten a dozen at least, so on the plea of washing started off to look for Jackechan's toldo, which I shortly found, and was received with open arms by my friend and El Sourdo. After his 'missus' had given me some food, followed by the luxury of a matè with sugar, Jackechan related his proceedings subsequent to leaving our party.

After a few days' march in the direction of the Chupat, he came across some cattle, which were caught and killed, and then, whilst in the same spot, he despatched the messenger to Chupat with the letter, who returned in fifteen days with an answer, but without any stores.

The letter, carefully wrapped in a piece of old linen which had served as the envelope to my own epistle, was ceremoniously handed to me by the light of a blaze produced by some grease thrown upon the fire. I read and interpreted the contents to Jackechan. The writer—Mr. Hughes, if I recollect rightly—expressed his pleasure at hearing of my safety, but regretted his inability to forward any stores or clothing, as the supply in the colony was extremely scanty, owing to the non-arrival of the ship with Mr. Lewis Jones on board, which had been expected for some months. It need scarcely be said that I had been quite unaware of the privations endured by these unfortunate colonists, which the despatches of Commander Dennistoun have made known to the public during the preparation of these pages for the press, and to which reference will be made in the ensuing chapter. Jackechan, after the return of his messenger, proceeded to Margensho, in the vicinity of which he met the parties under Teneforo, Patricio, Antonio, and other petty chiefs. These all united, and, sending into Patagones, obtained liquor and other stores, with which, as before mentioned, they had a drink for ten days, but no quarrels or fights took place—a fact which redounds to the credit of the chiefs. After waiting a month for our party, they, owing to the scarcity of game, had come by easy stages to this place (Trinita). Jackechan then explained that the first toldos were those of the Pampa Indians, under Teneforo and Champayo, the former being absent in Patagones, getting his rations of animals; his Indians are pure Pampas, and are often called Kerekinches,[1] or armadilloes, for some reason unknown to me. Some of them are in the service of the Argentine Government, and liable to be called upon by Linares, chief of the Tame Indians. The remaining toldos were those belonging to the Indians under Antonio and Patricio, who were composed of mixed Tehuelches and Pampas. The two encampments were situated about half a mile apart, separated by a winding stream, in some places concealed by most unusually high reeds. The position was entirely surrounded on the eastern, southern, and western sides by high rocky eminences; but to the north the valley apparently continued for some miles: its breadth was about three miles, and everywhere in the vicinity of the stream, which in some places had overflowed its banks and formed a marsh, the most luxuriant pasture was growing.

On returning to Patricio's toldo, I formally asked for the necessary horses to prosecute our journey, but was refused on the grounds of his having none to spare; so we determined, as our horses showed symptoms of fatigue and one was lame, to give them one day's rest before proceeding. We passed the following day with our friends, and I made acquaintance with the petty chief Champayo, for whom I wrote a letter requesting a ration which was due to him. He was very civil, and presented an Indian to me named Luiz Aguirre. This man had been brought up in Patagones, whence he had received his names, his parents, I believe, having been killed. He was a very intelligent man, and had formerly been in the troop of Linares, but had left disgusted with the quarrelling and generally mutinous state of those Indians, and taken to the Pampa, where he could live a free and happy life with his wife—at least so he affirmed.

After we had taken various matès together, Champayo, on my mentioning the cause of our not proceeding that day, said, 'Your people shall not want for horses. I will supply them, and send Luiz Aguirre in with you, and you can give him the answer about my ration.' I afterwards visited, at his own request, the Cacique Antonio, for whom I also wrote a letter requesting that his ration should be sent to him at the Guardia of Sauce Blanco, as, owing to having lost his troop of horses in a storm, he could scarcely reach the Upper Guardia. This was true, as at the first toldos we had visited in the neighbouring valley in Trinita we had been informed of Antonio's loss, which was most probably a gain to our well-dressed bandit friend; but he had some enemies on the road to Patagones, which was the real reason of his not going as far as the Upper Guardia.

After dinner, having asked me all about our proceedings, he commenced to give me advice as to what I should do on arriving at Patagones. He assured me that I should get employment readily, but especially cautioned me against drink, as the commandante disliked drunkards, and would not encourage them!

At a late hour I retired to Patricio's toldo, and coiled up in one corner. The next morning we were getting our horses ready for a start, when a boy galloped into camp with the news that people were coming in from Patagones. Everybody at once mounted and went to escort in the new arrivals, who proved to be Teneforo himself and two of his followers. They had brought a hundred head of horses and cattle as far as Valchita, two days' journey from Trinita, and had left them there, bringing on with them only some liquor and yerba, which were at once unloaded. After I had been presented to the newly-arrived chief, who hailed me as a brother, and honoured me by a place among the four caciques, who, pannikins in hand, walked round the lances in due performance of the ceremony of blessing the liquor, already described, the drinking commenced.

When the people arrived the sun had just risen, and by 10 o'clock most of the liquor, which consisted of some gin and caña, or white rum, had disappeared. Many of the Indians were intoxicated, but all after a merry, good-tempered fashion, which it had never been my luck to see before. After imbibing freely enough with my numerous friends—who, if it had been left to them, would have made me as drunk as themselves—I mounted my horse, and after a bathe amongst the tall reeds on the borders of the stream, returned to the toldo, where I found the aged Patricio singing to himself in a very maudlin state. By sundown all were sober again, and Patricio imparted to me that he intended himself to proceed with us, as well as some other friends, his wife, and two or three other women, but that we were to travel by the lower route, which, though longer, was easier and safer than the shorter and upper road, where the thorns grew higher and thicker: the latter is usually selected in summer, when water is scarce, of which at this season there was no danger.

The following morning, bidding adieu to Antonio, Champayo, and Jackechan—whose ration I had promised to procure—we started, eleven men and four women, taking plenty of horses, besides a troop of mares for an Indian called Hernandez, settled near the Guardia Chica, the mares being intended for the purpose of treading out his crop of corn. We were soon out of sight of the encampment at Trinita, and proceeding at either a gallop or a trot through an undulating country, in which incense, algarroba, and other shrubs abounded, arrived near sunset at a stream, on the north side of which we encamped, amongst some thick bushes. A little distance to the west lay a large salina, from which, several miles across, the place takes its name, being called Hitchin-kaik, or Salt Hill. The stream flows round one side of the salina, and is, I think, the same that we subsequently crossed near Valchita. This time we travelled in great style, the women having brought with them stores of horse-meat and yerba.

After dinner we all sat round the fire and took a matè, and some of an Indian sweetmeat, a yellow paste made from the algarroba bean pounded and mixed with water. Old Patricio, who had turned over a new leaf and grown quite frisky after the drink, said that I was a fortunate man, having a wife with me; alluding to one of the wives of the Cacique El Ingles, who was travelling with us to rejoin her husband near Patagones.

The following morning at daylight we again started, and, travelling over much the same description of country as on the previous day, arrived, about mid-day, at the place where Teneforo had left his cattle. Here we dismounted and refreshed ourselves off the round berries, about the size of a turnip-radish, the fruit of a small plant growing by the margin of the water, which had a very pleasant taste. The river here had a fringe of tussocks of pampa grass, under which we reclined and smoked.

The cattle were grouped about amongst these tussocks, and Golwin, Jackechan's son with the light hair, amused himself by vain attempts to count them. After half an hour's dawdling we proceeded, leaving behind one of Meña's horses which was done up, and, following more or less the line of the river, we arrived, about 3 P.M., at the encampment of Valchita. As it was early in the day, some of the party started to hunt, but returned empty-handed. We filled up the skins and water-bottles, in anticipation of entering the travesia the following day; and, after the usual meal and matè, sought out each his own particular nest in the Pampa grass, and went to sleep without fear of the horses straying far, the pasture and water both being of the best quality. As it was in this encampment that, according to Casimiro, the defunct Mendoza had discovered gold, I prospected carefully for any signs, but only noticed that parts of the adjoining pampa were strewn, amongst other pebbles, with pieces of quartz. At the usual hour we started to commence the ascent to the travesia, or desert, which rose above us to the north, in a high plateau. On ascending a short distance, we observed on our left hand (to the westward) a salina of several leagues in length, which bordered the edge of the travesia in about an east or west direction. I am inclined to think that the river Valchita loses itself in this salina. This river is subject to great floods, evidences of which were visible in the drift weeds and rubbish clinging to the bushes and shrubs throughout the valley, evidently left there by the spring inundation. By a gradual ascent we at length reached the level of the plateau, and saw before us an interminable dreary expanse strewn with small shingle, and covered with shrubs varying from four to twelve feet, or even higher, and here and there small tufts of grass. No signs of life were visible. The sky was bright and clear, although clouds were gathering on the southern horizon, and the wind (it nearly always blows in Patagonia) was cutting. I remarked to Luiz Aguirre that it would possibly rain; his reply, 'I hope it will—it will be splendid, then all the lagoons will be full,' told of the danger of drought, but found no assent from me, having had enough of wet weather during the excursion to Las Manzanas. During the ride he told me that he knew the difference between the Catholic and Protestant religions, and of the two he preferred the latter; he also asked me if I had ever been to China, where the tea came from, and various other questions evincing a considerable amount of information; and wound up by proposing that I should set up a trading establishment near the Chupat; Jackechan—who, if anyone can claim it, is the real lord of the soil—having volunteered to cede the ground to me. In the event of establishing a store in that neighbourhood, this astute Indian considered that all the Indian trade would be taken out of the hands of the people of Patagones, who notoriously used false weights, besides charging exorbitantly for all articles supplied to the Indians.

About 2 P.M., as the rough shingle had already begun to tell on our horses' feet, a halting place was found near a laguna containing rain-water of the colour of *café au lait*. The horses were for the present let loose, to pick up the best meal they could off the stunted grass near the borders of the lagoon. Before dark most of them were tethered, and a careful watch kept all night, lest they should return to Valchita in search of pasture and water. After a lengthened conversation by the fireside—in which I was informed that the track we were travelling was called Pig's-road, from wild pigs, or perhaps peccaries, having been killed near one of the lagoons in the route—we wrapped ourselves in our mantles and sheltered ourselves like hedgehogs under the bushes, from time to time getting up to look round for the horses. Next day we rode over the same interminable desert of stones, and bushes of the following descriptions:— Chañal or whitethorn; picayun, furnishing the best firewood; the osier-like switches before described; black bush, which is useless for burning, owing to the pestiferous smell it emits; algarroba, incense, which are, however, very scarce; and some others whose names I was unable to procure. The chañal is the only one that impedes the traveller's progress, as the thorns are large and sharp. In the other road (more to the west), which we had avoided, although the distance is shorter across the travesia, and therefore more used by the Tehuelches, who dread this crossing, especially in summer or for small parties, the chañal grows to the height of ten to fifteen feet, and, like the 'waitabit' thorns in Albania, renders fast riding impossible.

This day we were about to start hunting, when a demijohn of rum was discovered in a bush. This put an end to the sport, for, although it was hidden again in another place, enough was taken out to render most of the party talkative, a bottle or two also being reserved for discussion at the camp fire.

At 4 P.M. we camped by the side of a lagoon similar to the previous one, and, our Valchita water being finished, diluted the rum with meal and water about the consistency of Spanish chocolate. I forgot to state that in the excitement of the 'find' the horses were not looked after, and on mustering to proceed, one of Nacho's had disappeared, and, although carefully searched for, he was not found again.

The next day, despite the dissipations over night, we were in the saddle at daybreak, and had hardly traversed a league of this wearisome waste when we came suddenly upon seven wild horses. An effort made to surround them failed, owing to the difficult nature of the ground; but the failure was to me fully made up by the magnificent spectacle of these splendid creatures careering in their untamed strength and beauty across the plain.

We subsequently hunted and killed guanaco and ostrich, and also saw some hares and partridges. At about 10 A.M. our eyes were gladdened by the sight of the sea, and presently the level plain rose into more undulating country, and from the crests of the elevations at times a full view of the inlet called the Laco de San Antonio presented itself.

Smoke was visible ahead, and we accordingly pushed on, and made a long and rapid march, the surface being here altogether free from the small stones which had previously caused so much damage to the horses' feet. That night we halted, as usual, by the side of a lagoon, the water of which was not more than two inches deep.

Patricio during this day's journey pointed out to me a dry lagoon near which efforts had been made to sink a well for obtaining a permanent supply of water, but, although the shaft was of some depth, none had been reached, and the work had been given up in despair. It is a mystery even to the Indians where the guanacos, wild horses, puma, and other game that exist in this desert, find water, as these lagoons, depending entirely on the rainfall for a supply of water, must inevitably, in this country where little rain falls, be dry for many months in the year. No doubt springs exist in hitherto undiscovered places.

Before leaving the travesia, a few remarks, which cannot claim to be called a description, may be interesting.

This desert consists of a plateau about three hundred feet above the level of the valley of the Rio Negro, stretching to the southward more than thirty leagues to Valchita. Of its extent westward I have no precise information; but it narrows considerably in the interior, forming an irregular triangle, with its base on the coast, and its apex near the junction of the Rio Limay and the northern streams.

The soil is either clay or sand and gravel, with small stones strewn thickly over the surface; while the only vegetation met with consists of the bushes already mentioned, and scanty tufts of coarse grass.

It is much dreaded by travellers, and, after traversing it, I can well believe the stories current of people having perished on the passage; the track once lost would be very difficult to regain; while the want of water in the summer, and the danger of horses straying and leaving the traveller helpless, are both probable risks. With all our watchfulness, two horses strayed away and were lost. In the winter there is no fear of want of water; but the fatigue of travelling is at all times great, and the horses are almost worn out by the time that the desert is passed. It serves, therefore, as a barrier, protecting Patagones from all danger of attack by the Indians from the south, who in their forays must descend the river. A large troop of horses can scarcely find pasture, and, after the rapid journey, would not be in a condition for their riders to attack with success, if opposed vigorously by people able to defend themselves.

This district appeared to form a distinct and well-defined limit between the habitats of various animals; as for instance, the Rhea Darwinii, or smaller ostrich of Patagonia, and the Rhea Americana. The latter, according to my experience, is never found to the south of it, and I am at a loss to understand how Mr. Cunningham could have met with any specimens of it, as he seems to imply.[2]

The Tehuelches often described the larger Rhea as found north of the travesia, and as distinct from that hunted in their country. They also particularly insisted on the fact that the Gama, or deer—abundant in the Rio Negro valley and the country north of it—is never met with south of the travesia. The same remark is true of the Viscacha and the Aguarra (Lupus manatus), though the latter is probably to be met with in the spurs of the Cordillera.

Patagonia may thus be properly considered as cut off by the Rio Negro and the line of the Cordillera, and possessing its own races and a separate Fauna and Flora.

It may be added that only one species of armadillo, the Quirquincho (Dasypus minutus, Gay), occurs within these limits. The algarroba and other bushes, though found in and near the borders of the travesia, do not occur south of its immediate vicinity.

It was a joyful hour for all when, on the fourth day, after galloping from dawn till ten o'clock, we at length came in sight of the valley, still three miles distant, where large willows—which, by the way, are unknown in Patagonia, save a few at Chupat, probably introduced by the settlers—marked the winding course of the Rio Negro. We halted at the head of an abra, or lateral opening which ran up into the barranca from the main valley, and saw in the distance a solitary rancho, the first civilized dwelling beheld since my departure from Santa Cruz.

After a rest, to enable all to come up, some having lagged behind perforce, their horses being hardly able to limp along, we made our way down the slope and at length reached the river, in which our thirsty steeds soon drank their fill.

The rancho, which belonged to Hernandez, for whom the convoy of mares was intended, was then visited. The owner was absent, but his Indian wife did the honours, at least as far as serving us with matè, for no food was produced, though all were dreadfully hungry. I wished to stop and don what an American would call my citizen's clothes, thinking that we should immediately proceed to the Guardia I had heard so much of from Luiz Aguirre; but he told me not to be in a hurry, so in my dirty mantle I remained for the present.

After half an hour's delay we left the rancho and followed the south bank of the river, which here was a swift stream 200 yards wide, passing the farm of Hernandez, where a man was occupied in ploughing, and mares and cattle were grazing. The river here made a bend towards the southern barranca, which so nearly abutted on it as to compel us to ride close along the bank. Small partridges got up frequently, and I made a mental resolution to come and have a day's shooting at a future period in the magnificent willows bordering the river; blue pigeons were cooing in the trees; and through an opening we caught a glimpse, on the opposite bank, of a well-built, comfortable-looking estancia in the foreground of a wide extent of rich flat land, with corral, galpones, and the usual surroundings, which Luiz Aguirre informed me belonged to Mr. Kincaid. The feeling of having safely emerged from the desert into the settlements put us, though very hungry, into the best of spirits; and after a cheerful half hour's ride, passing on our road a tumbledown, unused rancho, we arrived at Sauce Blanco, or 'White Willow;' there the river, sweeping to the northern side, leaves a wide rincon, or expanse of rich alluvial ground. This is considered as belonging to the Indians, some of whom are always to be found encamped near the rancho, which belonged to the Cacique El Ingles, and three toldos were pitched in its vicinity.

We presented to the chief his wife, whom we had brought with us, and I was warmly welcomed as a relative, the cacique being a nephew of Quintuhual. This chief derives his name from his alleged relationship to some one or other of the officers of Fitzroy's surveying expedition, so that I was doubly welcome in my English and Indian character. Here we camped amongst the pajas, or pampa grass, and, having been presented with a mare and some pumpkins, soon had a good fire blazing and meat and pumpkins cooking; these latter being dressed by cutting them in halves, taking out the seeds, and filling the interior with hot ashes, and then placing them on the ashes, the result being, at all events as it seemed then to my taste, delicious. I wished to proceed direct to the Guardia, but, as Patricio and the others put it off till the morrow, in my ignorance of the road and usages of the place, I was forced to 'do at Rome as Rome does.'

A good wash in the river was one of the first things indulged in, and the enjoyment of getting rid of several days' accumulation of the dust and mud of the travesia can be better imagined than described.

The following morning, before daylight, we all bathed in the river, and after taking matè with the cacique El Ingles, and a warm by the fireside after sleeping in the frosty night air, we prepared to visit the Guardia. Casting off the Indian mantle, I assumed the usual dress of an Englishman of the period, shooting-coat, &c.; and having been provided with fresh horses by our friend, half an hour's gallop brought us to the north bank, opposite the Guardia—not, however, without misadventure, for as we made our way along the narrow uneven horse-path, full of ruts, and hemmed in by Pampa grass, Luiz Aguirre's horse stumbled and threw him, rolling over him and crushing his revolver into his ribs.

The mean appearance of the much talked of Guardia at once dispelled the ideas of it derived from the imaginative descriptions of the Indians, but previous experience of Spanish frontier towns saved me from disappointment. The settlement consists of a small fort mounted with one gun, a cuartel or barracks, and a few houses, one or two built of brick and the others of adobe, clustering round the fort. Almost, if not quite all, of these are 'pulperias,' or grog-shops and stores, intended for trade with the Indians, for whose transport a launch is kept. The usual object first seen in frontier towns—an unfinished church—is, here conspicuous by its absence, no provision for spiritual wants being made in the Guardia. After about half an hour's delay on the bank, a bustle on the other side was observed, caused by getting ready a large launch, which shortly crossed to our side; and having secured our horses with lazos and manéos, we jumped in, and I was greeted by a non-commissioned officer, who congratulated me on my arrival, stating that the Commandante, Señor Murga, had been expecting me for some months. We crossed over in great pomp, a soldier playing the cornet in the bows of the boat, and, landing, we proceeded to a store kept by a man named Don Fermin, where we were all ushered into a room behind the shop, and the Indians exposed their skins and plumes for trade. My friend the non-commissioned officer had left me, as I declined to surrender my letters to anyone but the Commandante in person, and he was at the time at Patagones, distant eighteen leagues from this Guardia. Meanwhile I watched the trade going on between Don Fermin and the Indians.

Now and again people came and contemplated us, as if we were some strange sort of wild animals; but as I was out of the trading, no one bid the stranger welcome, and I formed a bad idea of the politeness of the inhabitants, though perhaps my shaggy hair and dress, not altogether of the neatest, may have been against me.

The Indians were soon in full enjoyment of some grog and biscuits, which they naturally asked me to share. After a bite and a sup, finding the proceedings slow, I left the room, and shortly after met Mr. Alexander Fraser and Mr. Grenfell, the owners of an estancia a few miles lower down the river; and after introducing myself was most kindly received, and supplied with cash, a civilised medium of which I had not a sou to enable me to gratify the desire of treating my Indian friends to a bottle or two of wine and spirits and a few loaves of bread.

Mr. Fraser hospitably pressed me to come on to his establishment at once, but being desirous of handing the letters to the Commandante without delay, I returned across the river with the Indians.

A foretaste of Rio Negro manners was given us at the other side, as one of the horses, saddle, lazo and all, was missing—stolen by some of the civilised inhabitants. The horse belonged to El Ingles, and had been lent to Meña to go down from the encampment to the Guardia; the lazo belonged to me.

At the camp most of the people got more or less drunk, and Nacho received a richly-deserved thrashing for being pugnacious, after which he was lashed down, and left to cool in the frost for an hour.

In the morning I started for Patagones, accompanied by El Ingles and another Indian; but as our horses proved to be too tired to proceed into Patagones, we stopped for the night in a toldo at San Xaviel, the head-quarters of Linares and his Tame Indians.

I took up my quarters at the toldo of one Chaloupe, and after supper, being desirous of communicating the political arrangements to the chief, proceeded on horseback behind another horseman, who proved to be a brother of Rouque Pinto, to the chief's residence, a long low house.

After a little delay I was ushered into the Sala, where the two wives of the chief were sitting sewing. The usual matè was served, and I waited long in vain for the chief, who was away collecting his followers for an intended pursuit of some of Calficura's Indians, who had recently driven off cattle from the valley.

At last I bade good-night to my fair hostesses, and summoning my companion, who had been taking matè in the kitchen, set out to return. We had scarcely proceeded a hundred yards when the tramp of approaching horsemen was heard, and my companion enjoined strict silence, for fear of 'accidents,' and reined up our steeds under the shadow of some trees, till we heard the people pass. When their voices had died away in the distance we proceeded, and resumed our conversation, in the course of which he informed me that it was unsafe to meet people at night in this vicinity unless when well armed. I rather opened my eyes at this, and moralised considerably on the benefits conferred by civilisation on Indian races. At Chaloupe's toldo I found Antonio Linares, brother of the chief, who had brought with him a bottle of brandy, over a glass of which I told him my business, which he promised to forward, and after a nightcap he left in search of more boon companions. This young fellow was very well dressed in cloth ponchos and chiripas, leather boots and clean linen, and wore a revolver in his belt. He playfully informed me that he had been in search of some one he had quarrelled with all the afternoon, and would have shot him if he had found him.

Mrs. Chaloupe made me up a luxurious bed with ponchos and my own saddle gear, and indeed all the inmates of the toldo showed me the greatest civility.

At an early hour in the morning I started on my now jaded horse in the hopes of seeing Linares, but on arriving at his house was informed that he had already left for Carmen to have an interview with the Commandante, Señor Murga.

Refusing the proffered matè, I hastened on and speedily overtook him taking a stirrup cup at a friend's house. After introducing myself and joining in a social glass, I was glad to avail myself of his companionship, as our routes lay in the same direction, and transact my business on the road.

An hour's ride brought us in sight of Patagones, at which point I diverged from my companion to the chacra or farm of my expected host Don Pablo Piedra Buena, situated on the river bank. Half an hour's ride brought me to the house, but finding no one at home, with the exception of a big bull dog, I soon started in search, and shortly came on two men occupied in ploughing. After the usual salutations I inquired for Don Pablo, and was very civilly answered that he was shortly expected at the farm, but that if I went straight to Patagones I should probably meet him on the way. Accordingly, being very desirous of some breakfast, I spurred my horse into a gallop, and rode towards the town. Its aspect, as viewed from a distance, although it appeared rather irregular, was tolerably imposing; the fort and buildings on the northern bank, which are situated on a rise, showing out prominently, whilst on the southern shore the cathedral (unfinished, of course) and English mission station were the most noticeable buildings. After making a slight détour through ignorance of the track, I arrived at the immediate vicinity of the southern suburb, which, like all Spanish settlements, new or old, failed to bear a close inspection.

An extensive mud-hole, which a fall of rain would probably render impassable, bordered the outskirts, which, when reached, were found to be plentifully strewn with offal, heaps of bricks, and other *débris*, making it incumbent carefully to pick one's way along the paths.

As I had heard that it was possible the Commandante would come over to the south side to arrange about a race, I visited a pulperia, indicated as a likely place to learn his whereabouts, where I found Linares and his capitanejo (adjutant) taking a glass of brandy, and was introduced by them to the proprietor, Don José Real, who offered his services, and informed me that Commandante Murga was expected in about half an hour. I accordingly proceeded to the mission station, where, having introduced myself to Dr. Humble, I left my now tired horse in his quinta, and after a short rest returned to José Real's, and found the Commandante Murga, to whom I presented the letter from Casimiro and my own letter of introduction.

At first sight I was not prepossessed in favour of Señor Murga; he was about the middle height, dressed in Garibaldi shirt, uniform trousers and boots, and casquette with the lace bands denoting the rank of colonel. He disposed of my business by saying that he would attend to it 'mañana,' to-morrow, which is the answer to everything in the provinces of La Plata, and evidently dismissing the subject from his mind, resumed an argument with Don José about a race horse.

This Colonel Murga is addicted to field-sports of every description, is a good rider, in fact a perfect gaucho, and rarely misses a cockfight on Sunday after mass.

Somewhat disgusted with my reception I proceeded to the boatman's house with the intention of crossing the river to the north side, and knocking at the door asked in Spanish for Solomon. It was opened by a well-dressed woman, and inside I perceived a broad-shouldered, well-built man at his breakfast. I was about to retire with apologies, when he recognised me for an Englishman, and guessing who I was, immediately dragged me in and seated me at the table, whilst the good wife cut slices of bread and butter and brewed more tea. I was considerably hungry, as the Americans say, and enjoyed the bread and butter and tea as I never enjoyed a meal anywhere else. The kind, honest welcome of this Welsh family will always remain as a pleasant remembrance to me of Patagones.

Leaving the house with Solomon we met Don Pablo, who was equally hearty in his welcome, and we proceeded across in his company to the northern shore, where my friend placed his house at my disposal, and I took up my quarters with him; and after the necessary ablutions, and the reduction of a twelvemonth's growth of hair to a decent length, got into a new suit of clothes which were brought from Señor Aguirre's store, and felt that I was a civilised Cristiano once more.

That afternoon I was introduced by Don Pablo to several of his relations, who were all most kind and amiable, and their agreeable society dispelled the thoughts which I had entertained of returning to the Indians; instead of which I now determined to send Meña and Nacho out with the answers to the letters and some stores, and wait in Patagones until the arrival of the rest, employing the interval in reconnoitring the place and studying its chances in the future.

1. Quirquincho
2. *Natural History of the Straits of Magellan*, p.134

IX

THE RIO NEGRO SETTLEMENTS

AS it did not at the time occur to me that the rising settlements of the Rio Negro could have escaped being fully described already, I must candidly confess that the duty of keeping a diary was neglected during my stay; and recollections alone have furnished the materials for what has been peremptorily urged on me as a necessary supplement to my travels—a description of Patagones. This name, which seems intended to designate the future capital of Patagonia, has completely usurped the place of the original title El Carmen, conferred on this settlement in honour of Nuestra Señora del Carmen, under whose patronage it was placed.

The modern town, situated on a bend of the Rio Negro, about eighteen miles from the sea, consists of two parts separated by the river, here about 450 yards wide: the older and most important on the northern bank, where the authorities and principal people reside, and a new suburb on the southern bank, known as El Merced, which, though of recent growth, threatens to eventually rival the northern portion. The means of communication between the two is supplied by ferry-boats, which are procurable at almost all hours.

On the northern beach a wooden pier has been erected, opposite his store, by Señor Aguirre, the grand capitalist, banker, and factotum of the place, to allow the steamer to unload with greater facility. It is probable that the northern side will continue to preserve its importance for some time to come, owing to the want of equal facilities for landing goods on the other side, where at low tide an extensive mudbank is exposed, which has to be passed to reach the shore.

The position selected for Carmen by the founder combined security with easy access to the river. The barranca at this spot advances as it were to meet the river bend, and leaving but a narrow intervening space. A rather steep hill rises to a plateau, which again to the north, or rear of the town, falls by a step to the level of the pampa. The crest is crowned by the fort, and up the declivity climbs the town, laid out with scrupulous adherence to the prescribed pattern, the regularity of its streets and cuadros not being, however, very perceptible to a stranger, owing to the formation of the ground. Next to the fort, the most prominent buildings are the Commandante's house, a pretentious red brick building, and the old church of Nuestra Señora del Carmen, an insignificant edifice, both situated a little below the crest of the hill, and under the wings as it were of the fort.

The fort itself, crowning the crest of the hill, or barranca, is of imposing appearance when viewed at a distance, but a closer inspection dispels the illusion, and reveals its utter uselessness for defensive purposes. The walls are in wretched repair, and the whole edifice is so decayed that when one of the American gunboats stationed in the Rio de la Plata visited the place some four years ago, and duly saluted the Argentine colours, the reverberation of the discharge of her big gun shook down a portion of the wall fronting the river! The armament consists of a few field pieces of small calibre mounted *en barbette*, and of very little use, as a single well-directed shell would demolish the whole structure; but if advantage were taken of the position for the construction of a substantial battery mounted with modern artillery, the approaches to the town from all sides could be thoroughly commanded and easily defended.

The Plaza or square lies immediately behind the fort, which forms one side, and some comfortable houses are situated in it, several of which, however, were only in course of construction. The condition of the streets is very bad, especially those descending the hill to the river-bank; in some places the pedestrian sinks ankle deep in sand, and in others stumbles over rugged masses of sandstone. The pleasantest part of the town is the street running from the pier and store inland round the base of the hill: here a considerable tract of low land stretching from the rear of the houses on the eastern side to the river is laid out in gardens, or quintas, full of all kinds of fruit trees, backed by a row of tall poplars fringing the waterside.

One of these houses was the hospitable abode of my esteemed friend Don Pablo Piedra Buena. It was a long low house, built of sun-dried bricks and whitewashed. We occupied one end, consisting of three rooms, the next part being occupied by Don Ramirez, captain of the steam transport Choelechel (at anchor within hail, off the Quinta), and his wife. The remainder was tenanted by Don Domingo, an Italian, as a restaurant and hotel. Besides Don Domingo's hostelry, the town boasted another hotel, the property of Señor Aguirre, situated close to his store and pier, a fine well-built stone house, the only one of that material I observed in Patagones, almost all the other edifices being of brick, except in the Negro quarter of the town, where they were simple adobe houses. Whatever their material, many of the buildings in all parts of the town were, like the fort, in a most tumbledown condition, and a freer use of whitewash would, if the inhabitants only knew it, cover a multitude of sins, both against external decency and internal cleanliness.

On the southern shore a considerable tract of low land extends from the river, and is liable to be overflowed at high spring tides. This is devoted to the cultivation of wheat, ditches being cut to afford imperfect drainage; across these flats a causeway—the construction of which is chiefly due to the exertions of my friend the Welsh boatman Solomon—leads to the new town of El Merced, built on the higher ground, beyond the reach of floods. This, too, is laid out on the universal plan, and judging from the piles of brick and the numerous sites marked out for future houses, is rapidly growing in size and importance. The roads, however, were at the time of my visit as execrable as on the north side, and the outskirts were offensive with offal and rubbish, while the pantaño or mud-hole seemed to present an impassable barrier to friend or foe. The most noticeable buildings were—first, the new Church of Señora del Merced, in the Plaza, which, with its two towers, quite threw into the shade its elder rival del Carmen, on the northern side; and next the English Mission Station, a considerable building occupying two sides of a square, one wing containing the room used as a chapel, whilst the other constituted the residence and dispensary of the missionary, Rev. Dr. Humble. This gentleman, whose hospitality I frequently enjoyed, combined in his own person the functions of doctor and clergyman. As regards the mission, the converts did not appear to be numerous; indeed an Indian girl, who acted as servant and nurse, seemed to be the only specimen. The whole establishment was scrupulously neat and clean, and afforded an agreeable contrast to the surrounding buildings. In front a considerable tract of ground extended to the river bank, part of which constituted a pleasant garden, or quinta, the remainder being used for grazing the horses of the establishment, whilst a ditch cut at the lower end afforded a harbour for the medical missionary's boat.

Dr. Humble formerly had a school for children, but it was given up, I believe, on account of the opposition raised by the Padre. The church was generally pretty full on Sundays, when the British flag is hoisted to denote the hour of prayer; and as half the service was conducted in Spanish, a good sprinkling of the native inhabitants was generally present—some perhaps with a view to obtain advice from the pastor in his medical capacity, in which his skill and kindness made him deservedly popular.

According to Sir Woodbine Parish, the population of Patagones in 1832 amounted to no more than 800: although no statistical means of accurate information were at my disposal, I should be inclined to estimate the present number of inhabitants at not less than 2,000, and they may exceed that number.

They are divided into four very distinctly-defined classes:—1st. The descendants of the original and early Spanish settlers; 2ndly. The more recent foreign immigrants; 3rdly. The negroes; and 4thly. The convicts sent hither from the Argentine Republic. The descendants of the original settlers, who for some unknown reason are styled by their townsmen 'Malagatos,' both in name and character manifest their unmixed descent from the sturdy Gallegos, or settlers from Galicia. Closely united by intermarriage, they form, as it were, one family, almost every member of which is either a Crespo or a Real. Although hitherto jealously exclusive as regards any admixture of their 'sangre azul' by alliance with the foreigners—except perhaps Englishmen—the men are remarkable for their hospitable kindness and courtesy, whilst the ladies would vie with those of any part of Old Spain or the Argentine provinces in grace of manners or beauty. One noticeable feature of their character was that both men and women manifested a far more punctilious respect for religion than I had ever observed in other Catholic countries. Every one made it a point of being present at mass whenever it was celebrated. I was among the guests when Don Benito Crespo was entertaining a party at dinner, given to celebrate his daughter's birthday, which happened to fall during the period of the novena in honour of Santa Rosa, and when the bell sounded for vespers everybody rose from table and hurried off to the church.

The second part of the population—the foreigners—present a motley group of people of all nations, but the majority are Italians and Basque Spaniards. There are a few French, English, Welsh, Swiss, and Germans.

The negroes are the descendants of an importation of slaves, introduced when the slave trade was legal by the Governor, a Frenchman named Viba, Casimiro's patron, who appears to have entertained an idea of employing them to cultivate the public lands. They all live together in one quarter of the town—excepting, of course, those who go out as servants—and keep up many old traditions and customs. They are called by the Gauchos 'Blandequis,' which may be a corruption of Mandingo, and are a fine hard-working race, whose industrious habits and general character differ widely from the debased type of the negroes in the Brazils. Their exact numbers I am ignorant of, but was informed that they were once very much more numerous, their rapid decrease being caused by their being drawn as soldiers, and the ravages of the universal scourge of smallpox.

Lastly comes the convict element. Carmen, at an early period of its history, was made a 'presidio,' or frontier penal settlement, in this respect resembling Punta Arenas; but the strict discipline of the Chilian colony is altogether wanting in Patagones. There is a constant importation to the latter place of deserters from the army, robbers, and felons of every description, sent down from Buenos Ayres. These men are, on their arrival, either enlisted as soldiers, or turned loose on society, and allowed to work where and how they please, or otherwise obtain a livelihood. They cannot, it is true, escape, as there is no chance of getting away by sea, and the almost certain danger of death or captivity amongst the Pampa Indians is a sufficient safeguard against their betaking themselves to the interior; but beyond this there is no restraint exercised. Horse-stealing is, in the event of any animal being left unwatched, a moral certainty, and robberies of all kinds are frequent and go almost unpunished; while murder, in the rare cases in which the criminals are detected, simply involves being sent back to Buenos Ayres for a trial, which results in a sentence of transportation back to the Rio Negro. One man named Ruiz was pointed out as having been four times backward and forward to and from Buenos Ayres for murders committed: this man openly boasted that whenever he wanted a trip he had to kill a man. Another man, who had robbed the Bishop of Buenos Ayres of a jewelled clock, by presentation of a forged order, filled the position of billiard marker at the hotel, and was looked on as rather a clever fellow. The Commandante's orderly was also a man sent down for homicide. The state of society when these ruffians—every one of whom carries a knife, which is used on the slightest occasion—are allowed thus to remain loose may be better imagined than described.

My friend Don Pablo was attacked one evening close to his house, but fortunately escaped unhurt. Murder is of weekly occurrence, and it is necessary for everyone to carry some weapon of self-defence, while few people think of leaving the town without a revolver.

In the utter absence of legal protection, a project was mooted among some of the foreigners to establish a vigilance committee on the simple principle of mutual protection and agreement to avenge any injury to one of the society. As Sir Lucius consoled his friend by the remark that there is 'snug lying in the abbey,' the unprotected inhabitants of Patagones can pride themselves on their possessing an excellent new cemetery, situated to the north, about half a mile outside the town, which is surrounded by a brick wall, with iron gates, and kept in a neat and orderly condition. A little east of it, nearer the town, lies the old cemetery, the neglected state of which, when I visited it, offered a melancholy contrast: the mud wall was breached in many places; coffins appeared protruding from the sand, and in some cases were actually uncovered; skulls and bones lay exposed to view; and, as a climax, a cat jumped out of one coffin in which she had taken up her abode. I was extremely surprised at such want of respect being shown by the residents to the bones of their departed ancestors, and remarked on it to my companion, who shrugged his shoulders and muttered something which sounded like the inevitable 'Mañana.'

The most interesting relics of the first founders of the colony are a number of caves, or dwellings, excavated in the sandstone cliff, four miles below the town; they contain three or four chambers, leading into each other, and from eight to ten feet square. In one I remarked a sort of trough, hollowed out in the sandstone, which more resembled a manger than anything else. Tradition narrates that these were used as dwellings by the first settlers, or perhaps as hiding-places for themselves, or for their cattle, in times of war with the Indians.

Under the Spanish dominion the colony made but slow progress, notwithstanding the abandonment of all other attempted settlements on the Patagonian coast, which left the entire advantages to be derived from the valuable whale and seal fisheries in the hands of the people of Carmen; their inertness allowed this mine of wealth to remain unworked, and it fell into the hands of English and American fishermen, who worked them till a recent period. The Argentine Government has asserted its claim and granted a lease of the fisheries to Don Luiz Buena, with authority to warn off all intruders; but the fisheries do not, I fear, produce the profit deserved by his energy. The Carmen settlers alternately traded with, and were plundered by the Indians, preferring the profits of this doubtful commerce to the dangerous, though profitable, sealing and whaling. That the Indians' hostility had something to do with the concentration of the Spanish forces at the Rio Negro appears from a fact which has been studiously omitted from the Spanish records. The Indians preserve an accurate tradition to the effect that the first colonists at Port Desire aroused the anger of the natives, who made a successful attack: the colonists retreated into the church, where every soul perished at the hands of the natives. The buildings and fruit-trees still existing are the only monuments of the destruction of this colony.

From the time that the South American colonies asserted their independence, Patagones shared in the consequent increase of population and development of trade, as already pointed out. Since Sir W. Parish wrote, the population has largely increased and the value of property risen; and although the 'old inhabitants' complained to me of the want of progress, the growing demand and price given for land and houses at that time, compared with former years, proved the contrary. One item of its history must not be omitted. During the war between the Brazilians and the Argentine Confederation, the inhabitants of Patagones distinguished themselves by defeating and capturing a Brazilian expedition sent to endeavour to reduce the place. The story was told me as follows:—A strong force of the Brazilians landed near the sea-coast, and marched overland towards Carmen, halting about a league north of the town. The garrison, numbering about fifty regulars and some volunteers, sallied out, equipped with a large assortment of coloured ponchos. Taking up a position behind a hill which concealed them from the enemy, who were ignorant of their real strength, the cunning men of Carmen then displayed themselves as if for a reconnaissance, and retreated, but only to change their ponchos and reappear as a fresh detachment; the enemy was thus led by these repeated feints and transformations to considerably multiply the real numbers of the

Argentine troops, and hesitate to attack so seemingly large a force. After nightfall the herbage in the neighbourhood of the bivouac of the invading army was set on fire. Bewildered by the smoke, the Brazilians retreated, but were encountered by other fires in their rear, and, seeing themselves apparently surrounded and opposed by superior numbers, their leader capitulated. The story is substantiated by the existence of the wreck of a Brazilian man-of-war, still visible in the river.

The fertile valley of the Rio Negro must needs be described in order to convey a proper idea of the resources of Patagones as a colony. By far the greater extent of this valley is as uncultivated as when it was first explored by Don Basilio Villarino, who, under the orders of Viedma, ascended the river in order to ascertain its source, and whose diary is extant in the collection of De Angelis, a valuable abstract of it having been given by Sir W. Parish, though sufficiently long ago in our rapid age to be almost forgotten. He ascended with launches first as far as the Island of Choelechel, seventy leagues from Carmen, which he recommended should be fortified as an advance post against the Indians; thence, after incredible difficulties, he succeeded in reaching the foot of the Cordillera, always keeping on good terms with the natives. Here he met with the Araucanians (termed by me Manzaneros), and was in great hopes of reaching Valdivia through their aid, as they showed themselves friendly disposed; when, unfortunately, the Indians fell out amongst themselves, one of the chiefs being killed in the mêlée. The chief who caused this man's death came with his people to the Spaniards to implore their assistance, which was promised. This led to the whole of the remaining Indians forming a league and declaring war against the Spaniards, whose name up to the present they detest. Being obliged to abandon his intention of reaching Valdivia, Villarino reluctantly determined to return, and accordingly, after being supplied by his allies with a store of apples and piñones, descended the river and returned to Carmen.

From the description of this journey, together with the mention of the supplies of apples and piñones obtained at the farthest point reached, I am inclined to assume that this point was near, if not identical with, the place where we passed the Limay on our journey to Las Manzanas, a mile or two below the rapids where Mr. Cox was wrecked.

Villarino states that he entered in his small boat a channel where the river flowed over rounded stones to the S.W. Now the point where Mr. Cox's boat was lost was a rapid to all appearance impassable for a boat: however, it is possible that Villarino employed Indians on horseback to track his boat, and that the state of the river was more favourable for navigation at the period of his visit.

The mention of the friendly Indians who accompanied him on his return and settled under the protection of the Spaniards, suggests the idea that these may have been the ancestors of Los Mansos or the Tame Indians, at present in the service of the Government. Casimiro had a legend about Indians friendly to the first Spanish settlers, who were subsequently illtreated by them, and I believe revolted. Luiz Aguirre also asserted that his father was one of the original chiefs of the Rio Negro, who for a long time was friendly to the Spaniards, but at length, a revolt taking place, was imprisoned and kept in Carmen as a hostage, where he died. In the year 1832, when Rosas, for the protection of the southern frontier, made his great attack on the Indians, and driving them back to the neighbourhood of the Cordillera, forced them to submit to his terms, he established a military post at Choelechel, as advised by Villarino. His scheme was, I believe, to extend from this point a chain of forts as far as Mendoza, thus keeping the Salinas Indians quiet inside the chain, and driving the Araucanos up to their native valleys of the Cordillera.

This plan was never carried out, and the post, to which the name Isla de Rosas had been given, was abandoned. Rosas was, notwithstanding his having beaten the Indians back, very popular amongst them, and on his overthrow a relation of his, Don Pedro Rosas, took refuge in the Salinas with his artillery and battalion. Orkeke and several friends of mine often inquired after Rosas, saying that 'he was a good man,' &c.

The next expedition up the river occurred only a year previous to my arrival in the Rio Negro, when the steamer Choelechel ascended as far as the island, accompanied by a land force under the Commandante Murga. Indians were found occupying the island, and a European was reported as resident among them, and as exercising the authority of chief. Although he refused to hold any communication with the Argentine commander, it is most probable that this was the famous Frenchman Aurelie I., who was said to have obtained a supply of arms landed in the Rio Negro, and brought up to this island. The expedition did not think fit to disturb the Indians, and returned with little to show as the result of their journey.

It was in contemplation to despatch another expedition, but I have as yet heard no news of its progress from my Patagones correspondents, and it is probably postponed till 'mañana.'

The large island of Choelechel, which I know only by description, never having visited it, appears to be not only an important station in a military point of view, but also admirably adapted for cultivation; there are, however, some reasons against its occupation for that purpose: the first is the undoubted hostility of the Indians to any enterprise tending to occupy what they consider their country; secondly, its distance from Carmen or Patagones as a base of supply for bringing up implements and importing produce, supposing the first difficulties overcome. A railroad or tramway might, I am sure, be constructed at little cost to run down the whole valley of the river, or steam launches of good power, fitted to burn wood, would furnish an effectual means of communication. The present Government steamer Choelechel both draws too much water and is of too small power to render material assistance in the way of opening up the river. The Capitano Major Ramirez pointed out these defects to his Government previous to her being brought to the Rio Negro, but his opinion was overruled.

Foyel and a cacique named Limaron, who claims territorial rights over the island, had a scheme for cultivating Choelechel and other advantageous spots, importing for the purpose Valdivian settlers used to the labour from the other side of the Cordillera, and obtaining their supplies and implements from Carmen.

The present further limit of settlement in the valley is the advanced military post called La Guardia Chica, situated about seven leagues above the second Guardia, and about twenty-five leagues from Carmen. It has not, I believe, been in existence many years, and was two years ago the scene of an *émeute* amongst the garrison, which was graphically described to me at our watchfire in Las Manzanas by Rouque Pinto, who had evidently assisted, if not as an actor, at least as a spectator at the scene. The troops, who were mostly foreigners, according to his account, suddenly rose, shot or stabbed the officer in command, and then their lieutenant, who was killed whilst endeavouring to escape by swimming the river. The mutineers then sacked the place, getting of course intoxicated on the contents of the grog shops, and remained in possession for a day or two, when a party, headed by a man named Bonifaccio, a Government agent for treating with the Indians, rode in and took the ringleaders, who were, I believe, summarily shot. I tell the story as it was told me, and can only vouch for the truth of the fact that the officers were killed in a mutiny, which was afterwards suppressed by the determination and courage of Bonifaccio.

Woodcutters frequently come up the river thus far to procure the red willow timber. Their plan is simple: they ride up bringing their axes, ropes, and provisions, and when arrived at the scene of their labours turn their horses adrift, which readily find their way home. The men form their timber into a raft, and voyage on it safely down the river. This, although hard work, is a profitable occupation for men skilled with the axe. Perhaps at some future period their operations will be extended farther west, and rafts of Araucarian pine, apple, and other trees will be floated down from the forests of the Cordillera.

From the Guardia Chica or Little Guardia, still keeping on the north side, a wide flat plain extends to the Guardia described in the previous chapter; in this several farms are situated, most of them wheat-raising establishments. Nearly all this land is leased by Señor Aguirre from the Government, and he has at present a large number of men engaged in cutting a channel or ditch for the purpose of irrigating an extensive tract of land. The men employed in this work are nearly all of them natives of Santiago del Estero, and it is needless to state that it is a most expensive undertaking: it is only to be hoped that Señor Aguirre will find his labour and expense repaid by fruitful crops.

A few farms are rented by Welsh settlers, refugees from the Chupat, who wisely have preferred the valley of the Rio Negro to that luckless settlement.

A little above the Guardia is situated the estancia of Messrs. Kincaid, of which we caught a glimpse on our first arrival at civilisation. I had the pleasure of staying some days at this farm, where a good deal of land had been brought under cultivation, and flocks of sheep might be seen grazing on the rich plain.

The estancia, from its situation in what is termed a rincon or corner, namely, a peninsula nearly surrounded by a bend of the river, possessed great advantages, and as it is one of the most convenient places for passing cattle to the south side, the owner, who keeps a boat on the river, was enabled to do a profitable business with the Indians when they received their rations, by assisting them in ferrying their animals across.

The overseer, under Mr. Kincaid, was a Scotch shepherd, whose gude wife superintended the ménage; the house was a substantial edifice, built mainly by Messrs. Kincaid, the beams being taken from willow trees felled in the rincon. Up to the time of my visit these gentlemen had been working against fortune, neither of the yields of grain in the two previous years of their occupation having been even a good average.

Close to this estancia a number of ancient Indian burial grounds exist, where, besides skulls and bones, numerous flint arrowheads may be found, some of which, in my possession, have been exhibited to the learned members of the Anthropological Institute, and found to present the peculiar Indian type. Besides flint arrow-heads, pestles and mortars, fashioned out of a porous stone, are also to be found. These articles probably belonged to an old race of Indians who inhabited the Rio Negro previous to the advent of Spaniards and horses, and the pestles and mortars were probably used for pounding the algarroba bean into a paste like that at present manufactured by Pampa Indians under Teneforo; indeed, Luiz Aguirre gave me to understand that these Pampas were of an original stock formerly inhabiting the valley of the Rio Negro, but I leave these conjectures to the consideration of ethnologists more skilled than myself. Near these ancient graves I renewed my acquaintance with the old familiar vizcacha of the plains of Buenos Ayres, which I have previously pointed out does not exist in Patagonia proper, viz., to the south of the Rio Negro. Two other species of armadillo besides the quirquincho were described as being found in their neighbourhood, but I was not fortunate enough to meet with either description, as they were at this season hybernating. Puma have been killed in the neighbourhood of one of the sheep stations. The shepherd heard two outside the corral on one occasion, and giving chase the puma ascended a small tree. The shepherd was only lightly attired, but he stripped off his shirt and fastened it to a stick planted by the tree, which unknown white object so terrified the 'leones' that they remained quiet while he fetched his gun and shot them both.

The skin of an aguarra killed on the premises was also shown to me, but I had not the good fortune to see one alive. The rarity of the animal causes the skins to be highly valued, being worth 5*l*. each in Carmen.

From the second Guardia a short gallop past the advanced barrancas, near which the river flows in another bend, brings the traveller to another wide plain, which to the north runs up into an abra deeply recessed in the receding barranca: in this there are several farms; one of which, six miles below the Guardia, belonging to Messrs. Fraser and Grenfell, is named the Estancia San André, and is also situated (*i.e.* the house and parts intended for wheat growing) inside a rincon or corner partitioned off by a good whitethorn or chañal fence, resting at each end in the river. The sheep and cattle graze during the day outside, but the latter and the horses are invariably brought within the enclosure at night for fear of theft. This foresight of enclosing the cattle had saved Mr. Fraser a considerable loss a short time previous to my visit, as a party of marauding Indians rode along outside the fence, and finding nothing but sheep, which travel too slowly to be securely lifted, proceeded to the next estancia and drove off the cattle and horses, after stripping the shepherd of his clothes, but doing him no bodily injury.

When the news reached Mr. Fraser he got some men together and started in hot pursuit; although a stern chase is a long one, the cattle grew tired, and the Indians, probably some of Calficura's people, abandoned them, escaping with the horses only.

I passed several days at the Estancia San André, spending the greater part of my time in reading, first the papers, and then all the available books, and now and then sauntering about with a gun to shoot partridges or pigeon, whilst my companions were busy, each with his team of oxen ploughing in the seed, or carting bricks down to the new house in course of completion.

The house we occupied was of adobe, and getting rather into a tumbledown condition; but the new house was a substantial brick building, the bricks burnt by the future occupiers, and the walls run up by some Italian masons. This new house was situated on the extremity of the rincon, or corner, or where its apex touched the river: in front of it was a small island, rapidly undergoing conversion from its original reed-covered state to a fertile garden, in which a good crop of potatoes had already been grown and fruit trees were being planted.

The old house was to be given up to the Capataz, or head man, who then resided with his wife in a portion of it. This man was a native, named Medado; and I have since heard that, when pursuing the Indians who had invaded some stations near Bahia San Blas, he swam the river unaccompanied, and rescued two captives, for which he was made an officer of National Guards. His chief business consisted in looking after the cattle and horses, and training the race horse, of which Mr. Fraser was justly proud.

During my stay the San André crack was entered against a horse of Linares' over a short course, and won easily, landing stakes of about eighty head of cattle.

I noticed, whilst at San André, a very beautiful description of small hawk, which appeared closely allied to our merlin, and shot one specimen.

The San André people, like those at Rincon Barrancas, had been struggling against ill-fortune for two seasons; the last season their harvest was a fair one, but unfortunately they delayed thrashing out for a long time, waiting for a thrashing machine from England, which, when it did arrive, would not work properly, and made it necessary for them ultimately to resort to the native fashion of treading out with mares; bad weather ensued, and a considerable portion of the grain was spoiled: such are the woes of Rio Negro farmers, especially improving ones. During my visit the daily routine of tilling, marking cattle, bringing up the horses, &c., was carried on; but we found time to visit the next estancia, owned by a Swiss gentleman residing in Buenos Ayres, and managed in his absence by a Swiss countryman, known by the name of Don Juan. Here, as sheep at the present time hardly paid the cost of shearing, an experiment was being made of curing mutton hams for exportation to Buenos Ayres, and a large number had been already cured and were ready for shipment; but the result of the experiment is unknown to me, and the ingenious Don Juan has since died.

During my stay at San André and Rincon Barrancas I picked up a good deal of information regarding the relations of the Indians with the colonists, which perhaps may not be uninteresting to the reader. All the settlements and guardias previously described are situated on the north bank of the river, the south side being almost entirely, as far as this point, in the hands of the Tame and other Indians. The Indian parties who are most feared are the Araucanos, under the chief Rouque, and the Pampas of Calficura, who has his head-quarters at the Salinas near Bahia Blanca, while the former ranges from the neighbourhood of Choelechel to the Cordillera. I should be inclined to think that Rouque is a subordinate chief under Cheoeque, though I am not certain of the fact, as the latter chief, during my visit to Las Manzanas, mentioned Rouque as being with his people in the apple and pine groves, gathering the autumn harvest; but I subsequently met some of these Indians at the Guardia waiting for Rouque's ration, and recognised one as having been present at our council and subsequent festivities in Las Manzanas. The Government agent for Indian affairs, Bonifaccio, showed me a magnificent pair of stirrups sent from Buenos Ayres as a present to Rouque, the policy of the authorities being to keep him and Cheoeque from joining Calficura in the threatened raid on the frontier. The reason assigned for the declaration of war by this latter chief was the death—by which he probably meant the imprisonment—of one of his inferior caciques; but the real reason probably was that the Argentine

Government, on account of robberies committed by some of his people, had refused to renew his ration of animals. The outbreak in Entre Rios, resulting from the death of Urquiza, was then unforeseen, and it was intended to have despatched a large force, under the command of Señor Mitre, to reinforce the whole frontier, and if necessary crush Calficura; but the troubles caused by Lopez Jordan necessitated the despatch of all available forces at once to Entre Rios, and the meditated scheme of rendering the frontier secure was postponed. Calficura subsequently took advantage of this by attacking the frontier in various places, carrying off captives women and children, besides numerous herds of cattle, winding up by attacking and devastating the new settlements in the neighbourhood of Bahia Blanca, his Indians penetrating boldly, almost without resistance, into the very heart of the town, and returning with abundance of booty. Patagones was not attacked, which may partially be due to the arrangements effected in Las Manzanas, the unwillingness of the Tehuelches to join, and the gaining over of Rouque. The latter chief, however most probably played a double game, and whilst receiving rations and gifts with one hand, allowed his people to join the raids and received plunder with the other.

One reason for the Indians not committing great raids on the Rio Negro settlements is simply that cattle and horses hardly exist in sufficient numbers to reward a foray on a large scale. Small parties sometimes come in, as in the case described, when the horses were taken from the 'China Muerte,' the estancia of Mr. Fraser's neighbour; but these are rather robberies than hostile invasions— indeed, no important raids have occurred since the time of Lenquetrou, who united all the Indians for the purpose, and swept the valley in a raid which, it may be remembered, was described to me by Gravino, a participator in it, at Inacayal's toldos, near the Pass of the Rio Limay. The settlers were naturally anxious to know my opinion as to the probable safety of the Rio Negro, and I assured them that, from what I knew, there was little chance of a raid, but that on the contrary Bahia Blanca was sure to be attacked, and I especially warned one of our countrymen who was on his way to Bahia Blanca not to hazard himself by settling outside the town at the present juncture. Englishmen are apt to suppose that because they possess good weapons, rifles and revolvers, and are able and ready to use them, they can resist an Indian attack; but the whole system of their warfare consists in sudden surprises. They secretly collect their forces, and waiting at a safe distance during the night, come in at the early dawn, and perhaps the unsuspicious settler, going to the corral or looking for his horses, observes in the distance what appears to be a troop of horses, driven, according to custom, by one or two mounted men; these approach unchallenged, but in a second every horse displays an armed rider, shouting his war-cry. They then spread out, as if to encircle the game, thus presenting no front to the rifles of their opponents, and dash down lance in hand; and whilst some secure the animals, others set fire to the dwellings and carry off the women—if there are any—captives. In some cases they kill the men, but generally only when much resistance is offered.

Although their chief object in warfare is to carry off cattle and captives, the Indians will at times fight desperately, regardless of odds, and show little or no fear of death; and the survivors will never leave their wounded or killed on the field. The Indians in the service of the Government, mustering about fifty lances, and residing chiefly on the south side, are commanded by a man named Linares, previously mentioned as living at San Xaviel; he receives the pay and rations of an officer in the army, of what rank I do not know, and all his men regularly receive pay and rations. These are supposed to act as gendarmerie; but although Linares and his four brothers are probably to be depended on, I doubt very much if the rank and file could be trusted to remain true to their colours in the event of a united raid taking place, such as that organised by Lenquetrou.

They have all acquired, by their lengthened residence in the neighbourhood of bad characters, a rowdy, swaggering disposition not generally, according to my experience, common amongst uncivilised Indians; and frequent losses of cattle occur to people settled on the south side, no doubt attributable to these dubious allies and defenders.

Between San André and Carmen the winding course of the river twice approaches and recedes from the barranca, forming two successive wide alluvial plains, partly settled and partly in natural pasture, in one of which a mill turned by water-power was at this time in course of erection, the existing corn-mills being cumbrous, old-fashioned affairs worked by horses.

The barranca then abuts on the river, except in one place, where there is a farm and wharf used for loading salt, forming a cliff close to the river bank as far as Carmen. Above this farm and wharf an old fort, apparently untenanted, and armed with one gun, is situated; and away to the north-east, in an indentation in the plain, lies a large salina from which the salt is extracted.

From the immediate neighbourhood of this fort a fine view of the valley below presented itself: right in front, or nearly due south, on the other side of the river, lay San Xaviel, partially shrouded by trees; scattered farms occurred to the west of this, and along the bank as far as the south side of the town. In the river several delightful-looking cultivated islands were to be seen, the most noticeable forming the vineyard of Don Benito Crespo. Beyond the town, to the south-east, the eye ranged over unbroken plains, with dots here and there marking sheep stations or small farms. Of the south side little has been said: near the town there are many small estancias; but a great drawback, I am told, to settling there is the fact that no secure titles to the properties are procurable, and therefore there is no security of occupation in the event of acquiring a piece of land. An important establishment must not be overlooked, namely, the saladero of Señor Aguirre, situated about a league below the town of Carmen, whence a considerable amount of hides and tallow is exported to England. During my stay a North-German or Dutch barque was lying off the place loading a cargo. Besides these commodities, the exports of Carmen include salt, wheat, ostrich feathers, and peltries obtained from the Indians, and some few ponchos and saddle-cloths; while the imports may be placed under the head of sundries or notions, from imitation ponchos and cheap finery to Paraguay tea and bad spirits.

Although to my eyes, so long accustomed to treeless wastes, rocky spur-like mountains, and wild grassy valleys, the valley of the Rio Negro appeared almost a garden of Eden, no doubt to any new arrival from England it would not have the same aspect. The valley through which the river winds is destitute of any trees, besides the fringe of tall willows which belt the stream, extending (except perhaps in Sauce Blanco) nowhere more than a couple of hundred yards from the bank. The plains stretching on either bank to the chañal and scrub covered deserts in many places were so closely eaten down by sheep and cattle as to present the minimum of vegetation, at least in the winter season.

However bare and unpromising the land may seem, such is the fertility of the soil that wheat may be grown, crop after crop, and year after year, on the same land. Potatoes attain a very large size and are of excellent quality, but these are chiefly grown in the islands of the river.

The Government have lately issued orders that all islands belong inalienably to the State, and all present occupiers are obliged to pay a small head rent to the authorities, which seems to point at a future occupation of Choelechel.

Besides potatoes, all other European vegetables and fruit-trees grow well; tobacco seems to thrive, and vines promise to furnish a staple of export in the shape of Rio Negro wine. In one of the islands, occupied by Don Benito Crespo, and leased by him on shares to some Spaniards from the neighbourhood of Cadiz, a great number of vines have been planted and large quantities of grapes pressed out yearly. The wine, which is called 'Chacoli,' has the muscatel flavour and bouquet of Moselle, and is a thin pure wine, excellent to drink in the warm weather, as it is by itself not at all strong or heady. I should imagine that it would not bear exportation, but Don Benito has hopes that his Andalusians will shortly be able to produce a superior quality. Besides wine, I tasted at the table of this hospitable gentleman some brandy, the produce of the same grape: it was of course colourless, of good taste, but any number of degrees over proof.

A sportsman can always find amusement either in shooting ducks, partridges, geese, and other wild fowl, or mounting his horse and chasing ostriches or deer in the abras or openings running far up like inlets of grass between the scrub-covered promontories of the barranca. Fish may be caught in the river, chiefly, I believe, the delicious pejerey[1] or large smelt, and those perch-like fish described as existing in the rivers of Patagonia.

For guanaco, the pampas near San Blas must be visited, but the valley and the lagoons formed by backwaters of the river furnish abundance of black-necked swans, upland geese, red-headed ducks, widgeon, teal, flamingoes, and roseate spoonbills.

It will be evident that to any active and enterprising young men, prepared to rough it a little, and possessed of a small sum of ready money, who wish to invest in land and cultivate, there is much to be said for and against the Rio Negro as a home. The land may be had at a reasonable price, and little clearing is required. Implements may be brought from Buenos Ayres, either in a sailing ship or by the steamer which is supposed to run monthly, though rather uncertain in its movements. The climate is pleasant and healthy, and one good season of harvest would almost repay the outlay on a moderate establishment.

As to the drawbacks to be placed on the contra side, the river is subject at times to floods, at other times droughts prevail, and, unless artificial irrigation be resorted to, crops will fail, besides which occasionally a million of locusts will save the farmer the trouble of reaping his harvest; the cattle, of which most people keep enough to supply milk and meat for home consumption, may be run off by Indians; and last, but not least, the settler may lose his life by the hand of some felon. But no colony offers a certainty of making a rapid fortune.

The great mistake most English settlers make is going out to a place with the idea that they are going to make a 'pile' in a year or two and then return to Europe.

In my opinion the settler should go with the intention of making the place he has chosen his home: then if successful he can return, but he should not look forward to it. The Basque population are looked upon in the Argentine provinces as the best immigrants, as they generally stay in the country. The Italians, on the contrary, grub away for some years, starving and pinching, until they have amassed a small sum of money sufficient to enable them to live at ease in Italy, while English and all others are looked upon as people to be fleeced if possible. Sheepfarming in the Rio Negro is, I think, to be avoided, as in other places in the Argentine provinces. Señor Aguirre told me that he had lost a large sum of money in this investment, and many of my countrymen from the Rio de la Plata can sympathise with him.

Two sturdy Scotchmen are at present trying the experiment near Carmen, and as sheep were at a low price when they commenced, they may succeed.

It is a question in my mind whether larch or araucaria pines would not thrive along the flats bordering the river; perhaps the climate is too dry for the latter, but the experiment is almost worth trying for anyone possessed of means and inclination to take up his abode for a term of years in the Rio Negro. For my own part, were I a settler, I should be induced to confine my efforts to the cultivation of the vine, and perhaps tobacco, keeping of course the necessary stock of animals for home consumption.

It must be clearly understood that I am not recommending or interested in the Rio Negro as a place to which intending emigrants should direct their thoughts; it undoubtedly possesses great natural advantages, which are, as yet, insufficiently developed by most of the colonists. Their estancias, with the exception of those of my Scotch and English friends, are generally small, miserable-looking tenements, with offal scattered round the ill-kept corral; and their agriculture is as indifferent as the neglected appearance of the houses would suggest. But for all that, there is not a really poor man—except in consequence of his own laziness or drunken habits—in Carmen and its vicinity, and labour is in great demand at high wages, while living is cheap, which experience, since my return, has taught me to be a painful contrast to the state of our own population at home.

I was recalled from Rincon Barrancas and my speculations on the Rio Negro as a field for emigrants by the distant view of Indians, espied from the lookout on the top of my host's house, as they descended from the travesia, and hastened back to the town to receive them, according to promise. It will be remembered that on my arrival as chasqui I presented to Señor Murga my despatches, in which Casimiro detailed his arrangements for the protection of Patagones. A list of the chiefs to whom rations or gifts of cattle, horses, &c., were due, was also enclosed, and a request that a hundred mares should be sent out at once with the returning messengers. After some days' delay I was sent for by Señor Murga, who, it may be here remarked, is reputed to thoroughly understand the Indians, and to display considerable address in managing them. It was amusing to observe the natural suspicion and perplexity aroused in the mind of the Commandante concerning my position among the Indians; and my reply to his question as to what rank and influence I possessed among them, and how I was interested for them—that I was simply a guest and friend—did not seem at all sufficient to explain matters. But he discussed the question of the chiefs and their requests, and assured me that all the chiefs who should be found to be entitled to rations should duly receive them: he, however, absolutely refused to send out any mares, declaring that Casimiro should receive all his dues when he arrived.

As the grand Cacique had for several years not drawn his annual allowance, amounting to 200 cows, 100 mares, 500 sheep, and a quantity of clothes and yerba, it can be well imagined that with fair play and prudence he would, on this visit, become a wealthy as well as powerful Cacique, as a reward for his labours. At his previous visit he had left a quantity of cattle and sheep, under charge of some of the Tame Indians, to increase and multiply; but alas! on his arrival, in reply to his inquiries, only one small flock of sheep was forthcoming, the rest, instead of multiplying, having been gambled away by their guardians. The liberality of the Argentines and the largeness of the gifts may appear surprising; and indeed the nominal value, as charged to the Government for these annual gifts to the Indians, is very great. I saw myself 1,000 head of cattle pass on their way to Rouque, and Cheoeque was expecting 1,200. The cattle were brought down from the Tandil by purveyors, whose business must be as lucrative as that of American army contractors; for the Indians are sometimes when sober, or oftener when intoxicated, induced to part with their newly-acquired possessions for a mere trifle, and the cattle, reverting to the dealer's hands, thus do duty over again as a ration perhaps to the same Cacique. Thus the Indians benefit but little, while the Government pays a large amount and the purveyors and other agents grow rich, Indians and Government being esteemed apparently as lawful and natural pigeons, to be plucked by any safe means.

The Commandante's reply had been duly forwarded to Casimiro, together with some liquor and presents for my friends; and the morning following my return from the country I was awoke early by a knock at the door, and on opening it found five or six Tehuelches who had made their way over the river to my quarters. After giving them a matè we all proceeded to the store, and I gave one or two some small presents. Among these first arrivals was my friend Jackechan, the Cacique from the Chupat, who confided to me that he had been very drunk the night before. The Tehuelches had not, however, waited till they reached the settlements for an opportunity of abandoning themselves to the pernicious enjoyment of 'lum.' It soon came out that their delay at Valchita had been necessitated by a prolonged debauch on liquor procured from the Guardia. Casimiro had of course set the example, and the drink had, as usual, also led to quarrelling, which resulted in a general fight; several had been killed, including Cayuke, so often mentioned as a staunch friend; and I was greatly grieved at being unable to get any accurate tidings of my Herculean comrade the good-natured Wáki, who had, beyond doubt, been killed at the same time.

Such common occurrences were little regarded by my visitors, all of whom were caciquillos, and whom I presently dismissed rejoicing, with a promise to visit them on the south side in the evening. But my troubles had only just commenced. All day long Tehuelches kept arriving, and not knowing what to do with themselves, followed me about wherever I went, much to the amusement of some of my acquaintances.

In the evening I crossed to the other side, and remained for the night with my old hosts. All were in a great state of delight, as their rations were to be given them without delay—the yerba, sugar, and spirits from Aguirre's stores, and the cattle and mares from the Guardia in front of Sauce Blanco. Old Orkeke, who had not expected to receive rations, had been allowed, in consequence of my urging his claims, the same as other minor chiefs, and was consequently in high delight.

They were, on the other hand, very dissatisfied at the extremely low prices which their feathers and peltries had realised, and abused the dealers very roundly as a lot of rogues. False weights and other tricks of trade had been freely employed to cheat the Indians; and the storekeepers also charged exorbitantly for necessaries supplied to them. Their custom is to bivouac in the yards or corrals at the back of the stores, where they light fires and cook as in their own country, and pay in the end as dearly for their accommodation as if in a West End hotel. I delighted the heart of Mrs. Orkeke by presenting her with a long-promised iron pot and a shawl; and to Hinchel's son I gave a promised pack of cards, and to the children raisins, sweets, or bread.

Jackechan's wife and daughter, who had always shown me great kindness, I took into the store, and told them to choose whatever they fancied most; whereupon they both, without hesitation, selected two small bottles of scent to put on their hair. I must remark, *en passant*, that all this family were exceptionally clean in their habits and persons, and I promised, if I returned to Patagonia, to travel in their toldo, as I had then some idea of journeying by the sea-coast to the Chupat, and perhaps to Santa Cruz. Jackechan's son—the boy with light hair and complexion—volunteered to come to England with me, and I consented to take him; but on hearing that there were no ostrich or guanaco where we were going, he thought better of it.

Some of Quintuhual's and Foyel's people also arrived, but behaved themselves in a very different manner to the Tehuelches. Their women and children had all been left in Geylum, and the men walked about in a very independent manner, with a proud, superior bearing, not condescending to admire anything, or to ask for any presents. One of them, on the boatman requesting his fare for bringing him across the river, refused flatly, and then drew his revolver to enforce his denial.

Last, but not least, as became so great a personage, Casimiro arrived, attended by Meña, who acted as secretary. His costume had suffered considerably from his late pursuits, and his appearance was by no means improved by a gash in his face received from a Manzanero in a brawl at Sauce Blanco. He installed himself in the hotel, hired the fifes and drums of the garrison to play whilst he was at breakfast, and for two days kept open house for all comers, ending the day in an advanced state of intoxication.

At the end of this debauch a bill was handed to him which, I should think, took the value of nearly half his rations. This sobered him, and he, taking my advice, left the hotel, and crossing the river proceeded to Sauce Blanco to look after his rations and Indians. On the whole, the Indians behaved very well whilst in the settlement. I saw, of course, some drunkenness, but not nearly so much as I had expected. One and all parted from me with most cordial farewells, and pressed me to return to the Pampa, as they call it, as soon as possible. Jackechan was one of the last to leave. He, as well as one or two of the others, had found an old acquaintance in Mr. Humphreys, formerly of the Chupat colony, but now settled in Patagones as carpenter. We all met in Mr. Humphreys's house one Sunday after church, and had a long talk relative to this Chupat settlement, and to the answer received to my letter brought by Jackechan's chasqui. The statement in it that the settlers had no stores of any sort, and that of the Indian messenger that they were almost destitute of clothing, have been fully corroborated by the despatches of Commander Dennistoun, H.M.S. Cracker, published whilst these pages were being written. Mr. Humphreys considered himself and the few companions who had accompanied him to the Rio Negro fortunate in having left when they did; and all agreed that the colonists would do better if transferred to the Rio Negro, where those who were skilled in trades would be able to live in comparative ease, and the mere labourers find plenty of work, and be able at any rate to maintain themselves. I cannot but record my astonishment that Mr. Lewis Jones—who, although I am not personally acquainted with him, must, from the report given me by the Indians, be a man of no ordinary understanding—should endeavour to maintain the colony in a place which had formerly been tried by others and abandoned as hopeless, the distance of the harbour—thirty miles off—alone being a certain obstacle to its prosperity.

The visionary scheme of a Welsh Utopia, in pursuit of which these unfortunate emigrants settled themselves, ought not to be encouraged, likely as it is to end in the starvation of the victims to it. Had it not been for the charity of the Argentine Government, this must have been their fate ere now. Jackechan described to me that he had seen the settlers 'eating grass,' and had taught some of them how to hunt and furnished them with bolas. The Blue Book just published confirms the truth of this statement, and perhaps renders it needless for me to go more into the subject; but I must add that, though at that time friendly and well-disposed, this chief considered the settlers as intruders on his territory, and avowed his intention of demanding payment at a future time—a refusal of rent being in such a case sure to be followed by a very summary process of cattle driving and eviction.

The Rio Negro, with all its drawbacks of Indians, locusts, floods, and droughts, is certainly infinitely superior to the Chupat. If the Welsh wish to live as a separate community, I am sure that Señor Aguirre will only be too happy to let them settle on his tract of land between the Upper and Second Guardia, where already some of their countrymen—Messrs. Williams and Owen—have taken land.

After the Indians had left, I gave myself over to the enjoyments of social life in Patagones, which did not prove sufficient to reconcile me to the delay consequent on the non-arrival of the steamer. My days were spent in walking about, playing billiards, and taking maté; and a visit in the evening to Don Domingo's, where a party were in the habit of meeting to play 'truco' for sweetmeats. Sometimes we varied this by calling on some of the fair señoritas, or spending the evening at the house of Mr. Davis, the engineer of the Choelechel, in the company of his amiable señora. All the young ladies agreed that Patagones was very 'triste,' especially those who had been to Buenos Ayres, and had enjoyed the delights of the opera and bands of music in the Plaza.

On Sundays, after mass and service in the mission station, attended by all the English, a race would sometimes take place, or, in default, there would be sure to be a cock fight held on the south side; at either of which Commandante Murga invariably attended. There was also a fives court, where some Basque or natives were generally to be found playing. Once or twice I accompanied Dr. Humble—not, however, on Sunday—in a pull on the river. Every day we looked out anxiously for the steamer, which had been so long overdue as to make it appear probable that she had met with an accident. Tired of the delay, I had just negotiated my passage in a Dutch schooner laden with grain for Buenos Ayres, when one evening the steamer arrived, having been delayed in Bahia Blanca.

In the morning I was agreeably surprised by the size of the steamer, formerly the Montauk, of Boston, but re-christened the Patagones, and owned by Messrs. Aguirre and Murga. She was pretty well fitted up as regards accommodation, but all the decks, cabins, and every part of her presented a very dirty appearance.

After two days' stay she hoisted the blue peter, and, having taken my passage, together with Messrs. Fraser and Kincaid, who were going to Buenos Ayres on business, and Mr. Gibb, who was on his return to Europe, repaired on board, where we found a considerable number of passengers assembled; the distinguished billiard-marker who had annexed the clock amongst the number. About 4 P.M. we weighed, and, bidding adieu to Patagones, started down the river with the ebb tide, intending to anchor for the night in the Boca and cross the long line of sandbank, which forms a dangerous bar, with the morning tide. We steamed along smoothly enough until just well within sight of the ships lying in the Boca, when a sudden concussion announced that she was ashore on a sandbank, where she stuck hard and fast. We thought little of the misadventure, expecting to be off at high tide, and some of us went on shore and picnicked on the flats bordering the river. We returned about ten, and about midnight I was woke up by hearing one of the funnel guys snap, and, going on deck, found that, though the bow of the ship was high out of the water, the stern was in deep water, and the ship severely straining amidships in consequence. A few minutes after the main steam pipe broke: the steam had, however, luckily been turned off or the consequences would have been disastrous to those in the after part of the ship. The ladies were then landed, for fear of accidents, and the remainder of us held a consultation as to how we should get to Buenos Ayres, and ultimately went to sleep on it.

The following morning the Choelechel came down and succeeded in towing the vessel off, and the Dutch captain of the schooner came on board and agreed to take me and some others on to Buenos Ayres. We accordingly jumped into a boat, and proceeding down to the Boca, got on board the schooner, hoping to sail the next day; but were again doomed to be disappointed.

The captain went up to buy provisions, and did not return till late the following evening. Meantime the wind set in foul in the morning, and the line of roaring white breaker on the bar showed the impossibility of sailing; so we were compelled to wait, looking out on the dreary sand-dunes which narrowed the entrance to the river on either side. Some of us went on shore to visit the pilot station, and had a talk with the pilot, a brave old German or Dutchman. This veteran and his men had successfully defended his station against a large force of Indians in the raid of Lenquetrou. The enemy desired to get possession of a howitzer which is kept in the station, and the Indians rushed actually up to the enclosure, while the men fired on them almost muzzle to their breasts, at last succeeding in beating them off with immense loss.

The boat's crew consisted of men of all nations. I got into conversation with one, at first in Spanish, then in English. After lending me his pipe, he looked hard at me and said, 'I know you: I am Pat Sweeny, and ran away from the Sheldrake. What ship did you run away from?' I was not dressed in my best clothes, and looked doubtless weather beaten enough; but I recognised my friend, though he failed to remember me, and was not enlightened as to my identity. Several weary days were spent in drinking schnapps, and ineffectually trying to catch fish, when at last a fair breeze sprang up, which speedily wafted us out sight of the Patagonian shores, and after a boisterous passage of six days the anchor was dropped off Buenos Ayres.

1. *Atherinichthys Argentinensis*. Cunningham, p. 54.

Map of

PATAGONIA

Showing Captⁿ Musters Route

Author's Route

English Miles

APPENDIX A

A partial Vocabulary of the Tsoneca Language, as spoken by the Northern Tehuelches.

ENGLISH	AHONICANKA, OR TSONECA	ENGLISH	AHONICANKA, OR TSONECA
I or mine	ya		
you *or* yours	ma		
his or hers	ti	**EXCLAMATIONS**	
this one *or* he	win	of surprise	wati, wati, wati
who	hem	of anger	worrioo-wálloo
here	nanik	curse it	nourenk y sé
	mawoori	on erring with the bolas	wow
there	mawook		
	mon	on catching an animal or in fighting	kow
where	kinik		
when	kenoesh	jealous	ynaien
what	ket	foolish	chops
how, how much *or* many	kinkein kerum	quick	sourno
		good	ketz
above	eok	pretty	coquet
below	penk	bad	terosh
	wumka	ill	hammersh
immediately	marso	hot	yporsk
to-morrow	nush	cold	kekoosh
yesterday	nush	big	chaish
day after to-morrow	eounnush	little	talenque
quickly	gemmo	light	höppen
		heavy	pogelsh
		like	nourks

English	Ahonicanka, or Tsoneca	English	Ahonicanka, or Tsoneca
far	éouns	hat	kor
near	ekel	bolas	yatschiko
similar	wáks	(*three balls*)	
tired	wotysk	bolas	chume
hungry	pashlik	(*two balls*)	
difficult	wickemi	sinews	katz
hard	chornk	lazo	laso
soft	kattn	knife	paiken
ready	kush	gun	gilwum
yes	ahon (*very guttural*)	revolver	gilwinikush
no	kompsh	powder	tchampum
man (*Indian*)	ahonican	caps	kun
man (*Christian*)	háchish	lance	waike
people (*Indian*)	tchonik	pot (*for cooking*)	askem
woman (*married*)	karken	bottle	oëtre
father	yank	barrel	barr
mother	yanna	(bodkin) needle	hüllen
wife	ysher	*or* nail	
son	ykallum	bag	hüll
brother	yten	pipe	aniwee
sister	ystshen		conganou
children	coquetra	tobacco	golk
friend *or* companion	gennow	saddle	tusk
head	kittar	bridle	hum
eyes	ötl	bit	kankion
nose	tchal	stirrups	keshon
tongue	tal	spurs	wateren
lips	chum	girth	genig
teeth	oër	straps for	kaligi
hands	tsicc'r	securing horses'	
legs	noa	legs	
feet	shankence	whip	wakenem
toldo *or* house	kou	belt	wáti
poles for ditto	hö	sun (*or* a day)	gengenko
hides, ditto	wummum	moon	showan
thongs	cowan	(*or* a month)	
mantle	kai	stars	ááskren
fillet for hair	kotchi	a year	tsor
boots	tsuccre	fire	yaik
clothes	kakewit	water	léy

ENGLISH	AHONICANKA, OR TSONECA	ENGLISH	AHONICANKA, OR TSONECA
snow	gél	fish	oin
wind	hoshen	marriage	coyenk
rain	téwa	wild potatoes	appely
smoke	paan	sleep	shensk
clouds	páwall	a file	kikeriki
night	queyomen	council	aix
wood	kaki	ill	hammersh
hill	yorri	ship	youlel
place	hasik	gum *or* rosin	maki
land *or* country	yerroen	cards	bersen
river	koona		
road	nooma		

COLOURS	

ENGLISH	AHONICANKA, OR TSONECA
poncho	lecho
meat	yipper
stones	kátch
rocks	air
grass	kor
pasture	oet
broth or tea	áásleish
horse	ewoe
	cawall
cattle	choi
sheep	cámpān
large deer	shóen
guanaco	rou
ostrich (*or* rhea)	mikkeoush
puma	gol
fox	paltn
skunk	wickster
armadillo	áno
hare	paahi
fowls	peyou
fawn *or* colt	kooroo
skins	wummun
gold	wínki
eggs	oom
bones	kotsh
marrow	tcham
grease	am
a chief	gounok

Colours

ENGLISH	AHONICANKA, OR TSONECA
black	chorlo
white	golwin
yellow	waieken
green	arkum
red	kāōpen
blue	kaliken
brown *or* bay	soorsh
piebald	hogel
sit down	pespesh
catch	korigi
to be tired	ywotisk
I go	yschengs
he goes	wansk
he has	hell
give me	moyout
lend me	mon
write	aātkren
buy	amili
change	quewarien
I am tired	wotyskiya
I am hungry	pashlik ya
I am sleepy	yshensk
to kill	ymuck
to fight	ywowesk
to sing	yworrish
I like	yshorske ya

ENGLISH	AHONICANKA, OR TSONECA	ENGLISH	AHONICANKA, OR TSONECA
to mount on horseback	{ amcotts oin		NUMERALS
to race	káttern	one	chuche
to send messenger	wickeni coëto	two	houke
		three	aäs
to talk	ayensh	four	carge
I understand	ya omkes	five	ktsin
I do not understand	ytonkes	six	winikush
		seven	ouk
come along	heroschengs	eight	winicarge
to hunt	aoukem	nine	humanakoutsen
to speak	kinscott	ten	kake
to do a thing	micheten	eleven	chuche kor
make	máki	twelve	houke kor
to work	tirsk	thirteen	aas kor
to light	kaime		kor added up to twenty
to fill	meshawr	twenty	wommenikukikor
to eat	shehattu	thirty	aasenikski
march	wéen	forty	cargekaki
to break	charsk	fifty	ktsinkaki
to play	nayensh	a hundred	patack
		a thousand	huaranca

Thank you	Nouremi naki
Lend me the pipe	Mon aniwee—aniwee moyout
Catch my horse	Korigi ya
Come along, friend	Heroschengs gennow
Will you come out hunting? (*Lit.* Come out hunting, tell me.)	Heros aoukemshaw kinscott ya
The people are fighting	Ywowishk chonik
How many are killed?	Kinkeinkerum ymuck
Where are you going?	Kinek nis chengs
Cook some meat; I am hungry	Herósh yipper wummi pashlik ya
I understand Indian	Omkes Ahonicanka
I like your wife	Ma yshorsks ysher
What do you want?	Keterum karn?
It rains much to-day	Chaiske nush que tewa
We are going to see many people	Wushkaeye seonk chonik

We are going to see another country	Wushkaeye kaiok yerroen
Come here quickly	Gommo heout witka
What do you buy?	Ket, m amli

.

APPENDIX B.

Testimony of successive Voyagers to the Stature of the Patagonians.

A.D.

1520	*Pigafetta*	The least, taller than the tallest men in Castille.
1578	*Drake*	Not taller than some Englishmen.
1591	*Knyvet*	Fifteen or sixteen spans high.
1598	*Van Noort*	Natives of tall stature.
1615	*Schouten*	Human skeletons 10 or 11 feet long.
1669	*Narborough*	Mr. Wood was taller than any of them.
1750	*Falkner*	A cacique 7 feet and some inches high.
1764	*Byron*	A chief about 7 feet high, and few of the others shorter.
1766	*Wallis*	Measured some of the tallest: one was 6 feet 7 inches, several 6 feet 5 inches; the average height was between 5 feet 10 inches and 6 feet.
1783	*Viedma*	Generally 6 feet high.
1829	*D'Orbigny*	Never found any exceeding 5 feet 11 inches; average height 5 feet 4 inches.
1833	*Fitzroy and Darwin*	Tallest average of any people; average height 6 feet, some taller and a few shorter.
1867-8	*Cunningham*	Rarely less than 5 feet 11 inches in height, and often exceeding 6 feet by a few inches. One measured 6 feet 10 inches.

Also Available from Nonsuch Publishing

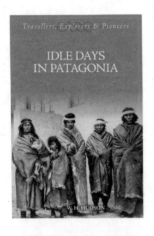

Written by the acclaimed novelist and naturalist William Henry Hudson, *Idle Days in Patagonia* is a detailed and unparalleled account of the kaleidoscopic wildlife of Patagonia, combined with lively anecdotes of Hudson's adventurous trips through the rugged and often inhospitable countryside.
£12
ISBN: 1-84588-024-2
160 pages, 27 illustrations

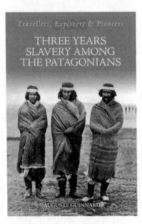

At the age of just 23 Auguste Guinnard was captured by Patagonian Indians and forced to live and work with them as their slave. *Three Years' Slavery* is a faithful record of Guinnard's brutal enslavement, surprising enlightenment and eventual escape and return to his homeland.
£12
ISBN: 1-84588-046-3
160 pages

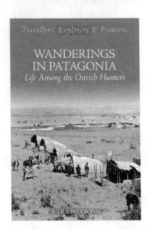

Setting out on what should have been a simple journey from Port Julian to Sandy Point the author and his companions find themselves facing unexpected dangers, from raging rivers to mutineers, in an adventure that turns out to be anything but simple.
£12
ISBN: 1-84588-062-5
160 pages, 9 illustrations